Mary Maxwell-Scott

The making of Abbotsford and incidents in Scottish history

Mary Maxwell-Scott

The making of Abbotsford and incidents in Scottish history

ISBN/EAN: 9783337234263

Printed in Europe, USA, Canada, Australia, Japan

Cover: Foto ©ninafisch / pixelio.de

More available books at **www.hansebooks.com**

The Making of Abbotsford

AND

Incidents in Scottish History

DRAWN FROM VARIOUS SOURCES

BY

THE HON. MRS. MAXWELL-SCOTT
OF ABBOTSFORD

CARVED PANEL AT ABBOTSFORD

LONDON
ADAM & CHARLES BLACK
1897

PREFACE

IN publishing this collection of hitherto scattered papers, my warm thanks are due to the courtesy of those who have permitted me to reprint them. To the Editor of the *Scottish Review* I owe thanks for permission to use the six articles which first appeared in that Review. To the Editors of the *Dublin Review* and of *The Month* I am indebted for leave to republish the Article on " Barbour's Legends of the Saints " and the paper on " The Ruthwell Cross." To the Secretary of Catholic Truth Society my thanks are due for the use of the little life of Mary Queen of Scots ; and to Messrs. Blackwood I am grateful for leave to reprint the paper on Claude, Duchess of Lorraine. I wish also to express my thanks to Messrs. A. and C. Black, and to Mr. William Gibb, for kind permission to republish the paper on " The Making of Abbotsford " which formed the Introduction to the beautiful book on *Abbotsford and its Treasures* published in 1893, and which owes its chief interest to Mr. Gibb's admirable drawings. One of these, the drawing of Abbotsford taken from the other side of the Tweed, is here reproduced as frontispiece to show Abbotsford as it now is; while the opposite vignette (taken from an early edition of Lockhart's *Life*) shows us the Abbotsford of 1812.

I wish also to express my warm thanks to the Marquis of Bute for his very valuable assistance and co-operation in the article on "St. Magnus of the Orkneys," which, owing to my being ill at the time, he kindly completed, adding at the same time much to its literary value.

These papers can claim unity of aim only in so much as they all deal with the history of my own country, or with that of our ancient ally—France.

M. M. MAXWELL SCOTT.

ABBOTSFORD, *August* 1897.

CONTENTS

		PAGE
1. THE MAKING OF ABBOTSFORD		1
2. BARBOUR'S LEGENDS OF THE SAINTS		23
3. THE LIFE OF SAINT MARGARET		48
4. ST. MAGNUS OF THE ORKNEYS		76
5. THE SCOTS GUARDS IN FRANCE		118
6. THE LENNOX		160
7. A SISTER-IN-LAW OF MARY QUEEN OF SCOTS		200
8. SCOTTISH CATHOLICS UNDER MARY AND JAMES		227
9. MARY STUART		248
10. THE CHEVALIER DE FEUQUEROLLES		297
11. WINIFRED, COUNTESS OF NITHSDAILL		325
12. THE RUTHWELL CROSS		352

I

THE MAKING OF ABBOTSFORD

O words of mine are needed to remind my readers of Sir Walter's love for his home. We know that, as in joy, so also in sorrow and loss, and to the very end, his thoughts turned constantly to Abbotsford. As Mr. Lockhart truly says, "to have curtailed the exposition of his fond untiring enthusiasm on that score, would have been like omitting the Prince in a cast of Hamlet." It was in his early youth that Sir Walter first saw the site of the future Abbotsford. "I have often heard him tell," writes Mr. Lockhart, "that when travelling in his boyhood with his father, from Selkirk to Melrose, the old man suddenly desired the carriage to halt at the foot of an eminence, and said, 'We must get out here, Walter, and see a thing quite in your line.' His father then conducted him to a rude stone on the edge of

an acclivity, about half a mile above the Tweed at Abbotsford, which marks the spot

> Where gallant Cessford's life-blood dear
> Reeked on dark Elliott's border spear.

This was the conclusion of the battle of Melrose, fought in 1526, between the Earls of Angus and Home and the two chiefs of the race of Kerr on the one side, and Buccleuch and his clan on the other, in sight of the young King James V., the possession of whose person was the object of the contest. The battle is often mentioned in the *Border Minstrelsy*. . . . In the names of various localities between Melrose and Abbotsford, such as *Skirmish-field*, *Charge-law*, and so forth, the incidents of the fight have found a lasting record; and the spot where the retainer of Buccleuch terminated the pursuit of the victors by the mortal wound of Kerr of Cessford (ancestor of the Dukes of Roxburghe) has always been called *Turn-again*."[1]

Sir Walter probably never forgot this incident, for when, in 1811, he determined to become a "Tweedside Laird," he fixed upon the little property which, though then "not a very attractive one to the general observer, had long been one of peculiar interest" to him.

On the 12th May 1811, Sir Walter writes to James Ballantyne upon business, and adds: "My

---

[1] *Turn-again* is situated in the wood to the left above the house. *Life* (in 10 vols.), vol. iii. p. 335.

attention has been a little dissipated by considering a plan for my own future comfort which I hasten to mention to you. My lease of Ashestiel is out . . . I have therefore resolved to purchase a piece of ground sufficient for a cottage and a few fields. There are two pieces, either of which would suit me, but both would make a very desirable property indeed. They stretch along the Tweed, near halfway between Melrose and Selkirk, on the opposite side from Lord Somerville, and could be had for between £7000 and £8000, or either separate for about half the sum. I have serious thoughts of one or both, and must have recourse to my pen to make the matter easy."

Of the two adjoining farms here mentioned, Sir Walter soon after bought the one comprising *Turn-again*. The person from whom he bought the property was a valued friend of his own, Dr. Robert Douglas, minister of Galashiels. He had never resided on the property, and the only embellishments he had effected had been "limited to one stripe of firs, so long and so narrow that Scott likened it to a black hair-comb. It ran from the precincts of the homestead towards *Turn-again*, and has bequeathed the name of *the Doctor's redding-kame* to the mass of nobler trees amidst which its dark straight line can now hardly be traced."[1]

[1] *Life*, vol. iii. p. 339.

Clarty Hole, as the farm was termed, seems to have deserved its inharmonious name; the haugh or meadow by the river and about a hundred acres of undulating ground at the back were alike in a most neglected state, "undrained, wretchedly enclosed, much of it covered with nothing better than the native heath. The farmhouse itself was small and poor, with a common *kail-yard* on one flank and a staring barn, of the doctor's erection, on the other." But, as Mr. Lockhart says, the Tweed was everything to Sir Walter, and from the moment he took possession, "he claimed for his farm the name of the adjoining *ford*, situated just above the influx of the classical tributary Gala. As might be guessed from the name of Abbotsford, all these lands had belonged of old to the great Abbey of Melrose."[1]

The neighbourhood of two antiquarian remains of interest lent an additional charm to the little property in Sir Walter's eyes. To the left of the site of the house we can still see the old Roman road leading down to the ford, while on the hill opposite Abbotsford may be traced the *Catrail*, so often mentioned in Sir Walter's early letters to Mr. Ellis.

In a letter to his brother-in-law Mr. Carpenter, dated 5th August, Sir Walter describes his new property, adding, "I intend building a small

[1] *Life*, vol. iii. p. 340.

cottage here for my summer abode, being obliged by law, as well as by inclination, to make this county my residence for some months every year. This is the greatest incident which has lately taken place in our domestic concerns. And I assure you we are not a little proud of being greeted as *laird* and *lady of Abbotsford*." And again, in a letter to Joanna Baillie, written the same week, the new Abbotsford is thus mentioned: "My schemes about my cottage go on; of about a hundred acres I have manfully resolved to plant from sixty to seventy; as to my scale of dwelling, why, you shall see my plan when I have adjusted it. My present intention is to have only two spare bedrooms with dressing-rooms, each of which will, on a pinch, have a couch bed; but I cannot relinquish my border principle of accommodating all the cousins and *duniwastles* who will rather sleep in chairs and on the floor, and in the hay-loft, than be absent when folks are gathered together."

Sir Walter lost no time in planning his future residence, and begged Mr. Stark[1] to give him a design for an ornamental cottage in the style of the old English vicarage house.

But before his wishes could be met, Mr. Stark died, and his building plans, checked for a time, expanded by degrees; and in place of the cottage the present Abbotsford gradually took form. Sir

[1] An Edinburgh architect of whose talents Sir Walter had a high opinion.

Walter's first plans for his house are sketched in a letter to Mr. Morritt: "I have fixed only two points," he writes, "respecting my intended cottage; one is that it shall be *in* my garden, or rather kailyard, the other that the little drawing-room shall open into a little conservatory, in which conservatory there shall be a fountain. These are articles of taste which I have long since determined upon, but I hope before a stone of my paradise is begun we shall meet and collogue upon it."

By the following year some little progress had been made, and such improvements as "a good garden wall and complete stables in the Haugh" are mentioned in a letter to Terry. In the spring of 1814 Sir Walter presses the Morritts to visit him. "I am arranging this cottage a little more conveniently," he writes, "to put off the plague and expense of building another year; and I assure you I expect to spare Mrs. Morritt and you a chamber in the wall, with a dressing-room and everything handsome about you. You will not stipulate of course for many square feet." In the autumn Sir Walter says, in a letter to Mr. Terry: "I wish you saw Abbotsford, which begins this season to look the whimsical, gay, odd cabin that we had chalked out. . . . I have made the old farmhouse my *corps de logis*, with some outlying places for kitchen, laundry, and two spare bedrooms, which run along the east wall of the farm-court not without some picturesque effect." Two years later a letter to the same friend, dated November 1816, and written from Edinburgh, reports further progress; after mentioning the arrival of Mr. Bullock and Mr. Blore, to both of whom Abbotsford was to owe much, Sir Walter continues: "I have had the assistance of both these gentlemen in arranging an addition to the cottage at Abbotsford, intended to connect the present farmhouse with the line of low buildings to the right of it. Mr. Bullock will show you the plan, which I think is very ingenious. He has promised to give it his consideration with respect to the interior; and Mr. Blore has drawn me a very handsome elevation both to the road and to the river. . . . This addition will give me first a handsome boudoir. . . . This opens into the little drawing-room, to which it serves as a chapel of ease; and on the other side to a handsome dining parlour of 27 feet by 18, with three windows to the north, and one to the south, the last to be Gothic and filled with stained glass. Besides these commodities, there is a small conservatory or greenhouse, and a study for myself which we design to fit up with ornaments from Melrose Abbey. . . . Abbotsford is looking pretty at last, and the planting is making some show."

By the July of 1817 the foundations of that

portion of Abbotsford which extends from the hall westwards to the square tower had apparently been laid, and in September Sir Walter writes to Joanna Baillie that the building is about to be roofed in, "and a comical concern it is," he adds.

The projected *tower* seems to have suggested some criticism from Mr. Terry, to which Sir Walter replies : " I agree with you that the tower will look rather rich for the rest of the building ; yet you may be assured that with diagonal chimneys and notched gables it will have a very fine effect, and is in Scotch architecture by no means incompatible." A few days later Sir Walter again writes to Mr. Terry detailing plans for the new house, of which he says : "Wilkie admires the whole as a composition, and that is high authority. . . . I do not believe I should save £100 by retaining *Mrs. Redford*[1] by the time she was raised, altered, and beautified ; for, like the Highlandman's gun, she wants stock, lock, and barrel, to put her into repair. In the meantime 'the cabin is convenient.'"

Some months later Sir Walter could congratulate himself on the strength of the new building. "I have reason to be proud," he writes, "of the finishing of my castle, for even of the tower, for which I trembled, not a stone has been

[1] The original farmhouse.

shaken by the late terrific gale which blew a roof clear off in the neighbourhood."

It was in the autumn of this year, 1818, that Mr. Lockhart first saw Abbotsford, and he confesses that it then had a fantastic appearance, being but a fragment of the existing edifice, and not at all harmonising in its outline with "Mother Redford's original tenement to the eastward." He continues, "Scott, however, expatiated *con amore* on the rapidity with which, being chiefly of darkish granite, it was assuming a 'time-honoured' aspect." Later in the same evening Mr. Lockhart tells us how the younger portion of the party, headed by Sir Walter, ascended the *tower* and viewed the Tweed and Melrose by moonlight.[1]

In the spring of 1820 Sir Walter writes to Lady Scott from London: "I have got a delightful plan for the addition at Abbotsford, which I think will make it quite complete, and furnish me with a handsome library, and you with a drawing-room and better bedroom, with good bedrooms for company, etc. It will cost me a little hard work to meet the expense, but I have been a good while idle." On his return from town, Sir Walter brought Mr. Blore's detailed plans for this, the completion of Abbotsford, including the wall and gateway of the courtyard to the south and the graceful arched and carved

[1] *Life*, vol. v. pp. 375, 376.

stone screen which divides the court from the gardens. The latter, however, had been originally devised by Sir Walter himself. "The foundations might have been set about without further delay; but he was very reluctant to authorise the demolition of the rustic porch of the old cottage, with its luxuriant overgrowth of roses and jessamines; and, in short, could not make up his mind to sign the death-warrant of this favourite bower until winter had robbed it of its beauties."[1] The building operations continued throughout the year, and in the summer of 1822 the house was, to use Sir Walter's expression, "like a cried fair," with the masons busy at work, and the numerous guests from the south, who, after engaging in the festivities of the royal visit in Edinburgh, hastened to Abbotsford.

In October Sir Walter writes to his son: "My new house is quite finished as to masonry, and we are now getting on the roof, just in time to face the bad weather." In the August of the following year Miss Edgeworth visited the almost completed Abbotsford, and her impressions are charmingly summed up in her greeting to Sir Walter, who received her at the archway to the courtyard. "Everything about you is exactly what one ought to have had wit enough to dream."

[1] *Life*, vol. vi. p. 388.

Thus by the beginning of 1825 Abbotsford was ready for the "house-warming," that joyous occasion so pleasantly described in the *Life*.[1] Who could then have foreseen that before the year was over heavy clouds of misfortune would hang over Abbotsford, and cause Sir Walter to write such words as these in his *Journal:*—18th December. "Sad hearts at Darnick and in the cottages of Abbotsford ... I have half resolved never to see the place again. How could I tread my hall with such a diminished crest? How live a poor indebted man where I was once the wealthy —the honoured?" And again, 22nd January 1826, "I have walked my last on the domains I have planted—sate the last time in the halls I have built. But death would have taken them from me if misfortune had spared them."[2]

Happily this foreboding was not fulfilled, and many tranquil days were to be spent at Abbotsford, and much happy work still to be done in the study so well known to all who visit Sir Walter's home, and of which he gives us the following description in the *Reliquiæ Trottcosienses*[3] :—

[1] See vol. viii. pp. 293, etc., 344.
[2] *Journal*, vol. i. pp.' 52, 89.
[3] "The descriptive Catalogue of the Abbotsford Museum, which he began towards the close of his life, but, alas! never finished, is entitled *Reliquiæ Trottcosienses—or the Gabions of the late Jonathan Oldbuck, Esq.*"—*Life*, vol. v. p. 143.

Sir Walter's Study

"The study is a private apartment 16 feet high, like the others, 20 feet long by about 14 broad, with a space of about 7 feet in height to the ceiling of the apartment, which affords room for a small gallery filled up with oaken shelves running round three sides of the study, and resting upon small protecting beams of oak. The gallery and its contents are accessible by a small stair, about 3 feet in breadth, which gains room to ascend in the southward angle of the chamber and runs in front of the books, leaving such a narrow passage as is sometimes found in front of the balustrades of old convents, and was certainly designed for the use of the lay brethren alone. In the south-east angle of the room a small door encloses a staircase which leads about seven paces higher, and by another private entrance reaches the bedroom story of the house, and lands in the proprietor's dressing-room. The inhabitant of the study, therefore, if unwilling to be surprised by visitors, may make his retreat unobserved by means of this gallery to the private staircase which unites his study with his bedroom,—a facility which he has sometimes found extremely convenient."

The door of the study opens upon a small hall

THE STUDY, ABBOTSFORD

communicating with the door of the entrance-hall, which is hung with armour. It was through these doors that Mr. Lockhart wheeled Sir Walter for his last visit to the study, so touchingly described in the *Life*.

These doorways are also connected with the story of Lord Byron's supposed apparition to Sir Walter, soon after his death. (August 1827.)

Those who have seen Abbotsford will remember that there is at the end of the hall, opposite to the entrance of the library, an arched doorway leading to other rooms. One night some of the party observed that, by an arrangement of light, easily to be imagined, a luminous space was formed upon the library door, in which the shadow of a person standing in the opposite archway made a very imposing appearance, the body of the hall remaining quite dark. Sir Walter had some time before told his friends of the deception of sight (mentioned in his *Demonology*), which made him for a moment imagine a figure of Lord Byron standing in the same hall. We quote Sir Walter's words—" Not long after the death of a late illustrious poet who had filled, while living, a great station in the eye of the public, a literary friend, to whom the deceased had been well known, was engaged during the darkening twilight of an autumn evening in perusing one of the publications which professed to detail the habits and opinions of the distinguished individual who was now no more. As the reader had enjoyed the intimacy of the deceased to a considerable degree, he was deeply interested in the publication, which contained some particulars relating to himself and other friends. A visitor was sitting in the apartment, who was also engaged in reading. Their sitting-room opened into an entrance-hall, rather fantastically fitted up with articles of armour, skins of wild animals, and the like. It was when laying down his book, and passing into this hall, through which the moon was beginning to shine, that the individual of whom I speak saw, right before him, and in a standing posture, the exact representation of his departed friend, whose recollection had been so strongly brought to his imagination. He stopped for a single moment, so as to notice the wonderful accuracy with which fancy had impressed upon the bodily eye the peculiarities of dress and posture of the illustrious poet. Sensible, however, of the delusion, he felt no sentiment save that of wonder at the extraordinary accuracy of the resemblance, and stepped onwards towards the figure, which resolved itself, as he approached, into the various materials of which it was composed. These were merely a screen, occupied by great-coats, shawls, plaids, and such other articles as usually are found in a country

Making of Abbotsford 17

entrance-hall. The spectator returned to the spot from which he had seen the illusion, and endeavoured with all his power to recall the image which had been so singularly vivid. But this was beyond his capacity; and the person who had witnessed the apparition, or, more properly, whose excited state had been the means of raising it, had only to return into the apartment, and tell his young friend under what a striking hallucination he had for a moment laboured."[1]

The desk so long used by Sir Walter, and "his own huge elbow chair," are familiar to us all. The former was copied from one at Rokeby, as we learn by the following passages in a letter to Mr. Morritt which bears the postmark of 23rd May 1810:—

"I have a little commission for you if you will be kind enough to accept of it. You know I fell in love with your library table, and now that the 'Lady' has put crowns into my purse I would willingly treat myself to the like. Only I think I have not much occasion for the space which holds accompt-books; in other respects it is quite a model, and in that respect I don't quarrel with it, for why should I not be a rich man some day and have accompt-books? And therefore I intrude so far on your time as to request you when

---

[1] Scott's Prose Works, *Letters on Demonology and Witchcraft.*

you are taking a walk to order me such a table as yours."

The desk cannot be better described than in Mr. Lockhart's words. They relate to it as he first saw it in the " Den " in Castle Street in 1818.

" The only table was a massive piece of furniture which he had had constructed on the model of one at Rokeby; with a desk and all its appurtenances on either side, that an amanuensis might work opposite to him when he chose ; and with small tiers of drawers, reaching all round to the floor. The top displayed a goodly array of session papers, and on the desk below were, besides the MS. at which he was working, sundry parcels of letters, proof-sheets, and so forth, all neatly done up with red tape. His own writing apparatus was a very handsome old box, richly carved, lined with crimson velvet, and containing ink-bottles, taper-stand, etc., in silver, the whole in such order that it might have come from the silversmith's window half an hour before."

And again what can be more pathetic than Mr. Lockhart's description of the opening of the desk on that sad day fourteen years later?

" But perhaps the most touching evidence of the lasting tenderness of Sir Walter's early domestic feelings was exhibited to his executors when they opened his repositories in search of his testament, the evening after his burial. On lifting up his desk, we found arranged in careful order a series of little objects which had obviously been so placed there that his eye might rest on them every morning before he began his tasks. These were the old-fashioned boxes that had garnished his mother's toilette, when he, a sickly child, slept in her dressing-room—the silver taper-stand which the young advocate had bought for her with his first five guinea fee—a row of small packets inscribed with her hand, and containing the hair of those of her offspring that had died before her —his father's snuff-box and *étui* case, and more things of the like sort, recalling

<blockquote>The old familiar faces."</blockquote>

In conclusion, it may perhaps be of interest to insert here an extract from a description of the house as it appeared during the year 1826. The account is taken from a magazine article published in 1829, written in the character of an imaginary American, supposed to visit Abbotsford during the summer of 1825, in Sir Walter's absence.[1]

After describing the changes wrought in the surroundings of Abbotsford by Sir Walter's patient plantings and judicious improvements, the writer continues: " But I am keeping you too long away from 'The Roof-tree of Monkbarns,'

---

[1] The paper on Abbotsford from which I give this extract was published in a keepsake, called the "Anniversary," and added by Mr. Lockhart to the second edition of his *Life of Scott* (in 10 vols.), vol. vii. p. 395.

which is situated on the brink of the last of a
series of irregular hills, descending from the
elevation of the Eildons to the Tweed. On all
sides, except towards the river, the house connects
itself with the gardens (according to the old
fashion now generally condemned);—so that
there is no want of air and space about the
habitation. The building is such a one, I dare-
say, as nobody but he would ever have dreamed
of erecting; or, if he had, escaped being quizzed
for his pains. Yet it is eminently imposing in its
general effect; and in most of its details, not only
full of historical interest, but beauty also. It is no
doubt a thing of shreds and patches, but they
have been combined by a masterly hand; and if
there be some whimsicalities, that in an ordinary
case might have called up a smile, who is likely
now or hereafter to contemplate such a monument
of such a man's peculiar tastes and fancies, without
feelings of a far different order? By the principal
approach you come very suddenly on the edifice;
—as the French would say, 'Vous *tombez* sur le
chateau'; but this evil, if evil it be, was unavoidable, in consequence of the vicinity of a
public road, which cuts off the *chateau* and its
plaisance from the main body of park and wood.
The gateway is a lofty arch rising out of an
embattled wall of considerable height; and the
jougs, as they are styled, those well-known emblems

of feudal authority, hang rusty at the side; this pair being relics from that great citadel of the old Douglases, Thrieve Castle in Galloway. On entering, you find yourself within an enclosure of perhaps half an acre, two sides thereof being protected by the high wall above mentioned, all along which, inside, a trellised walk extends itself— broad, cool, and dark overhead with roses and honeysuckles. The third side, to the east, shows a screen of open arches of Gothic stone-work, filled between with a net-work of iron, not visible until you come close to it, and affording therefore delightful glimpses of the gardens, which spread upwards with many architectural ornaments of turret, porch, urn, vase, etc. This elegant screen abuts on the eastern extremity of the house, which runs along the whole of the northern side (and a small part of the western) of the great enclosure. . . . The house is more than 150 feet long in front, as I paced it; was built at two different onsets; has a tall tower at either end, the one not the least like the other; presents sundry *crowfooted, alias zigzagged*, gables to the eye; a myriad of indentations and parapets, and machicolated eaves; most fantastic waterspouts; labelled windows, not a few of them painted glass; groups of right Elizabethan chimneys; balconies of diverse fashions, greater and lesser; stones carved with heraldries innumerable, let in here and there in the wall, and a very noble projecting gateway—a facsimile, I am told, of that appertaining to a certain dilapidated royal palace."[1]

The story of the building of Abbotsford now ends. A few more years and we come to the very affecting account, given by Mr. Lockhart, of Sir Walter's last return to his home. Let me conclude with his own words: "I have seen much," he kept saying, "but nothing like my ain house."[2]

[1] Linlithgow.   [2] *Life*, vol. x. p. 209.

II

BARBOUR'S LEGENDS OF THE SAINTS

THE discovery in 1871 of a hitherto unknown MS. containing a large collection of the unpublished writings of Barbour has not attracted the attention it deserves, and yet the fact is one not only of national interest, but, as we venture to think, has a very general interest. The name of the author of *The Bruce* is familiar to us all, and famous in Scotland as that of one of her earliest poets and historians, and we welcome the discovery in our own generation of another work from his pen—one calculated to sustain his fame as a man of great piety and learning, and as affording a fresh example of the purest style of the early Scottish language.

We owe the discovery of the Legends to the late Mr. Bradshaw, librarian of the University of Cambridge, and for the publication of as much of the MS. as has as yet appeared in print we are indebted to the zeal of M. Horstmann, who has brought out an edition in Germany.[1]

That the Legends should have attracted some attention abroad is gratifying, but we cannot but regret that as yet no edition has appeared in England; and while we trust that such an edition will eventually be published, we are tempted in the meantime to lay before our readers a specimen of the Legends, together with a few words regarding the author himself and the scanty historical facts known in connection with him. The Saint whose legend we have chosen to illustrate our subject also deserves some more special notice.

The exact date of Barbour's birth is uncertain, but it is conjectured to have taken place probably in or about the year 1316; and he is supposed to have been a native of Aberdeenshire. He is known to have studied both at Oxford and in France, and to have become a priest. He was raised to the dignity of Archdeacon of Aberdeen by the year 1357.[2]

---

[1] Barbour's *Des Schottischen Nationaldichten Legendensammlung*, C. Horstmann, Heilbronn, 1881. The legend of St. Machar is, however, not included in the collection of Scotch Legends, but is bound up in M. Horstmann's edition of the *Altenglische Legenden*, Heilbronn, 1881.

[2] The Cathedral of St. Machar, in Aberdeen, in which the nave now remains almost entire, was commenced in 1366. Bishop Henry Leighton (1422-40) erected the two western towers and founded the north transept. Bishop Lindsay (1441-59) paved and roofed the church, and Bishop Elphinstone built the central tower and the wooden spire.

In 1560, when the fury of the mob had wrecked this stately church, the leaden roofing, bells, and other church property were shipped for Holland by the sacrilegious robbers, but the ship laden with these ill-gotten goods sank

From the evidence of his writings, Barbour must have been a man of childlike faith and simplicity, but combined at the same time with a deep knowledge of the human heart. His poem of *The Bruce* shows him to have been a devoted patriot, animated by that zeal for Scotland's freedom which has at all times been one of the chief characteristics of his country.

It has been asserted that Barbour wrote *The Bruce* at the request of King David II. to honour the memory of his heroic father; but a comparison of dates proves this to have been impossible. The poem was evidently written in the latter years of the reign of Robert II., who likewise granted a certain pension to Barbour in token of his gratitude. Barbour's death took place in the year 1395-96, and it must have been during the last few years of his life that he wrote the legends we are considering. Of this we have his own testimony in the prologue to the Legends. The author tells us that he is debarred by his great age from continuing his priestly duties, and so to escape the dangerous vice of idleness he intends writing stories of the Saints.

> To kene us how we suld do
> Tharefore in lytil space here
> I wryt the lyf of Sanctis sere,

---

near the entrance of Aberdeen Harbour. Besides the cathedral, two parishes still bear the name of our Saint—Old, and New, Machar.

How that mene ma ensample ta
For to serwe God, as did thai.

M. Horstmann thinks it possible that the Legends were composed in the shape of familiar instructions to be read from the pulpit, but we incline to the belief that they were more probably intended as pious reading for the use of the faithful in general.

The author, as he tells us in the prologue, commences with the legends of the Twelve Apostles, giving each Saint in the order of his dignity instead of in the order of the Calendar. These are followed by legends of the immediate disciples of our Lord, and after them we find the story of the two penitents—St. Mary Magdalen and St. Mary of Egypt. These again are succeeded by the lives of four martyred Saints, whose history is followed by that of four confessors, representing the three states of life—Matrimony, Continency, and Virginity. In compiling the remainder of the legends, Barbour does not seem to have followed any definite plan, but would appear to have grouped together the stories of the Saints with regard to the interest merely of particular legends and their reference one to another, as will be seen by the following list:—

St. Margaret	St. Eugenia
St. Placid	St. Justina
St. Theodora	St. George

St. Palagia	St. Agatha
St. Thadea	St. Cæcilia
St. Baptista	St. Lucy
St. Vincent	St. Christina
St. Adrian	St. Anastasia
SS. Cosmas and Damian	St. Euphemia
St. Ninian	St. Juliana
St. Agnes	St. Thekla

St. Katherine.

The chief source from which Barbour has taken the legends appears to be from the *Legenda Auræa*, and they are as a rule free translations, interspersed, however, with the author's own reflections and comments; and he seems also to have introduced some matter from other sources now lost. Again, some of the legends claim other origin than the " Legenda Auræa "; for instance, that of St. Thadeus, which is taken from the *Vitæ Patrum* itself, the original source of the " Golden Legend." Another great exception is the legend of St. Machar of Aberdeen. This legend is taken from the *Vita Sancti Macharii*, now lost, from which life the six lessons for the Saint's feast in the Aberdeen Breviary were likewise probably derived.

As it would be impossible to consider in full the whole of these interesting legends, we have selected for illustration the story of St. Machar ; and this for several reasons. As the friend and companion of the great St. Columba, and as being with him one of the earliest apostles of the North of Scotland, the life is historically interesting, and in the absence of any other full account of the Saint, Barbour's legend is of peculiar value.

That Barbour should have given us this life, the only one of a Scottish Saint in the collection (with the exception of that of St. Ninian), shows his special desire to honour the memory and spread the fame of the patron Saint of Aberdeen, of whom he complains that even in his day too little was known, and portions of whose cathedral now alone remain to remind the inhabitants of Aberdeen of their great apostle. We have, of course, followed Barbour entirely in our short sketch of St. Machar's life and labours; but there are several points in the legend to which we would wish specially to call attention. It will be observed that Barbour distinctly states that St. Machar spent the last few years of his life at Tours, and that he died Bishop of that city. In this his account agrees with that given in the Aberdeen Breviary, where we are told that the Saint was buried at Tours—"His body the Church of Tours in reverence retains." But of this fact, unfortunately, no proof now remains. St. Machar's name does not occur in the list of the Archbishops of that diocese, either under this name or under that of Mauritius, the name given to the Saint by the Pope just before the journey to Tours, and on occasion of his consecration. Nor again can we find any historical evidence that the shrine erected, as Barbour tells us, over St. Machar's body and close to the tomb of St. Martin, existed.[1] At first sight therefore it seems difficult, if not impossible, to reconcile Barbour's statements with facts; but there is one way in which we think it is possible to prove that Barbour was not mistaken, or only partially mistaken, in his statement. We know that the Archdiocese of Tours possessed several suffragan Sees, whose Bishops were under the jurisdiction of the Archbishop of Tours. Among these Sees we find mention of Le Mans, Rennes, Vennes, and other Armorican Sees.

The inhabitants of these suffragan dioceses, being a Keltic-speaking race, would have a community of language with our Saint, and may we not conjecture that when, as Barbour describes, the clergy of Tours earnestly besought St. Columba to leave them one of his companions to preach the knowledge of God, they were seeking to give the Bretons a Bishop whose language would be almost familiar to them? And therefore it is possible to conclude that, although at present we cannot certify that St. Machar was Bishop of Tours itself, he very probably occupied one of the Sees subordinate

---

[1] The fact of the Saint being buried in "St. Martin's Chamber," and the miracles which occurred at his tomb, are likewise commemorated in the Hymn for the Saint's Office in the Aberdeen Breviary.

to that diocese. Writing, as Barbour did, seven centuries after the Saint's death, and with but scanty written records to bear out the traditions which had come down to him, such a confusion of facts would not be unlikely to occur. As regards the statement that St. Machar was buried at Tours, we think that a possible explanation may have been that, his sanctity being so well known and honoured throughout the diocese, a commemorative shrine, possibly containing some of the relics, was erected in the church of St. Martin, believed by succeeding generations to be the actual burying-place of the Saint.

The whole story of the Saint's connection with Tours and his devotion to St. Martin is especially interesting, and affords another proof of the peculiar veneration felt by our early Scotch missionaries for that great Saint. Our readers will recall the affection evinced by St. Ninian for St. Martin, and the interesting details of their mutual friendship to which the church erected in Galloway by St. Ninian long bore witness. This church, which St. Ninian caused to be built by workmen brought from Tours, was in course of erection when St. Martin died, and St. Ninian dedicated it to him, the first of many churches in Scotland which were placed under the invocation of the Saint of Tours. If we consider also the long friendship that was so happily to unite France and Scotland for many generations, it is pleasant to trace the commencements of this sympathy in those early days of our national history, and to connect it with the mutual friendships of the Saints of the two countries. In conclusion, we would suggest that the legend of St. Machar is but one of the many gems of saintly biography contained in these volumes of Barbour, which we earnestly recommend to the study of our readers.

Legend of St. Machar.

Born of a noble race, Machar was the son of Syaconus, a king or chief in Ireland, and Synchene his wife, and being baptized by St. Colman, was named "Mocumma." From his infancy God's grace shone in him brightly, and angels watched over him. The king, his father, saw one day these gracious visitants hovering over the house where the child lay, singing heavenly music, and, entering, saw them watching round the infant's cradle. Filled with joy, he praised God for the gift of such a son, and prayed that he might be kept from all evil, and grow up in God's service; and he and the queen, in token of their gratitude to Heaven, redoubled their prayers and alms-deeds.

Before long, a great sorrow came upon them; another son was born, who died without the grace of baptism, and the country was plunged into mourning; but the king, calling to mind the privileges granted to his eldest son, commanded that the body of the dead child should be taken to Mocumma and laid beside him, trusting in God's mercy that the elder brother might win grace for the younger; and his faith was rewarded, for the child was restored to life, to the joy and wonder of the whole people.

Other marvels are recorded as having occurred during Mocumma's childhood, and so he grew in strength and virtue, showing gracious promise of his future holiness.

When his boyhood was passed, Syaconus, who had a special veneration for St. Columba, besought that Mocumma might join his disciples, and, Columba consenting, the youth quickly became one of his most devoted followers, and was specially beloved by his master, whose teaching he kept ever in his heart. Making rapid progress, he soon surpassed his fellow-disciples as well in knowledge as in virtue, and he was especially remarkable for his great humility. Lest we should wonder at the perfection attained by Mocumma in so short a space of time, Barbour reminds us that Solomon became wise in a single night—" For to God as we ma se, Naething may impossible be."

Columba, perceiving how clearly God's grace shone in his pupil, spoke of him in these terms to his other disciples :—

> Zone mane that schenis as a zeme,
> I ame nocht dingne to lere, trewly
> Fore angelis of tyme sene haf I
> Repare til hyme I kene hyme al
> That he wald lere, gret and smal,
> & namely, hou he huly wryt
> Sal understand & expond It.

The others, hearing these praises of Mocumma, were filled with envy, and strove to disparage him, but Columba, knowing the jealousy of their hearts, was unmoved, and continued to cherish Mocumma singularly. Meanwhile the fame of Mocumma's virtues spread through Ireland, and crowds flocked to visit him from all parts of the country. Mocumma, desiring to escape this homage shown to him, and feeling that wish which comes to all Saints of ridding himself of earthly ties, and devoting himself more entirely to God's service and the good of souls, determined to leave his native land and go whither he should be unknown, and where his royal birth might not stand in the way of the work he contemplated. Therefore, opening his heart to his master, he declared to him his wishes. Columba rejoiced at his resolution, and confided to him his own determination to seek another land wherein to preach God's truth, but counselled Mocumma to endeavour in the first place to gain the consent of his family and friends, who might naturally be displeased at his project. Mocumma, however, replying in the touching words of Ruth, assured Columba that in the future he should consider him as his earthly father, and Holy Church as his mother, and so he should follow his master, "Fore quhare thu gays wil I ga, Til ded tak ane of ws twa."

Columba, rejoicing at the perfection to which his pupil had attained, declared to him that as in youth he had borne the name of Mocumma, the time was now come when, as he had attained to manhood in Christ, a more appropriate name should be his, and called him from that time forth Machar. Then Columba, desiring a boat to be prepared and provision to be made for the voyage, he entered it with those who were willing to accompany him, and Machar in his eagerness was the first to place himself in the boat. The voyage was prosperous, and after sailing for a time they reached in safety the shores of Hy (Iona), where one called Melumma hospitably received them. After a time Columba, seeing that the island was fair, adorned with trees, and "spryng and well is fare and clere," chose it for the place of his abode, and caused huts to be erected for himself and his monks—the lowly commencements of the world-famed monastery of Iona. Machar meanwhile was sent to preach the Gospel in the Island of Mull, hard by, and after accomplishing this mission he returned to his master and devoted himself to the study of Holy Scripture. Miraculous assistance was granted to him in his work, and his brother monks began to murmur at the favours received by their comrade, and accused him to Columba as a sorcerer, declaring that their master must choose between them and him. Columba, grieving at their hardness of heart, and at the necessity either of banishing that disciple (or, as Barbour quaintly calls him, Printyse) whom he most loved, or those whom he had cherished from their youth upwards, besought the brethren to hold their peace for a time, and, deliberating within himself, decided to send Machar from him to preach the Gospel on the mainland of Scotland. Sending for Machar, therefore, he reminded him of our Lord's words to His disciples: "Go, therefore, and teach all nations," and of the impossibility of continuing this work on the island on which they dwelt; and telling him that as his own age forbids him journeying far to spread God's seed, Machar, as younger, "Scharpare of wyt and mare mychtty," should carry the tidings of the faith to the many lying in darkness. Machar agreed willingly to his master's wishes, answering that it was good for him to do his bidding. Then giving him twelve companions to assist him, Columba made him presents of a bishop's staff, a belt, and two of his own garments, together with some books, and ordered a galley to be provisioned for the voyage. When therefore Machar was ready to pass the sea, Columba called the other brethren together, and reminding them how he had fostered them for so many years, and how earnestly he had striven to inculcate charity among them, he reproached them for their unbrotherly conduct to Machar, who had never wronged them. Touched by his words, they repented of their wickedness, and implored St. Columba to reconcile them with him whom they had injured, and Machar willingly consenting, they separated in all peace and charity. Machar, after receiving his beloved master's blessing, embarked on his perilous voyage, and after sailing for three days he and his companions disembarked on the coast of Aberdeenshire. Near where they landed they found dwelling a certain "Cristine man" named Farcare: a man of wealth and position, who, when he had discovered who they were, greeted them with great joy, and knowing by fame of Machar's holiness, besought them to enter his town (or dwelling?) and pressed them to accept all that was needful to them. Profiting by the Saint's teaching, Farcare made great progress in the spiritual life, and praised God that he was considered worthy of harbouring such a guest. Full of love for his instructor, he desired to make over to him his lands in that part, in order that they might be devoted to God's service. Machar accepted the gift, and, remembering St. Columba's prophetic words regarding the spot upon which he was to build his church, sought till he found a piece of ground on the banks of the river, round which the water flowed in the shape of a bishop's staff. Seeing this, Machar called his disciples and declared to them that he had found the place foretold him by his beloved master, announcing to them—"Lo, here myne dwelling-place for ay." Then he caused the ground to be prepared and a costly church to be erected—that church which was hereafter to be called after its saintly founder, and on the site of which there still remains entire the stately nave of the cathedral built in later years to honour the patron Saint of Aberdeen. While the church was being built the workmen suffered much from thirst, and in their distress appealed to Machar, who, always full of sympathy and pity, by his prayers caused a spring of fair water to flow. This spring still existed in Barbour's time.

This is the first miracle recorded of St. Machar in the new land of his apostleship—that country which Barbour quaintly describes as "now the name is Scotland, bot Pychtis then in it were duelland." Near by our Saint's dwelling-place there lived a holy man named Dewynik, who had served the Lord from his youth. Between him and St. Machar a loving friendship grew up; but they were not long to enjoy this mutual comfort. One day Dewynik, coming to his friend, represented to him how many were still living in spiritual darkness in other parts of the country, and proposed that, while Machar should remain to instruct the Picts, he himself should go into Caithness to preach the Gospel. Machar was grieved to lose him, but Dewynik replied that they would meet in the heavenly kingdom, and knowing that his own days were numbered, besought Machar to promise that when tidings of his death should reach him, he would cause his body to be brought back and buried in the country in which he had so long dwelt. Machar promised, and they parted, to meet no more in this life—Dewynik to go into Caithness, and Machar to continue his work among the Picts, where his apostleship was greatly blessed, many of the leading men and the greater part of the people being converted to Christianity by his means. The temples and idols were destroyed, and his mission was blessed by many miracles and graces : among others, we are told how the Saint restored a person to life, delivered another from the power of the devil, and gave sight to the blind. We select one of the last-named miracles as an example :—

> Ane vthir tyme Sanct Machor zed
> Prechand & sawand Godis Sed,
> Mene brocht a mane that was blind-borne
> & seit hyme Sanct Machor beforne

& prayt hyme ful fare that he
Thru his prayere wald gere hyme se,
& he, that reucht ay in hert had,
Tuk wattir & blissit it but bad
& there-with-all ennoyntit richt thane
Oure-corce the eyne of that blind mane
& sad till hyme "luk vpe and se"
& as he bad, richt saw did he:
& saw als clerly all-kine thinge
As he of sicht had neur merring,
And that na tyme saw befor,
Saw thane, & lowyt Sanct Machor,
Quhame thru the sieht God swa hyme gefe.

The fame of Machar's holiness spread abroad, and people came from other countries to gain his blessing. Among these are specially mentioned two young men from Ireland, who, after long search, discovered Machar's abode, and being, as Barbour says, "sume dele lettryt," anxiously desired his assistance in the study and understanding of Holy Scripture. The Saint received them with much kindness, and instructed them in Christian knowledge, and in all that concerned their soul's health; but his words fell on barren soil, and these young men took their departure, reviling the learning and admonitions of the Saint, and calling him a hypocrite. But their irreverence did not pass unpunished; sudden death overtook them, and their bodies, falling into a morass, were never recovered.

Meanwhile Machar's fellow-workman in the Lord's vineyard, St. Dewynik, was approaching the term of his labours in Caithness. On his deathbed Dewynik desired his disciples, as soon as he should be dead, to bear his body to one of Machar's churches, and remind his friend of his promise on the occasion of their sorrowful parting. When all was over, therefore, the disciples hastened to fulfil their master's bidding, and bore the sorrowful news to St. Machar. The latter was deeply grieved at the tidings, but strove to resign himself to God's holy will, and spent the night in prayer. During this vigil he was consoled by a vision of angels watching over St. Dewynik's body. Rejoicing at this testimony to his friend's beatitude, Machar, when day came, summoned his disciples to accompany him, saying they must hasten to perform the rites of burial, and sing the Office appointed for those who die in the Lord. Machar buried his saintly friend at Banchory, and the place in Barbour's own day was still known as Banchory-Dewynik. It would be pleasant to linger over this period of our Saint's life : but for a fuller account of the miracles, and for a pretty story of the visit of St. Ternan, a neighbouring Bishop, to Machar, we must refer our readers to Barbour's graphic description, and follow the Saint's life in its concluding years.

A few years before his death Machar was

consoled by a visit from his beloved master, St. Columba, and so rejoiced were the Saints to meet that they shed tears of joy. Then, as on a former occasion, St. Columba had confided to Machar his intention of leaving his native country to evangelise Scotland, he now told him that he was again bent upon a long journey, and that he purposed to make a pilgrimage to Rome. Machar implored that he might be allowed to accompany him, to which St. Columba consented, and the two Saints set forth on their way to those foreign lands from whence Machar was not destined to return.

Their journey was long and toilsome, but God watched over them singularly, and many wonders were wrought on their behalf, and so at last they came to the Eternal City, and hastened first to the churches of St. Peter and St. Paul, as is the pious practice of all pilgrims on first reaching Rome. The Pope (St. Gregory the Great), hearing of the arrival of the two venerable pilgrims, sent for them to his presence, and received them with great kindness and reverence, inquiring the object of their journey, and asking many questions about the distant land from which they came. They, in a few words, making known the cause of their journey, thus replied :—

> The cause of this trawall
> That we haf tane one hand but fale
> Is for-to wyne lestened renude,

Till our sawlis eftire our dede.
Ane uthir cause als haf we eke
Petire and Paule here for-to seke,
And mony ethir in this stede
For Godis sake that tholit dede,
& for till haf zoure benysone
& zoure gud informacione.

The Pope then calling Machar to him, told him that he should create him Bishop of the Picts, and bade him change his name. Thus he who had been called in his own country Mocumma, and in the land of his apostleship Machar, was hereafter, by the bidding of the Holy Father, to be called Morise. On a day fixed the Pope consecrated Morise, after instructing him in all the duties of the episcopal state, and then addressed him in this strain :—

Lo, bruther & in Criste sone dere
Thru wefcheyng of our handis here
The haly gast als callit the
Of bischape to the dignite
That is schofine & to the hicht,
Trawale that for all thi mycht
In Goddis wyne-zarde forto vyne
Fule folk that bundine ar with syne
The wark of wangeliste tha do,
& the office, that is the to
Committit, fulfill ilke day
& unreprofit kepe the ay.

> & gaynand & unchangeabili,
> As thu se nid is, thu chastly
> In pacience argw, and pray
> & in doctrine be besy ay.

After this ceremony the new Bishop and St. Columba received again the Pope's blessing, and then set forth on their return journey. According to Barbour's narrative, the two Saints had no settled plan of visiting Tours on their way home, but Providence would seem to have led them to that town, dear to them as containing the shrine of St. Martin. While they were approaching Tours, the Bishop of that town—to whom God made known the holiness of His servants—came forth to meet them, accompanied by his clergy, and made them welcome, entertaining them most hospitably. Not content with thus honouring the pilgrims, the Bishop urged them to remain and dwell at Tours, but St. Columba, whom nothing could tempt to abandon Scotland, could not be persuaded to comply with this request. Then the clergy implored him that he would at least leave them, in his place, one of his disciples to preach God's word to them.

Columba was disturbed at this request, and he and his companions remained silent till St. Morise spoke, and addressing St. Columba as his " fadire dere," said whatever the Saint thought needful to command he would undertake as being God's will, however hard or painful it might be. Columba, blessing his resolve, declared he should remain at Tours to work in God's cause, and comfort Holy Church for three years, and that when this was accomplished he should receive the heavenly reward, and be with himself and St. Martin fellow-saints in God's kingdom. The tender friendship which united the two Saints made the parting a hard one, and Morise affectionately reproached his master for leaving him thus alone amongst strangers; and to console him Columba promised always to be near him in spirit. Then they repaired together to the Bishop to ask his blessing before Columba should set out on his journey. After this leaving-taking was accomplished, Columba spent the night in prayer in the church of St. Martin, where it is said the great Bishop appeared to him and gave him the book of the Gospels, which had been buried with him. This book, preserved as a great treasure by Columba, was left by him at his death to his church.[1] When the night was passed, Columba left Tours, accompanied by Morise and many of the clergy and laity, who, after escorting him for

[1] It will be observed that Barbour's version of this occurrence differs from the account given by O'Donnell, who says that the people of Tours having lost the remembrance of the place of St. Martin's sepulture, begged Columba to discover it for them, which he consented to do on condition that he should be allowed to take whatever was in the hallowed tomb, except the bones of the Saint, and became in this way the possessor of the precious book.

some distance, took leave of him with much sorrow, or as Barbour has it,

> With oft blissing and regrat bath,
> For it is a full noyus thing
> Of dere friendis the departying.

The night after St. Columba's departure, the Bishop of Tours had a vision regarding the new teacher who had been given to his flock. St. Martin appeared to him, and bade him praise God for the grace done to Tours in possessing so great a servant of God as its apostle and intercessor: one whose heavenly reward would be equal to that of the patriarchs and prophets, whose example he had followed on earth, by leaving his mighty kindred and all this world's goods to undertake for God's sake this long pilgrimage. The Bishop lost no time in consulting his clergy upon this vision, and so impressed were they all with its heavenly character, that the Bishop, with the unanimous consent of his flock, gave St. Morise full jurisdiction over himself and his diocese.

The Saint's work at Tours was greatly blessed; he himself was the most beautiful example of the virtues he preached, and the clergy and people rejoiced at possessing such a pastor. Temporal blessings were likewise granted to Morise's prayers, so that during the time of his episcopacy no pestilence troubled man or beast, and the seasons were fair and fruitful. When three and a half years had passed, the time of his exile, as foretold by St. Columba, was accomplished, and his reward was at hand. Falling into a "lytill fewire," the Saint was soon in danger, and after six days, so rapid was the disease, death was at hand. He caused his grave to be made, and had himself carried to his oratory, and then desiring his disciples to come to him, he bade them a loving farewell, exhorting them to continue in the practice of all virtues and of brotherly charity; and as they weeping implored him not to leave them desolate, he assured them that he would always be near them, making intercession for their needs before the throne of God. As God had blessed his life with many supernatural blessings, so in his death these graces continued. The Bishop and religious who surrounded Morise's deathbed saw our Lord and the twelve Apostles standing by him, and St. Martin and St. Columba also present to receive the soul of their brother in Christ. Our Lord, addressing Morise, welcomed him in loving words to heaven. At these gracious words Morise rose, and throwing himself on his knees, said in a strong voice, " In manus tuas Domine, my saule I gyf," and so saying he yielded up his soul to his Maker.

The legend goes on to tell us that the people of Tours, in token of their reverence for St. Morise, laid his body by the side of St. Martin, and erected a costly shrine over the tomb ; and from the date of the Saint's death till Barbour's own day the miracles wrought by his intercession continued to show forth his glory.

III

THE LIFE OF SAINT MARGARET[1]

T has long been matter for regret that so little should be known of the life of our great Saint and Queen, and that the only authentic record of her virtues should exist in a form unavailable to the general reader. We therefore rejoice to see "St. Margaret's Life," written by her confessor, the learned and pious Turgot, Bishop of St. Andrews, in the admirable translation of Father Forbes-Leith. This little work is not only interesting from the simple and beautiful description of the Saint's daily life by one who witnessed it, and instructive from the light it throws on the state of Scotland and the Church towards the latter part of the eleventh century; it is also one of the first really authentic

---

[1] *The Life of St. Margaret, Queen of Scotland.* By Turgot, Bishop of St. Andrews. Translated from the Latin by Wm. Forbes-Leith, S.J. Edinburgh, 1884. As regards the question of the authorship of the *Life*, we refer our readers to F. Forbes-Leith's preface. We have followed his decision in ascribing it to Turgot.

Life of St. Margaret

histories we possess, and as such has been often referred to by later historians.

Turgot appears to have been a Saxon of good birth, who, during the troubles in England, was offered as a hostage to William the Conqueror, by whom he was imprisoned in the castle of Lincoln, from whence he escaped and fled to Norway. In his exile he was employed to instruct the holy king and martyr Olave in sacred literature. The example shown by his royal pupil greatly influenced Turgot, so that he also strove to withdraw his heart more and more from the world. Having on his return to his native land lost all his worldly goods, and been in great danger of losing his life, he realised still more deeply the nothingness of this world. Having resolved to devote his life to God in the cloister, he asked for admittance into the monastery of Durham, where his great piety and learning led to his being eventually chosen as prior. After Margaret Atheling had become Queen of Scotland, she prayed him to be her confessor, and he remained her constant guide and adviser until close upon the end of her life. After the Queen's death Turgot continued to devote himself to the service of her family, remaining with Matilda of Scotland after her marriage with Henry I. It is to this princess, the worthy inheritor of her mother's virtues, that we owe the *Life* in which Turgot committed to writing his recollections of the Saint. He prefaces his narrative by a letter to Matilda, in which, after saluting her with wishes for her welfare, spiritual and temporal, he thus continues:—

"You have by the request you made to me commanded me—for a request of yours is to me a command—to offer you in writing the story of the life of your mother, whose memory is held in veneration. How acceptable that life was to God you have often heard by the concordant praise of many. You remind me how in this matter my evidence is especially trustworthy, since (thanks to her great and familiar intercourse with me) you have understood that I am acquainted with the most part of her secrets. These your commands and wishes I willingly obey: nay, more, I venerate them exceedingly and I respectfully congratulate you—whom the King of the Angels has raised to the rank of Queen of England—on this, that you desire not only to hear about the life of your mother, who ever yearned after the Kingdom of the Angels, but further, to have it continually before your eyes in writing, in order that, although you were but little familiar with her face, you might at least have a perfect acquaintance with her virtues. For my part, my own wish inclines me to do what you bid, but I have, I do own, a lack of ability: as the materials forsooth for this undertaking are more than my writing or my words can avail to set forth."

He concludes by again stating the difficulty he finds in doing justice to the greatness of his subject, and assuring Matilda that, far from exaggerating the Saint's virtues, he omits many things, fearing that they might be thought incredible, and he himself accused of "decking out the crow in the swan's plumage."

Margaret, this precious pearl, as Turgot styles her, came of a kingly race, and many of her ancestors were famous as wise and valiant rulers of their people, as well as for holiness of life. Grand-daughter of Edward Ironside, she was the eldest of the three children of Edward Atheling, surnamed Outre-Mer, from the fact that the chief part of his life was passed in exile in a foreign land. In his infancy Edward had been sent by the usurper Canute to Volgar, who governed part of Sweden, in order that he might be made away with; but Volgar, more merciful, determined to save the child's life, and sent him secretly to the court of the King of Hungary, who received him with great kindness and charity, and had him brought up as if he had been one of his own children. When Edward had attained to manhood he so distinguished himself as to obtain the hand of the Princess Agatha, who, it is conjectured, was the niece of the Emperor Henry II. of Germany. Of this marriage was born a son, Edgar, and two daughters, Margaret and Christina; Margaret's birth probably took place in the year 1046, at Alba the Royal, the chief residence of the kings of Hungary.

For nine years our Saint had lived in the foreign court, which yet was a very home to her, when her father, being recalled to England by his uncle, St. Edward the Confessor, returned to his native country, accompanied by his wife and children. At the court of Edward this noble family were received with all honour and affection, and the years that followed must have been peaceful and happy. Margaret, early instructed in piety and knowledge, thus grew up in the unworldly court of her uncle, whose influence, united with that of his Queen, Editha, must have greatly strengthened the pious teaching of her own parents; and we may conclude that it was there that she learned by such noble examples how to show love and reverence to God's poor in their wants both of soul and body. From her infancy Margaret had shown that she was no common child; endowed as she was with many mental gifts, clearness of intellect, and great facility in expressing her thoughts in elegant language, her studies presented few difficulties to her, and she became one of the most accomplished princesses of her time. But her chief wish and aim was to serve God as perfectly as she was able; and so, even in her earliest years, "loving God above all things," as her biographer tells us, she spent much time in prayer and the study of Holy Scripture, and, in the midst of a court, led a very strict life. In all this she was preparing herself unconsciously for the high duties which awaited her.

And now, leaving the Saint for a while, it may be well to learn what we may of the character of the King of Scotland, her future husband. Malcolm, eldest son of Duncan, spent his childhood in retirement and obscurity, concealed by faithful friends from the vengeance of the usurper, and the murderer of his father, Macbeth. As he grew up, however, he was received at the court of St. Edward the Confessor, who showed a paternal interest in his welfare; and it was, no doubt, owing to his care that Malcolm became proficient in those knightly exercises which enabled him in after life to distinguish himself as a valiant warrior as well as a wise and able monarch. It is probable that it was during these years that Malcolm first saw his future bride, and it is not unreasonable to conjecture that he had thus already become attracted by her many graces of mind and person, before the time came when he could beg her to share his throne.

Some years had gone by since Malcolm had been restored to his father's throne, and England had passed through stormy days, when the successes of William the Conqueror forced Edgar Atheling, the last Saxon prince of the royal line, to leave the country with his mother and sisters. Taking ship, they, together with many of their followers, intended passing to Hungary, to which country many grateful ties still bound them; but Providence had other views for the royal fugitives. Meeting with adverse weather, and being unable to proceed further on their voyage, they were forced to take refuge on the shores of Scotland, where the place of their landing still bears the name of St. Margaret's Hope.

As soon as Malcolm received news of the arrival and destitute condition of his royal friends, he hastened to assure them of his sympathy and bid them welcome to his kingdom, entertaining them most honourably at his palace of Dunfermline.

We learn that the King soon became most desirous of making the Princess Margaret his wife: but at first he met with strong opposition to his suit, not only from Edgar and his nobles, but also from Margaret herself, who wished to consecrate her life to God in the cloister. However, it would appear that Edgar did not dare eventually to refuse his friend and benefactor's wishes, for, being so urged, the Saxon chronicler says, " he answered yea and durst not otherwise, for they were come into his power." And no doubt Margaret submitted herself humbly to her brother's decision, perceiving that it was the will of God that she should serve Him in the married state.

The exact date of the marriage is uncertain, but

it seems most probably to have taken place in 1068-69. The ceremony was performed at Dunfermline, where the Queen afterwards founded the stately Church of the Holy Trinity to commemorate the event; it was to be in after years the last resting place of herself, her husband, and many of their descendants.

Margaret, being now raised to the greatest earthly dignity, was not on that account moved to alter her former desires of serving God in every way possible, and set herself, to this end, to perform those duties most suited to her new state. She desired to find a wise and prudent adviser to aid her in ruling her daily life, and in Turgot she found one who worthily performed this office, as we know, for many years. The Queen's first care was to perform her duties as a loving wife and helpmate to the King, her husband, and it is beautiful to see how she used her gentle influence for his good and that of his people, to whom she was ever a very mother. She persuaded the King to be more attentive to the care of his soul; and, although his early life had not been blameless, he became from this time more earnest in prayer and good works, especially those of mercy, justice, and alms-deeds, and showed such sorrow for his sins, that Turgot says it was a marvel to see such repentance in one living in the world. The description of Malcolm's devotion to his Queen is so charming and simple that we must give it in the words of her biographer :—

"There was in him [the King] a sort of dread of offending one whose life was so venerable, for he could not but perceive from her conduct that Christ dwelt within her; nay more, he readily obeyed her wishes and prudent counsels, in all things. Whatever she refused, he refused also; whatever pleased her, he also loved for the love of her. Hence it was, that although he could not read, he would turn over and examine books which she used either for her devotions or her study, and, whenever he heard her say that she was fonder of one of them than the others, this one he too used to look at with special affection, kissing it, and often taking it into his hands. Sometimes he sent for a worker in precious metals, whom he commanded to ornament that volume with gold and gems, and when the work was finished the King himself used to carry the volume to the Queen as a kind proof of his devotion."

The Queen, being thus encouraged and aided by the support of her husband, soon effected great changes at Court, and so regulated the conduct of those who surrounded herself and the King that the palace offered the highest example to all the nation.

By her sweet and gentle manner and mild reproof, she acquired such influence that all, "Men as well as women, loved her while they feared her, and in fearing, loved her; and in her presence no one dared say or do ought that was wrong."

Skilled in the use of the needle and embroidery of all kinds, the Queen devoted some of her time to adorning vestments for the churches, and Turgot tells us that in her chamber were always to be seen such tokens of her industry. The charge of these works was confided to ladies of high birth and approved conduct.

Nor was Margaret neglectful of the outward customs and ceremonies of royal pomp so necessary to maintenance of the kingly dignity. She it was who so arranged that a nobler class of persons should attend the king whenever he went abroad, and this was carried out with so much order that none were ever suffered to injure or take anything belonging to the poor people of the country. The Queen also encouraged the nobles of the court to dress in a manner more suitable to their rank, causing merchants from other countries to introduce materials for this purpose, such as had been hitherto unknown in Scotland. Anxious that the royal table should be served with becoming splendour, she also introduced the use of dishes and cups of precious metals. But, although the Queen made these changes from the sense of what was right and suitable for her royal husband's Court, she herself was not uplifted, but remained humble in heart, despising the things of this world, and, as her biographer tells us, even while she appeared in regal state, "She, like another Esther, in her heart trod all these trappings under foot, and bade herself remember that beneath the gems of gold there was but dust and ashes." She meditated constantly on the shortness of life and on the judgments of God, and used to urge her Confessor to spare no pains to point out to her, her faults; and, as he did this less often than she wished, she would reproach him for what she termed his slackness in this respect, urging him to reprove her and to use no flattery in her regard.

Malcolm and his Queen were blessed with eight children, and the Saint so trained them that they were the worthy children of such parents. They were instructed in all virtue from their earliest years, and no pains were spared in their education; and, desiring that they should not be unduly indulged, the Queen charged the governor of the royal nursery to see that they were punished when they were naughty, "which," as remarks Turgot, "frolicksome childhood will often be." Owing to their mother's care, the royal children were loving and peaceable with each other, and in good behaviour surpassed many who were their seniors in years, and everywhere the younger paid due respect to the elder. The Saint often spoke to her children of the things of God in a manner suitable to their age, and urged them to love Him, saying, "Oh, my children, fear the Lord, for they who fear Him shall lack nothing, and if you love

Him, he will give you, my darlings, prosperity in this life and everlasting happiness." This was her dearest wish for her children, and she ceased not to pray that their lives might be acceptable to God and that they might be worthy to attain to eternal blessedness.

Not content with doing her duty to her own family, the Queen showed herself a true mother to her subjects. Persuaded that one of the surest ways of testifying love of God is shown by tender charity to His poor, she spent herself in their service. She desired that the poor should ever have access to her, and when she went abroad they were encouraged freely to approach her. There is still shown a stone on the road to Dunfermline which bears her name, and which tradition points out as being one of the spots where she used to sit and receive all who needed her compassionate assistance. The news of the great charity shown by their Queen was soon noised abroad in the whole kingdom, and crowds of distressed persons hastened to the royal palace, where they were treated with the greatest kindness.

Like another saintly princess, St. Elizabeth of Hungary, it was the Queen's joy, for the love of God, to attend in person to the wants of the sick and suffering, and in these deeds of mercy the King cheerfully joined. In Lent the royal pair redoubled their acts of charity, and Turgot tells us how each morning they washed the feet of six poor persons, and daily fed three hundred in one of the halls of the palace, waiting on them themselves. The Queen daily supported twenty-four poor people throughout the year, and spent her substance in relieving the wants of all who came near her, so that she was herself as poor as her own poor subjects, not having even the desire to possess aught. When her own means failed she was wont playfully to take money from the King's purse, which he as pleasantly permitted, sometimes pretending, when he caught her in the act, that he would have her arrested for these pious thefts. The Queen had the greatest sympathy for captives, and all those who were exiles from their native land, and it is impossible to say how many she restored to liberty; for this purpose she employed trustworthy persons to discover the most miserable among the prisoners and slaves, and having done so, hastened to ransom them. Doubtless her mother's heart yearned in a special manner to poor and helpless children, for we learn that she often had little orphans brought to her own chamber, where she would feed them herself.

The many duties of her state and these acts of charity in no way interfered with the Saint's devotion to prayer and meditation. In the midst of so much external occupation her heart was full of the thought of God, and she spent her spare time in prayer, not only by day, but by night, rising to devote hours to praise and adore her Lord in the church, and in this she was often accompanied by the King. Devoted to the study of Holy Scripture, she used earnestly to urge Turgot to procure for her copies of the sacred volumes; no less for her own benefit than for the comfort and instruction of those around her. Turgot relates a pretty story of what befell one of her books, for which she had a special affection. It was a copy of the Gospels beautifully bound and enriched with gold and precious stones. During one of the Queen's journeys, the attendant who was carrying this book let it fall into a stream, and, not knowing what had happened, proceeded on his way. When the loss was discovered, diligent search was made, and the book was found lying in the bed of the river, whence it was taken up "so perfect, so uninjured, so free from damage, that it looked as if it had not been touched by the water." When it was restored to the Queen she returned thanks to God, and valued the book more even than before.[1]

Margaret, whose tender heart was moved with such charity for the bodily wants of her people, had a still greater desire for their spiritual good. Being pained at perceiving certain grave abuses in her new country, such as the neglect of the

[1] This precious MS. is now in the possession of the Bodleian Library, Oxford.

Sunday, the practice of unlawful marriages, and divers other points in which the Church in Scotland did not conform to the universal Church, she so wrought with the King, that he, agreeing willingly to all her desires, and understanding the necessity of reform, held councils of the chief ecclesiastics and nobles of the realm for the purpose of discussing these grave questions. The Queen was present on these occasions, and full of zeal for the greater glory of God, stated what she observed; the King acting as her interpreter, having himself an equal knowledge both of the English and Scotch tongues.

The chief subjects discussed were those connected with the observance of the Lenten Fast, the Liturgy, and the non-observance of the commandment of the Church that all should receive Holy Communion at Easter. As regards the Fast of Lent, it appears to have been the custom at that time to begin the Fast from the first Monday of Lent instead of the previous Wednesday, thus reducing the time to thirty-six days instead of forty. This custom, apparently tolerated in the early ages of the Church, was abrogated towards the close, at least, of the sixth century; and the full period of forty days was generally observed in the Western Church. St. Margaret, then, showed that, as they agreed in faith, so they should unite also in discipline with the Holy See.

As regards the question of Easter Communion, our Saint persuasively pointed out how sad and deplorable a thing it was to refrain from approaching the altar at the season appointed by the Church. To the argument advanced that sinners were unworthy of such a grace, and that they feared to offend God, and, in the words of the Apostle, dreaded to eat and drink judgment to themselves, she showed how this did not apply to those who rightly prepared themselves by prayer, penance, and confession. Her words so touched her hearers that from that time they failed not to communicate devoutly at the holy season. It is difficult to say in what the "barbarous rite," alluded to by Saint Margaret's biographer, and which she strove to alter, consisted. The expression does not appear to apply, as some have thought, to the use of the vulgar tongue in the celebration of Mass. If it is the ancient Ephesian liturgy which is referred to, and which was in use in some parts of Scotland, it seems probable that the Keledei or Culdees were alone permitted to retain it after St. Margaret's efforts had caused the Church of Scotland generally to follow the Roman rite.

The endeavours of the Queen to promote the holiness and progress of the Church of Scotland in these and in all other matters were greatly blessed; so that Baronius says of her, "that having found the Church of Scotland like a wild desert, she left it at her death in so flourishing a state that it resembled a well-cultivated beautiful garden."

Having now briefly considered the life and exalted virtues of the Queen, we approach the end of her holy career; and, as suffering in this life is ever the portion of those chosen souls who strive most nearly to imitate their Divine Model, so we find that Margaret's last days on earth were overshadowed with trials and afflictions. Sorrowful days for Scotland were at hand, and Turgot says that the Queen had a foreknowledge of the evils to come, and of her own death. Some months before the end, she summoned Turgot to her, and related to him the history of her whole life, shedding as she did so floods of tears. Her compunction was so wonderful, and the tenderness of her conscience so manifest, that Turgot says he felt unworthy of being admitted to so intimate a friendship with one so holy; he thus concludes his account of this his last interview with the Saint—

"When she had ended what she had to say about matters which were pressing, she then addressed herself to me, saying: 'I now bid you farewell. I shall not continue much longer in this world, but you will live after me for a considerable time. There are two things which I beg of you. One is, that as long as you survive you will remember me in your prayers; the other is, that you will take some care about my sons and daughters. Lavish your affection upon them; teach them before all things to love and fear God; never cease instructing them. When you see any one of them exalted to the height of an earthly dignity, then, as at once his father and his master in the truest sense, go to him, warn him lest through means of a passing honour he become puffed up with pride, or offend God by avarice, or through prosperity in this world neglect the blessedness of the life which is eternal. These are the things,' said she, 'which I ask you—as in the sight of God Who now is present along with us two—to promise me that you will carefully perform.' At these words I once more burst into tears and promised her that I would carefully perform her wishes; for I did not dare to oppose one whom I heard thus unhesitatingly predict what was to come to pass. And the truth of her prediction is verified by present facts; since I survive her death, and I see her offspring elevated to dignity and honour. Thus, having ended the conference, and being about to return home, I bade the Queen my last farewell; for after that day I never saw her face in the flesh."

This parting with her valued friend and adviser must have been a trial to the Queen, but a far sadder one was before her. Malcolm had now reigned for thirty-five years, and the country had been prosperous under his wise and beneficent rule; and as the even course of a peaceful reign leaves little scope for the historian, so we find but few facts of the domestic history of this period, save that the King gradually incorporated the different provinces, of which the kingdom had hitherto been composed, into one monarchy, and at his death left Scotland in possession of the same southern frontier ever after retained. With regard to Malcolm's dealings with England, it would be foreign to our purpose to enter into the details of the various causes which led him to invade that country on five different occasions. The English chronicler speaks with bitterness of the savage way in which the Scottish King and his troops devastated the Border country, and of the many captives carried back to Scotland. We have seen how Malcolm's gentle Queen endeavoured to mitigate their hard lot. The immediate cause which led to Malcolm's final and fatal breach with England appears to have been a refusal on the part of William Rufus to fulfil the conditions of a treaty with the Scottish King, and the insult offered to the latter by requiring him to do homage as vassal to the English crown. In consequence of this affront, Malcolm once more prepared to invade the English border, and although the Queen, as if foreseeing the fatal issue of events, strove to dissuade him from accompanying the troops in person, he on this occasion remained deaf to her entreaties, and they parted to meet no more in this world.

Margaret had been for some months in failing

health, and, indeed, was seldom able to leave her bed. The account of her last days was preserved and given to Turgot by a priest who remained with her to the end, and to whom for his simplicity and holiness of life the Queen was much attached. He relates that one day, some time after this painful separation from her husband, and three days before her own death, the Queen became sadder than usual, and, turning to him, uttered these words: "Perhaps on this very day such a heavy calamity may befall the realm of Scotland as has not been for many ages past." Words only too surely realised, for on that day Malcolm and his son and apparent heir Edward were slain. Although accounts differ as to the place and manner of the Scottish King's death, all agree that there was treachery on the part of the English. The Scottish army perished partly by the sword and partly by the inundations of the rivers, swollen by the heavy rains of winter, and as none of his faithful followers were left to do honour to their lord's remains, Malcolm's body was placed in a cart by the English, and buried at Tynemouth. Meanwhile the holy Queen was drawing near her end; united as they had been in life, so were they in death; but three days were to elapse from the day of Malcolm's death before his Queen should follow him. He was slain on November the thirteenth; and on the sixteenth, Margaret's weakness having slightly decreased, she was enabled to rise and assist at Mass in her oratory, strengthening herself for her passage by receiving Holy Communion. Then, returning to her bed, her former pains attacked her with renewed force. The disease increased, and death was at hand. The Queen desired that the chaplains should remain near her reciting psalms; and, sending for the Black Cross, for which, as it contained a portion of the True Cross, she had a special devotion, she, despite her excessive weakness, attempted to kiss it, and, signing herself with it, continued steadfast in prayer. A short time had elapsed, and the Queen had apparently become unconscious, when her second son, Prince Edgar, entered the room, the bearer of heavy tidings. Coming to announce the news of the death of his father and brother, what must have been his grief to find his beloved mother on her death-bed! Rousing herself at her son's entrance, the Queen inquired for the King and Prince Edward. Edgar, loth to tell her the truth, and fearing to hasten her death, answered that they were well, but she, replying, said with a deep sigh, "I know it, my boy, I know it. By this holy cross, I adjure you to tell me the truth." Thus urged, Edgar related all, and concealed nothing from her, and Margaret, making her last great sacrifice, accepted the trial in all patience and resignation. Raising her eyes to heaven, she exclaimed, "I give praise and thanks to Thee, Almighty God, for that Thou hast been pleased that I should endure such deep sorrow at my departing, and I trust that by means of this suffering it is Thy pleasure that I should be cleansed from some of the stains of my sins!" Then, as death visibly approached, Margaret began to recite one of the prayers used by the priest during Mass: "Lord Jesus Christ, Who, according to the will of the Father, through the co-operation of the Holy Ghost, hast by Thy death given life to the world, deliver me." As she repeated these words, "deliver me," her soul passed to the judgment seat of her God, whom she had striven to love and serve above all things. After her death a great beauty was observed upon her countenance, all traces of suffering having passed away, and she appeared rather as one who calmly slept than as a dead person.

The Chronicle of Mailros, one of the most authentic records we possess, states that the Queen's blessed death took place in Edinburgh Castle. From thence her body was removed to the church erected by her at Dunfermline, and interred, as she had herself desired, opposite the altar. Later, the bodies of Malcolm and their son Edward were brought from Tynemouth and placed beside her.

Turgot's memoir ends here, and while we regret that he should not have entered more fully into many details which would have been of great interest, yet we have, in his vivid and truthful pages, as charming and edifying a picture of the life of a great and holy Queen as perhaps exists anywhere; and no doubt this little volume will be read with interest as revealing the inner life of one with whose name we are so familiar; a name graven as it were on the history of our country, and even yet borne by many of the spots connected with her memory.

It may be interesting, before concluding, to cast a glance upon the history of Margaret's children, and to see how her teaching bore fruit in their lives. Five of her sons survived her, but Ethelred died shortly, and Edmund, the only one who appears to have been—and this for a short time only—unworthy of his family, died a penitent in an English cloister. The other three, Edgar, Alexander, and David, succeeded each other on their father's throne. Of the two princesses, their sisters, Matilda, the eldest, became the Queen of Henry the First of England, thus uniting the royal Saxon line to that of the Norman dynasty. Her sister Mary was married to Eustace, Count of Boulogne. Of her little is known, save that she was "a princess of singular piety towards God, and charity towards her neighbour." Her only child, Matilda, became the wife of King Stephen of England.

Of Matilda (Queen of Henry the First) much more is known, and those who study her life cannot fail to be struck with the resemblance she bears to her mother, especially in those practical acts of mercy to the poor for which she was famous. A story is told which well illustrates this. One day her brother David, whilst visiting the English court, saw his sister employed in washing the feet of poor lepers, and kissing them: he asked her how the King, her husband, could bear to touch her lips after she had put them to such usage, to which she replied with a smile, "that she preferred the feet of the Eternal King to the lips of any mortal prince."

It would not be within the scope of the present article to enter fully into the history of the reigns of Margaret's sons, rather let us, following the same course in which we have endeavoured to treat of their mother's life, state briefly the special personal characteristics of each. Of Edgar, who, after some years, succeeded his father on the throne, Ailred tells us that he greatly resembled his kinsman, Edward the Confessor; his nature was sweet and amiable, and, incapable of harshness or tyranny towards his subjects, he ruled them with the utmost gentleness. Of Alexander, who succeeded his brother on the throne, Ailred gives a different account. Although kind and humble to the clergy, "he was to the rest of his subjects beyond everything terrible, a man of large heart, exerting himself in all things beyond his strength"; a man of learning, zealous in erecting churches, enriching them with the relics of saints, and in supplying them with sacred books; generous to strangers, and so full of love to the poor that he seemed to like nothing so much as feeding and clothing them, and attending to their wants in person. Alexander dying like Edgar, childless, the youngest brother, David, ascended the throne. He was in all respects the most distinguished of the royal brothers, and perhaps the one who bore most resemblance to his mother. Like her, he showed a special love to his poor and suffering subjects, and on certain days he, like the kings of old, "sat at the gate" giving audience to the poor and aged, and would defer a hunting expedition without a murmur to attend to some poor suppliant. In compliance with the policy pursued by Malcolm and Margaret, he encouraged foreign merchants to frequent the Scottish ports, at the same time preserving to native traders the advantages possessed by them during Malcolm's reign. Many noble buildings owed their foundation to David's pious zeal, among them notably Melrose, Jedburgh, and Kelso. We may gather that he had a special love for the beautiful Abbey of Holyrood, erected by him to enshrine the "Black Rood," for which his mother had so great a veneration; and on his death-bed his last wish was to be carried to pray before this representation of his crucified Saviour.

While her descendants continued worthily to fill their parents' throne, the love felt for the memory of their holy mother by her adopted country had grown in strength and reverence; and all felt that in losing her visible presence they had gained an advocate in heaven. Miracles were wrought at her tomb, and throughout Britain she was considered to be a saint. In the year 1250, during the reign of the Saint's great-grandson, Alexander, the public recognition of her sanctity was formally sanctioned by Pope Innocent IV. Her body was removed from the grave where it had hitherto lain, in the Church of the Holy Trinity, Dunfermline, and enclosed in a silver shrine richly adorned with jewels, which was placed under the high altar in the same church. The young King, together with his mother, Queen Jane, and many bishops and nobles, was present at this ceremony, which was performed with great solemnity and splendour.

The Feast of St. Margaret was originally kept upon November the 16th, the day of her death, but in the seventeenth century it was transferred to the 10th of June, at the request of James II., probably from the fact of that day being the birthday of his son, the Prince of Wales. At the same time, our Saint was declared Patroness of Scotland, together with St. Andrew. Her shrine continued to be the object of the greatest veneration until the time of the Reformation, when it was plundered and desecrated; the relics were, however, preserved. The head was brought at Queen Mary's desire to Edinburgh Castle where she then was, probably when, exposed to many dangers, she took refuge there to await the birth of her son. After Mary's flight to England the Saint's head was removed to the house of the Laird of Drury, where it was for some years preserved by a Benedictine Monk. Confided by him to the missionary Jesuits, it was by one of them, John Robie, taken to Belgium, and after due authentication was publicly exposed for veneration, first at Antwerp, from whence it was removed to the Scots College at Douay; there it remained till the days of the French Revolution, when it disappeared amid the general spoliation of the churches. George Carruthers, the historian, saw this relic at Douay in 1785, and describes it as being in a state of extraordinary preservation, and with a quantity of fine hair, fair in colour, still upon it. It was enclosed in a bust of solid silver, larger than life; the crown, and chain about it, richly adorned with pearls and other jewels. With regard to the other remains of the Saint and her husband, they are stated to have been sent to Spain at the earnest request of Philip the Second, and placed by him in the Escurial. Some years ago Bishop Gillies, in the hope of restoring St. Margaret's relics to a Scottish shrine, applied for this purpose to the Spanish Government, but they could not then be identified. It is, however, possible to hope that these relics still exist, and that the day may come when they will be brought back to the land which still glories in the memory of its illustrious Queen.

IV

ST. MAGNUS OF THE ORKNEYS

"PRAISE, glory, and reverent honour be unto God Almighty, our Maker and Redeemer, for His manifold goodness and mercy, which He hath granted unto us, who dwell in the uttermost parts of earth, and as the learned have written that it seemeth unto them, as though we were gone out of the world. But though it be so, it hath pleased God to show forth His goodness upon us in this thing most excellently, that He hath suffered us to come unto the knowledge of His Blessed Name and hath given unto us thereafter those who were strong pillars, the holy standard-bearers of His Church, with whose sanctity the whole North, both afar off and near at hand, is lighted up and shineth. These are holy King Olaf, and his august kinsman Halward, who adorn Norway with their sacred relics; Magnus, the illustrious Earl of the Isles, who enlighteneth the Orkneys with his holy power, and to whose honour this history here following hath been written; with whom are numbered the blessed Bishops, John and Thorlac, who have illuminated Iceland with the glory of their famous and worthy acts. Whence it is manifest that albeit our dwelling in this world be set far apart from other nations, we are not far from the Mercy of God; and unto them we owe thanks, honour, and reverence all the days of our lives."

Such is the commencement of the Greater of the two Sagas which record the life of the martyred Earl of the Orkneys. His name is still a familiar one in his native land, and the magnificent pile raised in veneration of his memory strikes and impresses the eye of every traveller who approaches Kirkwall. The Cathedral of St. Magnus is indeed one of the architectural glories of Scotland, and possesses a special and mournful interest as being one of the two Cathedral Churches which alone remain entire in their original grace and beauty; but, by too many, little is known of the Saint in whose honour this glorious fabric was raised by his loyal and grateful people.

Until lately, the history of the Martyr was little known save to the readers of Torfæus—not as numerous a body as even that author, especially in the absence of better authorities, might well have found. The Greater Magnus Saga—an Icelandic text which is in great part a translation of the life written in Latin by Master Robert twenty years after the martyrdom, on the occasion of the enshrinement of the relics, was again translated into Latin and published at Copenhagen in 1780, and was republished in London by Pinkerton in his *Vitæ Sanctorum Scotiæ* in 1789. The public has since been indebted to Messrs. Hjaltalin and Goudie for their learned and interesting translation of the Orkneyinga Saga, edited by Dr. Joseph Anderson in 1875; and another most valuable addition has now been made to English literature by the publication, in 1894, of Sir George Dasent's new translation of the same Saga, and also of both the Greater and Lesser Magnus Sagas, with Appendices, containing, among other things, a collection of the liturgical monuments connected with the martyred Earl. It is to the personal courtesy of the late eminent scholar last mentioned that the present writer was indebted, in 1886,—when this paper was published,—for the use of the materials upon which the following pages are mainly founded.

In order to follow the story of St. Magnus and to gain more knowledge of the country he ruled, we must first glance briefly at some of the chief events in the history of the Northern Islands. Up to the middle of the sixth century, but very little is known of them. Classical writers, it is true, mention their existence, but their allusions only serve to show that hardly anything else was known about them. Julius Solinus, in the first century of the Christian Era, remarks that they are uninhabited. It is supposed that the wave of Celtic population which swept over the North of Scotland gradually extended to them, and this theory is corroborated by the similarity of weapons and other remains found in the Orkneys and Shetlands to those discovered on the mainland of Scotland. If the language of the poet Claudian is to be taken seriously, there was also a Saxon occupation of them, at least temporarily, in the middle of the fourth century, but Nennius records that a hundred years later they were harried by the Teutonic pirates Octa and Ebissa.

Although it appears probable that the Northern Archipelago was evangelised at a very early date by Irish missionaries, we have no record of this fact, and it is in Adamnan's Life of St. Columba that we first find distinct mention of the Orkneys, and of the mission of Cormac and his fellow-monks to these islands. They were at that time subject to the suzerainty of the King of the Picts, from whom Columba besought protection for the missionaries. From this date up to the time of the Norse conquest in 872, it seems certain that a great portion at least of the inhabitants embraced the Christian faith. The evidences of this are fourfold—1. The dedication of the early ecclesiastical foundations; 2. The discovery of monumental stones, sculptured in the style peculiar to the earliest Christian monuments of the North of Scotland, and inscribed with the Ogham character; 3. The bells found in the Islands, of the square form belonging to the early ages of the Church; 4. The names that occur in the local topography, and which bear witness to a previous Celtic Christian settlement—for example, in Rinansey (St. Ninian's Isle), Daminsey (St. Adamnan's Isle), in the Orkneys; St. Ninian's Island in the Shetlands; and in the constant recurrence of the name *Papa* in different places. That the memory of St. Columba was fresh in the hearts of the people may be inferred from the fact that in the parish of South Ronaldsey alone—the spot where probably his monks first landed—there were three chapels dedicated to the Saint. From the scanty records that have survived, we gather that the Islands remained under the alternate sway of the Pictish and Dalriadic kings from the time at least of St. Columba until the Norse invasion. In 872, with Harald Harfagri and his Northmen, a flood of heathenism swept over them, and for more than a hundred years Christianity was banished from their shores. At length, about the year 994, Earl Sigurd—fourth in succession to that Sigurd on whom Harald bestowed the Earldom of the Islands—was converted by Olaf Tryggvisson, King of Norway, and his people with him. Although it would appear from the history of this event that their conversion was at first due to policy rather than to conviction, yet after some years the faith was firmly re-established.

The first church known to have been built in the Orkneys after the Norse conquest is Christ Church, Birsay, hereafter to be mentioned as the first burial-place of St. Magnus. This church, of which some existing foundations are possibly the remains, was erected by the Saint's grandfather, Earl Thorfinn, one of the most famous of the Earls in the Norse line. He reigned, according to the Saga, for "seventy winters," and about the year 1050 made a pilgrimage to the Holy Land. It is supposed that the church was built after his return from Palestine. Earl Thorfinn died in 1064, and was succeeded by his sons Paul and Erlend as joint rulers of the earldom. Earl Paul and his wife Ingibiörg had but one son, Hakon, while Erlend and his wife Thora were the parents of four children, St. Magnus, Erling, and two daughters. Paul and Erlend ruled peaceably for many years, and were brotherly and well agreed in the joint exercise of their power, until their sons grew up. Then troubles began. Hakon and Erling were turbulent, overbearing youths; and Hakon, in especial, showed early signs of the havoc his proud selfish nature was to cause in after days. In right of his mother's royal descent, he considered himself superior to his cousins in rank, and strove to rule over them.[1] In consequence, dissensions arose not only between the cousins, but also among the people, as Erlend's many friends could not bear to see his children despised. At length Paul and Erlend interfered to settle matters between the disputants, and a meeting was held in order that peace might be made, but it soon appeared that, as was natural, each Earl supported his own son's interests, and they could not agree, but parted in anger. The Earls, however, soon made friends, and things went well for a time. Then fresh troubles arose, till at last Hakon was persuaded to leave the islands, and in his absence peace was restored to the land.

As some of Hakon's doings during his wanderings resulted in events of deep importance to his cousin, we must follow him to Norway before considering the early days of the Saint. Hakon "first fared east to Norway" to visit his kinsman, King Olaf the Great. He did not remain here long, but proceeded to Sweden, where he was well received by King Ingi, and made welcome by his maternal grandfather, Hakon, and his other kinsmen. Christianity was still young in Sweden, and although King Ingi was earnestly endeavouring to

---

[1] Earl Paul's wife was a grand-daughter of King Magnus, the son of St. Olaf.

root out every vestige of heathenism, the people clung to some of their ancient superstitions, and Hakon, who appears also to have had some little leaning to the practices of his forefathers, determined to seek the assistance of a certain spaeman of the country, to learn what the future had in store for him. The account of the interview is curious. After ascertaining Hakon's name and kindred, the wizard suggested that it might be better for him to ask the assistance of his kinsman, King Olaf, instead of coming to one in whom his relations no longer believed. Hakon answered by owning plainly that he was not worthy to receive help from Olaf, adding, that in the point of merit, he did not think there was much to choose between himself and the wizard. "It hath come into my mind," said he, "that here neither of us twain will need to look down upon the other for the sake of matters of virtue or belief." The wizard then bade him return in three nights' time to receive his answer. In the second interview the sorcerer stated his belief that Hakon would become sole ruler over the Orkneys, though the time might seem long in coming, and that his children also would probably rule there; he added that Hakon would "let that wickedness be done for which he must either make atonement, or not, to the God in whom he believed," and concluded by saying that his querent would take a journey farther out into the world than he could get to see, but would probably return to die in the North. After this Hakon remained a short time longer with King Ingi, and then returned to Norway. During his absence Olaf had died, and had been succeeded on the throne by Magnus Barelegs. At his Court Hakon heard news from the Orkneys, to the effect that Earl Erlend and his sons were now the chief rulers in the islands, and greatly beloved of the people, so that Earl Paul had little authority. Hakon thought also that he perceived that his own presence was not greatly desired by his countrymen, and he feared that if he returned, his kinsmen would hold the earldom against him. He therefore determined to seek help from King Magnus, hoping, according to the warlike ideas of his age, that if he could persuade Magnus to conquer the islands for the glory of the thing, he would place him in power. So he took opportunities of saying before the King what a fine thing it would be for a prince to call out his forces and take possession of the islands as Harald Harfagri had done, hinting that once in possession of the Southern Islands, it would be easy to make harrying expeditions into Scotland and Ireland, and from thence to try the power of the Northmen against the English. As often happens, ambition brought its own punishment — King Magnus heartily agreed to the proposed expedition, but by no means intended to gratify his kinsman's wishes, of which no doubt he had his own suspicions. He spoke out plainly, bidding Hakon understand that if he conquered the Western Islands he should probably keep them for himself. At his words Hakon "grew cold, and said little more about it," but the deed was done.

Before relating the results of this expedition, so disastrous to St. Magnus's family, it is needful to turn to the few details we possess of the Saint's childhood and youth. It would be difficult to fix the exact date of Magnus's birth, but, judging from after events, we may conjecture that it took place probably about the year 1075. From his earliest childhood he was remarkable, and showed promise of his future sanctity. He was, as his biographer tells us, "old in good behaviour, shareless of childish life in his deeds, gladspoken and blythe, gentle in his loving words, and yielding and reasonable in his conduct and in all his doings." Docility and obedience seem to have been his ruling characteristics as a child, for the Saga dwells on the obedience and attention he paid to his parents and masters. He was sent to school at an early age, to receive religious instruction, and to learn the secular knowledge considered necessary for a lad of his time and rank. As he grew up, he continued also to advance in virtue, "in sweetness of temper and soberness of life," so as to be a cause of edification to all about him. But this youth, who was destined to be so brave a soldier of Christ, was allowed, like many other saints, to pass through a time of sin and humiliation between his innocent childhood and the steadfast virtue of his manhood. When Magnus was "about full grown of age" he for a time suffered from the influence of bad companions, and for some winters joined in their life of robbery and plunder, and, to use the words of the Saga, "stood by at manslaughters along with others." It is supposed that this most probably occurred at the period when Magnus and his brother and cousin were all together in the Orkneys before Hakon's voyage to Norway, and the narrative which now commences certainly shows us that, by the time of the Norwegian invasion, Magnus had turned aside from all unlawful pursuits, and had begun again to tread the narrow path from which he never afterwards strayed. The words of the Greater Saga concerning his conversion are an ascription which is everlastingly true. "This is the change of Thy right hand, O Thou Most High. Thou art strong to strengthen, gracious to help, ready to better, mighty to save."

In pursuance of the design above mentioned, King Magnus Barelegs presently came from the

St. Magnus of the Orkneys

east out of Norway with a great multitude of ships and force of warriors. When he came to the Orkneys he seems to have effected his purpose without difficulty, for we have no record of any battle, but simply of the fact that "he seized the Earls Erlend and Paul, and forced them away from the isles, and sent them east to Norway; but he set his son Sigurd over the Orkneys, and gave him councillors, for he was not older than nine winters. King Magnus settled that the sons of the earls should fare with and attend him: Magnus and Erling, the sons of Erlend, and Hakon, Paul's son. Magnus, the son of Earl Erlend, was a tall man of growth, quick and gallant, and strong of body, fair to look on, light hued, and well limbed, noble in aspect, and the most courteous in all his behaviour; him King Magnus made his waiting-swain, and he always served at the King's board." The King made the three cousins, Hakon, Magnus, and Erling, thus accompany him on his southward voyage.

On his way south, the Norwegian monarch devastated the islands of Harris, Lewis, Uist, and Skye. He also landed at Iona, and, as it would appear, with no friendly intentions, but the Holy Island was saved from his plunder. One of the Sagas tells how, going to the little chapel of Columcille (St. Oran's), he opened the door and was about to enter, when he suddenly stopped, either struck by remorse or by some supernatural wavering, then closing the door, he forbade any one to enter, and gave the inhabitants peace.

After his expedition to the islands, the King proceeded south to the Welsh coast and fought a great battle in Anglesea Sound against the Earls of Chester and Shrewsbury, the latter of whom was killed, probably by an arrow shot by Magnus Barelegs himself. This battle is chiefly interesting to us from the following incident. Whilst the King's men were arming themselves for action, the young Magnus took his seat on the fore-deck as was his custom, but did not arm himself. The King inquired wherefore he did not prepare for battle like the others, to which the Saint replied that he had no quarrel with any man there, and therefore would not fight. Then the King bade him go below out of men's way if he was afraid to fight; but Magnus remained where he was, and taking a psalter, sang out of it while the battle raged, seeking no shelter from the storm of shafts and arrows that fell around him, and although many close to him were killed or wounded, he received no hurt.

The King did not enter into the high motives which influenced his young kinsman's conduct on this occasion, and from that day took a dislike to him. This was so evident, that after a time, Magnus, seeing that "it would neither be for his honour nor his soul's sake" to remain longer with the King, took counsel with himself, praying that God would direct him. Having determined to escape, he left the ship one night and swam to shore. The fleet had now returned to the coast of Scotland, and there he lay hid for some time in the woods, to elude the search made after him, but ultimately made his way in safety to the Court of the King of Scots.

We know very little about the period of Magnus's exile. All we can gather is, that his time was spent partly at the Scottish Court, and partly in visits to a certain Bishop in Wales, whose name is not recorded. The monarch of Scotland at this time was Edgar, the fourth son of Malcolm Canmore and St. Margaret, who had only recently been placed upon the throne with the assistance of William Rufus, who became his brother-in-law in the November of the year 1100. The character of Edgar is thus described by St. Ailred of Rievaux: "He was a sweet-tempered, amiable man, in all things resembling Edward the Confessor; mild in his administration, equitable and beneficent." It is not an improbable conjecture that these features may have endeared him to the Martyr, and, in the absence of greater certitude as to dates, it is possible that Magnus may have remained with him until his death, 8th January 1106, when he was succeeded by his brother Alexander I., a man of a very different temperament. It is certainly to this period that the writers of the Northern histories ascribe the most remarkable advance made by Magnus in the spiritual life.

In the meanwhile, great political and personal changes were passing in the world to which the Orkneys belonged. The Earls Paul and Erlend both died in exile in Norway, and in the spring of 1099 King Magnus Barelegs gave Gunnhilda, daughter of Erlend and sister of Magnus, in marriage to Kol Kalisson, with a considerable dowry. In the year 1102 the Norwegian King was killed in battle in Ulster, and it is supposed that the Saint's brother Erling fell at the same time. When the young Prince Sigurd received news of his father's death, he left the Orkneys to take possession of his paternal throne conjointly with his brothers Eystein and Olaf. The opportunity sought for by Hakon seemed now at hand. He accordingly visited the Norwegian Court, and obtained from Sigurd the title of Earl and such authority in the Islands "as his birth might claim." This expression shows that the King did not intend to deprive Magnus of his share of the earldom; but Hakon thought little of his cousin's rights, and, sailing for the Orkneys, took possession of the whole realm, slaying the steward of the King of Norway who had charge of the half of the Islands which by inheritance belonged to Magnus. The latter made his way into Caithness, where the people received him with joy, and chose him to be their ruler, giving him the honoured title of Earl. When the Saint heard of his cousin's conduct, he took counsel with his friends and agreed with them to wait for a time, until Hakon's anger and greed had cooled, before taking any steps to obtain his rights, desiring only to seek his inheritance in the spirit of right and justice. When, however, the time arrived that it seemed prudent for him to return home, he went to the Orkneys attended by a goodly company from Caithness, and was well received by his friends and kinsmen. Then he asked to take his inheritance in the Islands, and this pleased the people, who bore him much affection, but Hakon prepared to fight, rather than give up the realm. However, by the aid of mutual friends, it was agreed that if the King of Norway approved Magnus's claim, Hakon should give up half the country to his cousin. Magnus therefore went over to Norway, and the King made him welcome, and willingly granted his petition. After this decision, Hakon was contented to share the rule with Magnus, and for some years peace was restored to the Islands.

These years form—from an earthly point of view—one of the most prosperous periods of the

Martyr's life : a resting place, as it were, between the trials of his youth and the later conflicts which awaited him. What he was as a Prince and a ruler of men, is written in the Orkneyinga Saga :—" The holy Magnus, Earl of the Islands, was a most excellent man. He was of large stature, a man of noble presence and intellectual countenance. He was of blameless life, victorious in battles, wise, eloquent, strong-minded, liberal and magnanimous, sagacious in counsels, and more beloved than any other man. To wise men and good he was gentle and affable in his conversation; but severe and unsparing with robbers and vikings. Many of those who plundered the landowners and the inhabitants of the land he caused to be put to death. He also seized murderers and thieves, and punished rich and poor impartially for robberies and thefts and all crimes. He was just in his judgments, and had more respect to divine justice than difference in the estates of men. He gave large presents to chiefs and rich men, yet the greatest share of his liberality was given to the poor. In all things he strictly obeyed the divine commands ; and he chastened his body in many things, which in his glorious life were known to God, but hidden from men." [1]

Very different in character from his holy cousin, Hakon cared little to punish evil among his

[1] Orkneyinga Saga, xxxiv.

followers, and, greedy both of money and power, he rather urged them to warfare than restrained them. Hakon was filled with envy at the popularity of his cousin, and when, after these years of peace, wicked counsellors, especially two named Sigurd and Sighvat, endeavoured to sow discord between the Earls, Hakon lent a willing ear to their suggestions, and began to plan with them to overthrow Magnus's power, and even to plot against his life.

At this point the Greater Magnus Saga makes a circumstantial and detailed statement, which is supported neither by the Orkneyinga nor the Lesser Magnus Sagas. It is to the effect that when Magnus became aware of the designs against him and saw that his cousin desired his ruin, he determined to absent himself from the Islands, thinking it best for a while to give place unto wrath. He chose therefore some of his most trusty men to accompany him, and travelled to the court of Henry of England. Here he made known his history to the King, who welcomed him, and soon grew to love and revere his saintly guest, and took advice with him in affairs of State, listening willingly to his advice. Magnus was loved and honoured by all at the English Court, so attractive was his cheerful kindliness of demeanour and the marked holiness of his life. He and his followers remained as Henry's guests for a year, but the atmosphere of the Court was uncongenial to Magnus's pure soul, and "may be," says the writer, "that God had revealed to him that he should close his toils within a short time, and so offer to God the pure flower of his chastity by the triumphant death of his martyrdom. For to be set free from the body, and live with Christ, is far more glorious than to be held in the defilement of this world." After taking an affectionate farewell of Henry, Magnus visited the holy shrines in the neighbourhood, and then turned his steps homeward. In his absence Hakon had once more usurped his cousin's place, and had taken forcible possession, not only of the Islands, but also of Caithness. He was established at the latter place when news reached him that Magnus had returned to the Orkneys and sought to win back his possessions. His cousin's return aroused all Hakon's worst feelings, and he planned to come unexpectedly upon Magnus and slay him; but the day when, through the apparent triumph of evil, Magnus was to win his crown, had not yet come. According to his biographer, God still saw some "rust of worldly behaviour" in His chosen servant, and left him a little longer in his exile, till earthly trial and temptation should have purified him entirely and fitted him to enter into his reward. It came about, therefore, that peace was once more made between the cousins, and for some time longer

Magnus ruled his people and redoubled his efforts in the service of God; but Hakon, under the cover of friendship, let the bitterness of anger and envy take root in his heart, so that when the moment of temptation came he fell an easy prey to the suggestions of his own evil heart and to the counsels of others no less wicked than himself.

Among Hakon's followers, two have already been named as taking the lead in striving to make mischief between the Earls, and these men, Sigurd and Sighvat, with their companions, by their wicked reports, brought about so great a misunderstanding that Hakon and Magnus called out their followers, and met each other in warlike guise at Hrossey. This meeting took place in Lent of the year 1116, and ended without bloodshed, as the well-disposed friends of the Earls interposed to make peace.

It was arranged that Hakon and Magnus should have a final meeting on the Island of Egilsha after Easter. Each Earl was to come with only two ships and the same number of men on each side, and they bound themselves by oath to keep the agreements their friends should make for them at the Easter meeting. After this was determined upon, the cousins and their men returned home. Magnus, well pleased with these preliminaries of concord between them, being himself "thoroughly whole hearted and of good conscience, without all mistrust," but Hakon, who had made the agreement with treachery in his heart, did not intend to fulfil the conditions, and was even now plotting his cousin's destruction. On Easter Monday, which fell that year on 15th April, the Earls and their followers set forth for the place of meeting. Magnus had summoned to his aid the men he knew to be most friendly both to Hakon and himself, and embarked his company in two long ships. The weather was fine and the sea calm, but as they rowed towards Egilsha, on a sudden a large wave rose close to the ship in which the Saint was, and broke over the place where he sat. All who were there marvelled greatly that such a wave should fall on them when the sea was smooth and the water deep, but Magnus said, "It is not strange though ye wonder at this, but my thought is, that this is a foreboding of my life's end; may be that may happen here which has before been spaed, that Earl Paul's son would work the greatest wickedness, may be that Hakon is plotting treachery against us at this meeting." The Saint's comrades were greatly alarmed at his words, and implored him to beware of Hakon, and not to expose his life by continuing his voyage; but Magnus replied that he must certainly proceed to the place of meeting as agreed, and not have to reproach himself with having broken his word for a mere foreboding of evil; and then, expressing his desire that God's will might be done in their voyage, he added that if he had a choice, he would rather suffer wrong himself, than do evil to another, concluding with these words, "So may God let my kinsman Hakon get forgiveness, though he may do wrong to me." While the Saint and his followers were making their way to Egilsha in this wise, Hakon was making his preparations for the coming interview in very different dispositions. He summoned a numerous band of warriors to accompany him, and filled seven or eight large war-ships with his followers. The Earl did not conceal his intention that this meeting should so settle matters between himself and his cousin that in future one of them alone should enjoy supreme power over the realm. Many of his men, and in especial Sigurd and Sighvat, were all pleased at Hakon's words, but there was one man on board, the son of Havard Gunni, and an intimate friend of both Earls, who, when he heard of Hakon's evil intentions, leapt overboard, and swam to a little island where no man dwelt, for he was determined to take no part in any treachery against Earl Magnus.

Magnus and his company were the first to reach Egilsha, but as they approached the island, they could see Hakon's ships in the distance, and the

Martyr then perceived that his cousin indeed intended to break the conditions and make him the victim of his treachery. The Saint's followers also, fearing that in very truth their master's foreboding was about to be realised, offered to fight Earl Hakon's men, but Magnus would not let them imperil their lives for him, repeating that if peace could not be made between himself and Hakon, he would be willing to suffer himself rather than to do injury to others.

On landing at Egilsha, Magnus's first act was to seek the church, and there he spent a large part of the night in earnest prayer, committing his case to Almighty God, and begging for light and grace to do His will. The church which thus witnessed the last earthly hours of the Saint, and in which he received the Holy Communion upon the following morning in immediate preparation for the conflict of martyrdom, appears to be almost certainly that which is still standing, although in a roofless and mutilated condition. Professor Münch is indeed of opinion that it dates from the earliest days of Christianity in Orkney.[1] If so, it is not improbable that the island may have been selected for the meeting of the Earls on account of its sacredness, as containing one of the earliest memorials left in Orkney of the preaching of

[1] The learned Professor also inclines to the opinion that the very name of *Egilsba* is a mere corruption of *ecclesia*.

the Gospel of peace on earth as well as of glory to God in the highest. And this consideration, along with the fact of its being committed almost in the very light of the Resurrection morning, adds a peculiar circumstance of horror to the crime about to be perpetrated.

The church of Egilsha affords one of the only three instances in Scotland of a round tower after the Irish manner, the others being Brechin and Abernethy. This tower has been partially pulled down, but was then at least sixty feet high. At the top were four windows facing the cardinal points, and it was roofed with a conical stone roof; its external diameter at the bottom is about fourteen feet. The towers of Brechin and Abernethy are, at least at present, isolated, but that of Egilsha is built into the west end of the church, with which it seems to be contemporary. This church, which is known to have formerly been roofed with stone shingles, consists of a nave and chancel, the former almost thirty and the latter nearly sixteen feet in length.[1] The construction of the chancel, which has a stone vault, above which has been an attic entered from a door over the chancel-arch, suggests the probability that the nave had a flat wooden ceiling.

On the following morning,[2] being Easter

[1] See Dr. Anderson's *Scotland in Early Christian Times*, pp. 34-37.
[2] The authors of the Sagas tell us, that for the account of the Saint's

Tuesday, Earl Magnus, as already mentioned, caused Mass to be sung, and at it received the Holy Communion. What must have been the feelings of the Saint on this occasion it would seem like an impertinence, were it not an impossibility, to conjecture. As the earthly warfare was now drawing to such a close, the Martyr must have listened with an emotion altogether indescribable to the words of the risen Saviour read by the Church in the Gospel for that day :[1] " Peace be unto you ; it is I, be not afraid."

The Mass was hardly ended when four of the followers of Hakon arrived at the Church. The authorities differ as to whether they found the Saint still there. The Greater Magnus Saga states that they entered with great tumult and violence, seized him, and carried him bound before their master. This account is accepted in the Aberdeen Breviary. On the other hand, the Lesser Saga and Orkneyinga Saga agree with the living local tradition of Egilsha, that the Martyr had left the church, seemingly in an attempt to conceal himself, accompanied by only two companions, one of whom was Holdbodi. It is said that he was engaged in prayer, but that as the search for him

last day and his conversations with Hakon, we are indebted to the report of one of Magnus's followers, a trusty and truthful man called Holdbodi, who was with the Earl to the end.

[1] So in the Arbuthnott Missal, and the same seems to have been the immemorial custom of all the Latin Churches using a Petrine Liturgy.

proceeded (probably when discovery had become inevitable), he came forward and surrendered himself. All are agreed as to his demeanour at this moment. In contrast to the fury of his captors the Saint was calm and cheerful, "as glad and merry when they laid hands on him, as if he were bidden to a banquet, and with such steadfast heart and soul that he neither spoke to his adversaries with any bitterness, wrath, or broken voice."

When they reached Hakon's presence, Magnus was the first to speak, and addressed his cousin in these words—"Thou doest not well, kinsman, that thou holdest not thine oaths, and it is much to be looked for that thou hast done this more by the ill-will of others, and their egging on, than by thine own badness. Now, I will offer thee three choices, that thou may'st take one of them, rather than that thou should'st spoil thine oaths and let me be slain, thy kinsman, and guiltless, as some will say." Hakon agreed to hear his cousin's proposals. Then Magnus suggested three ways in which he himself should be sacrificed and Hakon gain supreme power, the object of his ambition. First, he offered to make a pilgrimage to Rome or to the Holy Land, to make atonement both for himself and Hakon, taking with him two ships manned by trusty followers, and containing necessary provisions, and promising never to return to the Orkneys. This proposal was immediately rejected by Hakon and his men. Then the Saint said, that knowing his life and the lives of his companions were in their power, and considering that he had been guilty in many things against Almighty God, and must make reparation to Him, he would propose that he should be sent to their mutual friends in Scotland, and kept there in ward, with two of his own men to bear him company, and never return to the Orkneys unless Hakon gave him leave to do so. The Saint's enemies found many objections to this second proposal, and refused to act upon it. Magnus then offered them one more alternative, hoping to save his cousin from the guilt of bloodshed, and here we will use his own words, "Now is that one (choice) alone left, which I will offer thee, and God knows that about this, I look rather to the salvation of thy soul than to the life of my body, for after all it beseems thee less to quench my life. Let me be maimed in my limbs, or let my eyes be plucked out, and set me in a dark dungeon, from which I may never come out." To this, surely one of the most heroic proposals ever made by one man to another, Hakon replied that he was well satisfied, and desired nothing further, but his men declared that they would not agree to torture Earl Magnus, but that they would either kill him, or their own lord, Hakon, so that from that day one only of them should rule the earldom. When Hakon heard these words, he said that, for his part, he would rather rule the country than die so quickly; and Magnus knew that his hour was come. He betook himself therefore to prayer, covering his face with his hands, and offering his whole self and his life to God.

A scene now ensued between Hakon and his standard-bearer, whom he commanded to play the part of executioner. The man, whose name was Ofeig, indignantly refused. The Earl then forced Lifolf, his cook, to do the bloody work. The poor wretch began to cry. But the Saint said:— " Thou shalt not weep, for there is fame for thee in doing such deeds. Be thou of steadfast heart, for thou shalt have my clothes, as is the wont and law of the men of old. Thou shalt not be afraid, for thou doest this by force, and he that forces thee to do it hath greater sin than thou." So speaking, he took off his kirtle and gave it to him; after which he asked and obtained a few minutes for prayer. These he spent lying upon his face upon the ground. He prayed earnestly for the pardon of his murderers, as well as for the forgiveness of his own sins, and finally commended his spirit into the hands of his Maker, whose angels he invoked to meet it. He then rose from his knees and faced Lifolf with the words, "Stand thou before me, and hew me on the head a great wound, for it beseems not to behead chiefs like thieves. Strengthen thee, O man, and weep not, for I have prayed God that He will pardon thee." So speaking, he made the sign of the Cross, and bowed himself to the stroke. Lifolf gave him a heavy stroke upon the head with the axe. Then Hakon bade him strike again, and Lifolf hewed another blow in the same place. The Saint thereupon fell forward, first upon his knees, and then upon his face, dead.

Hakon, whether from hatred of his cousin's memory, or from shame at his own evil deed, would not allow Magnus's body to be buried in a Christian manner, but apparently caused it to be hidden in the ground on the spot of his martyrdom. It did not long remain there, however, as the Saint's mother, Thora, of whom we hear too little in the Saga, so dealt with Hakon that he granted her leave to remove her son's remains. It had been settled that after the peace-meeting at Egilsha, the two Earls should go together to a feast at Thora's house on the island of Paplay, and, strange as it may appear, Hakon proceeded thither with his followers as if nothing had occurred. Thora, seeing, no doubt, that she was powerless to prevent this ill-timed visit, and hoping to win the favour of Christian burial for her son, put aside her own feelings and welcomed her guilty nephew. During the feast, and when the wine had taken some hold on Hakon, Thora approached him, and beseeching him so to deal with her petition as he would have Almighty God to deal with him at the day of judgment, implored him to give her leave to bury Magnus in church. Hakon seems to have been touched at the moment with sorrow at what he had done, and shedding tears, bade Thora bury her son where she wished. Thora chose Christ's Church, Birsay, as the place of her son's sepulture. Soon after the holy body was laid there, it was told that a heavenly light was often seen to shine over the tomb, and a sweet fragrance perceived by those who approached it. Those who invoked the Saint obtained their request, and the sick who visited his grave were cured of their ailments; but as long as Hakon lived, the people feared to spread these wonders abroad.

Hakon, meanwhile, for some time showed no symptoms of repentance for his sin, but took possession of the whole earldom, and made those who had been Magnus's followers swear fealty to him, laying heavy burdens on those who had been most devoted to his cousin's interests. It is said that the men who had taken the most prominent part in treachery against St. Magnus met with sudden and terrible death, and possibly Hakon took warning by their fate, for after some years had elapsed, he made a pilgrimage to Rome and to the Holy Land, in atonement for his sin; and that his repentance was sincere, we may gather from the fact that he returned to the Islands a changed man, and for the remainder of his life appears to have ruled his people well and peaceably. When Hakon died, he was succeeded by his son Paul, and during his reign the glory of St. Magnus was fully manifested and his sanctity recognised. William, called the Old, who was then ruling as first Bishop of Orkney, invited all the chief inhabitants of his See to meet him in Christ Church. A large multitude joyfully obeyed the summons, and in their presence the remains of the Saint were removed from the lowly grave in which they had lain for twenty years, and placed in a shrine over the altar. This took place on 13th December, St. Lucy's Day, and the Bishop appointed that this day and also the anniversary of the Saint's martyrdom, 16th April, should both henceforth be kept holy throughout the diocese. From Birsay the shrine was shortly afterwards removed to Kirkwall, and placed over the altar in the church there. This church must have been that dedicated to St. Olaf, said to have been built by Earl Rögnvald Brusison, in honour of his sainted foster-father.[1] It appears to have been the only

[1] The fact that the Saint's body was placed in St. Olaf's Church derives additional interest when we consider that the names of these Saints seem to have been specially united by the devotion of the people. In the account of one of St. Magnus's miracles, we find St. Olaf invoked conjointly with

church then existing in Kirkwall, and it seems probable that the town owes its name to the sacred building, Kirkwall being derived from Kirkiu-vagr or Creek-of-the-Kirk. Kirkwall was but a poor hamlet at this time, but the fame of the Saint's shrine attracted people to the place, and the town rapidly increased.

Less than forty years had passed from the date of St. Magnus's martyrdom, when the first stones were laid of the church erected in his honour. The founder of this glorious pile was Earl Saint Rögnvald II., his nephew and ultimate successor. In his endeavour to secure that half of the earldom to which he considered himself the lawful heir, Rögnvald met with much opposition. In one of his seasons of greatest difficulty, his father Kol recommended him to make a vow to his kinsman St. Magnus, promising that if he should obtain his rights he would build a stone church in his honour at Kirkwall, "more magnificent than any in these lands," and endow it, so that it should be fitly established, and the Saint's relics removed to it, and likewise that the Bishop's See should be removed thither from Birsay. Rögnvald's prayer was granted, and when he came to power he generously fulfilled his vow. It is said that Kol

him, and one of the reasons tending to prove that the ancient Church of St. Magnus the Martyr in London was dedicated to our Saint Magnus is the fact that in close neighbourhood to it is the Church of St. Olaf.

himself designed and superintended the building, and that after his death Bishop William continued the work till his own decease. After this time we have no record of the progress of the building till the sixteenth century, when it is said that Bishop Edward Stuart (who succeeded in 1511) added the pillars and pointed arches of the east end, and Bishop Robert Reid, who came to the See in 1540, has the reputation of having completed the western extremity of the nave, with its porch and windows.

This traditional history, however, is rendered extremely unsatisfactory by a contemplation of the actual building. To enter here into a disquisition on these points, or even an architectural description, is of course impossible. It may be said that if Kol was indeed the designer, his abilities were very remarkable; and even if the plan was not his own, he deserves almost equal credit for his judgment in the selection of an architect. The whole building, as it at present stands, is only 217 feet long, by 47 broad (89 in the transepts), and 71 from the floor to the vaulting; the nave between the pillars is only 16 feet broad. And yet, "the first thing," says the late Dr. Neale, "which strikes the visitor, on entering the Cathedral, is its enormous size. I do not think that either York or Lincoln gave me the idea of greater internal length"—an effect which must have been very much greater when not obstructed, as at present, but enhanced by the successive vistas of the rood-loft, the altar-screen, and the shrine.[1] The earliest portion of the building seems to be the west part of the chancel, which, with an apse, must have had an internal length of about 50 feet, but the apse has been destroyed and the church prolonged in the Gothic style. Similarly, the five easternmost bays of the nave, giving an internal length of about 80 feet, may be of the time of Bishop William. But here, again, the church has been prolonged. It may therefore be conjectured that the Cathedral, as originally designed, would have consisted of a nave and chancel, ceiled with a flat wooden roof, intersected by transepts and a lantern surmounted by a square tower, and ending in an apse covered by a semi-dome, the whole being about 130 feet long internally. The front of the altar was probably designed to coincide with the chord of the apse, and the shrine to stand upon pillars behind it. After the prolongation of the church, it would appear as if the site of the altar (perhaps already consecrated) had not been changed, but that the shrine was moved somewhat eastward, so as to stand under the centre of a very remarkable piece

[1] According to a section given by Sir Henry Dryden, the effect is enhanced by a sham perspective in the choir, caused by the vaulting sinking a little eastward—a rather base trick, of which the Cathedral of Poitiers probably offers the main example.

of oblong vaulting which here forms the ceiling. The relative positions must therefore have been very similar to those of the altar, and the shrine of the Confessor, with an aisle round behind, in Westminster Abbey.

Unfortunately no details have come to us of the consecration of the Cathedral, or of the solemn translation of the Saint's remains to their stately shrine. It seems probable that this took place previous to Rögnvald's visit to the Holy Land in the year 1152, and Bishop William, as we know, assisted at the ceremony. The Episcopal See was removed to Kirkwall also during his lifetime.

Both the Magnus Sagas contain a long and detailed list of miracles believed to have been wrought, up to the time of their compilation, upon those who commended themselves to the prayers of the martyr. The usual method seems to have been, if possible, to make a pilgrimage to Kirkwall, and to remain all night at the shrine. Sometimes we hear of the beautiful and beneficent figure,[1] clad in glistening raiment, appearing to

---

[1] Such is the unvarying description of the appearance of St. Magnus which attests the constant tradition of his noble and winning comeliness. One of the latest, however, is subsequent to the probable date of the composition of either of the Sagas, and is that belonging to the dream said by the Norwegians to have been dreamt by Alexander II., just before his death, in 1149. "King Alexander, then lying in Kiararey (Kerrara) Sound, dreamed a dream, and thought three men came to him. He thought one of them was in royal robes, very stern, ruddy in countenance, somewhat thick, and of middling size. Another seemed of a slender make, and of all

the sick as in a dream and laying its hands upon them, and thereupon they awoke healed.

The Bishops of Orkney of course continued to belong to the Scandinavian hierarchy, as long as the islands remained under the dominion of Norway. When, on the marriage of James III. with the Princess of Norway, in 1468, the Orkneys and Shetlands came into the possession of the Scottish crown, the bishopric became one of the suffragan Sees of the Archbishopric of St. Andrews. For a short hundred years from this time Scotland continued to honour her Saints, and the glory of St. Magnus remained unchanged, but when the storm of the Reformation swept over the land, St. Magnus' shrine was destroyed, like so many others; and though the church itself was spared and still bears witness to the faith of the early Orcadians, the story of its origin has fallen into the background, and among his fellow-countrymen the Saint's memory has grown dim.

men the most engaging and majestic. The third, again, was of very great stature, but his features were distorted, and of all the rest he was the most unsightly. They addressed their speech to the King, and inquired whether he meant to invade the Hebrides. Alexander thought he answered that he certainly proposed to subject the islands. The genius of the vision bade him go back; and told him no other measure would turn out to his advantage. The King related his dream, and many advised him to return. But the King would not; and a little after he was seized with a disorder, and died. The Scottish army then broke up; and they removed the King's body to Scotland. The Hebrideans say that the men whom the King saw in his sleep were St. Olave, King of Norway, St. Magnus, Earl of Orkney, and St. Columba."—*Norwegian Account of Haco's Expedition against Scotland in* 1263.

Nature, however,—more faithful than man,—still seems to testify to the glory of St. Magnus, upon the ground watered by his blood. "That spot on which Saint Magnus was smitten," says the Saga, "was stony and mossy; but a little after his worthiness towards God was revealed, so that since there is there a green field, fair and smooth; and God showed by this token that Earl Magnus was slain for righteousness' sake, and that he had gotten the fairness and greenness of Paradise in the land of the living." Mr. J. W. Cursiter, F.S.A. Scot., visited Egilsha on 7th December 1886, and writes from Kirkwall, on the same day, the following description of the spot :—" It is slightly above the surrounding ground, the rock almost at the surface, which is closely covered with green moss, short natural grass, and very short young heather. . . . The spot, and for at least six yards all round, has never been cultivated, and shows certainly green among the surrounding shorn fields. In addition to the murder, the only story attaching to it which survives is—" That one will *always* find an *open flower* growing there" —and to-day, after ten days of occasional snow and strong gales, we found there several daisies, *fresh*, but not so numerous as to be striking in describing the herbage of the spot."[1]

[1] Mr. Cursiter's letter, for which the writer of these lines desires here publicly to acknowledge deep obligation and to offer the most grateful

St. Magnus of the Orkneys

Certainly to few memories seems more applicable the exquisite passage from the Book of thanks, is so extremely interesting and valuable, that it seems well to give here the following additional extracts from it :—

"We had a bitterly cold day in a large open boat . . . and found that there are at present two spots pointed out as the site where St. Magnus was beheaded. We were accompanied to both places by one of the oldest and most intelligent natives of the island, David Robertson, tenant of South Tofts, over eighty years of age.

"The spot of which I sent you the bearings, as given me by Mr. ——— some time ago, we have no hesitation in characterising as the fictitious one, and was never associated with the tradition until about twenty years ago, and that was fixed by ———, we believe, on insufficient evidence, . . . without consulting the natives, but by his interpretation of the accounts which he had read.

"The only spot previously pointed out, and believed in by the inhabitants, is a good way farther from the church, very similar in appearance, and in somewhat similar direction from the church, and in our opinion the correct one. I shall try to describe it.

"[It is slightly above the surrounding ground, the rock almost at the surface, which is closely covered with green moss, short natural grass, and very short young heather.] It is not so much a 'knoll' as the termination of a short ridge which slopes more abruptly on the east and south sides ; along the crest of this ridge a shallow zig-zag cut was made long ago, to convey water to a mill on the south end of the island ; which mill was demolished or disused some few years ago. The tradition states that St. Magnus from the church saw Hakon's ships off Vaady on the S.W. of the island, tried to make for Howan, S.E., and when thus far on the way saw Hakon's men come over a slight rising-ground at Warsett (to the S.W.), and in the hope of being unobserved lay down on the east side of the termination of this ridge, which is the only place near at hand where hiding might have been obtained (I consider an elevation of two or three feet might thus be interposed between them and him), but he was perceived, set upon and killed there.

"It is situate about 350 yards S.S.E. $\frac{1}{4}$ S. of the church, and 250 yards W. by S. of the farm-house of Feally Ha'. The wart on the top of Knitchenfield (a hill) in Rousay lies W. $\frac{1}{2}$ N.—and the top of Kierfea (another hill in Rousay) N.W. $\frac{1}{4}$ N. These bearings taken to-day exactly *by compass.* . . .

"From inquiries to-day we were able to fix 1792 as the year in which the top of the round tower was removed, and were informed that the top

Wisdom (iv. 7-15), assigned during the Middle
Ages to be read on the anniversary of his death—

But if the righteous be cut off early by death, he shall
    be at rest.
For honour standeth not in length of days,
Neither is it computed by number of years.
The understanding of a man is his eldership,
And the spotless life is venerable.
He pleased God, and was beloved,
And he was taken away from living among sinners.
His place was changed, lest evil should mar his under-
    standing,
Or falsehood beguile his soul.
For the bewitching of folly darkeneth goodness,
And wandering desire leadeth astray the guileless under-
    standing.
He was made perfect in a little while,
And finished the work of many years.
For his soul pleased God,
And therefore He made haste to lead him forth out of
    the midst of iniquity.

---

of it was of quite a different sandstone from that of which its wall is built, and the stones taken away to be used as whetstones for the old shearing-hooks of that period.

"The schoolmaster told me that his inquiries led him to think, with regard to the *two* spots, that St. Magnus was killed at the southerly one, and buried for some time near the northerly one. . . ."

Mr. Cursiter, in a later communication, says that all sources of information which he has been able to consult are unanimous in supporting the authority of Mr. David Robertson as to the local tradition, and the correctness of the opinions transcribed above. Mr. Cursiter is indeed inclined to doubt whether it may not be by a mere mistake that Mr. ——— is locally credited with having advocated the substitution of the new spot north of the school for that which has always been recognised as the true one by the natives of the island.

St. Magnus of the Orkneys 115

And the people saw it and understood it not ;
Neither considered this,
That the grace of God and His mercy are upon His saints,
And His regard is unto His elect.

In his own day, and for long afterwards, the blessed example of this servant of God shed its brightness over all that part of the world to which his native islands belong. It is not for the sake of the merely antiquarian interest attaching to a sermon which was esteemed in the Orkneys more than seven centuries ago, but as a monument of the feeling which the martyr evoked among his own contemporaries, that these pages are closed by extracting, in its entirety, from the Greater Magnus Saga, a discourse delivered upon St. Magnus's Day by the same Master Robert who compiled his earliest biography on the occasion of the enshrinement of his relics twenty years after his victorious death.[1]

This day, dearest brethren, is the day of the death of the blessed Earl Magnus the Martyr, the day of his rest, and of his eternal gladness. Let us rejoice and be glad upon this illustrious day. He, beside whose holy remains, and under whose care and guardianship we dwell, and for

---

[1] We have not extracted this sermon from Sir George Dasent's translation, but have made it from the Latin version in Pinkerton, as we think that Sir George, from want of familiarity with the Vulgate, has failed to recognise several of the Scriptural quotations or allusions.

whose sake we hope, doth invite us unto solemn kindliness and especial thanksgiving; for it was on account of the nobleness of the example and the holiness of the life of this glorious martyr that the seemly ordinances of his own bright kindliness and holy laws first flourished in the coasts of the kingdom of the Orkneys, and brought forth manifold fruit in good living. He it was who cast down the throne which Lucifer had exalted for himself in the sides of the North, and who raised up instead thereof the tabernacle of the God Almighty. He it was who by his exhortation utterly plucked up the tares, and caused green things to spring up unto a sweet harvest of life-giving fruit. He it was who turned the bitter leaven of the Orkneys into the praise and sweetness of holy living. And upon this day he overcame this world and the prince of this world, and went up above this world a radiant conqueror, gifted with a crown of glory from the hand of his and our Holy Lord Jesus Christ. Upon this day he was set free from the bondage of fleshly corruption, he was received up into the heavens, and entered into the joy of [his Lord], being in all things made like unto the saints. Upon this day he laid aside the earthly garments of this changeful life, and went up higher than man's weakness may reckon. Upon him, therefore, is bestowed greatness in heaven, honour and blessedness in the presence of all the saints. So did the blessed Earl Magnus, this illustrious witness for God, go up bright with worthiness, rich with the fulness of happiness, triumphant in glorious victory, adorned with a crown of his own blood. . . .[1] It remaineth, my dearly beloved, that

---

[1] A few words are here omitted in which the existing texts give the date wrongly, doubtless through a mistake of copyists.

we lay aside fleshly lusts, that we beware of loving things unlawful, that we vanquish and overcome the assaults of sin. Let us with all the strength of our mind follow after the footsteps and life of this glorious martyr. As far as our weakness will allow, let us walk in the way of his life, let us keep firm hold upon the example of his doings, let us try to make our lives like his life, albeit it appeareth and is made manifest day by day, by those great and wondrous works and famous marvels which God Almighty doth grant unto the North, both by land and by sea, for the sake of his excellent prayers and praiseworthy works, that his life and holy righteousness are things more meet for us to honour and wonder at than to compare with our own weakness. He hath appeared on earth to guard us and to ask for us healing and grace from God Almighty. We, therefore, who are pressed down under the heavy load of our own sins, ought constantly to honour him for his excellent leaning to due obedience and thanksgiving, so that it may please this illustrious martyr, Earl Magnus, to beseech for us, for the sake of his worthy deeds and prayers, that we also may come to be made partakers of the eternal glory whereon he entered upon the day of his suffering, through the gift of the Lord Jesus Christ, who is Himself the glory and the salvation, the help and the health, the joy and the honour of all His own holy and righteous servants, and who liveth and reigneth with the Father and the Holy Ghost, One God in Three Persons, world without end. Amen.

V

THE SCOTS GUARDS IN FRANCE

"*IN omni modo fidelis.*" "Ever faithful." Such is the device emblazoned on the standards of the famous companies whose history is contained in the volumes before us. A proud motto truly, but one fully justified by the deeds of those who bore it.

Few things can be more interesting than to trace through three hundred years the career of those brave men—many of them, perhaps, bearing our own names—who, leaving their country, devoted themselves with unswerving fidelity to the service of a foreign king united to their nation by ancient alliance.

We are indebted to Father Forbes-Leith for these most interesting volumes,[1] in which he has spared no pains to enable us to follow the history of the Scots Guards, from the first detachments

[1] *Scots Men-at-Arms and Life Guards in France.* By William Forbes-Leith, S.J. Two vols. Edinburgh.

sent to France at the request of Charles VII., till the moment when this faithful bodyguard of the French kings disappeared with the Monarchy itself, swept away by the torrent of the French Revolution.

We propose to give a slight sketch of this curious and valuable book, making free use, with this object, of the author's own words. But we feel how inadequately any such attempt can represent the stores of research and learning contained in these volumes. We must refer the reader also to the original work itself, to gain a just idea of the various etchings, beautiful in themselves, and historically interesting, which illustrate its pages.

To understand the reason that led so many of our countrymen to devote their services to a foreign land, we must revert to the ancient alliance between France and Scotland. Some historians trace this back as far as to the days of Charlemagne; but, however gratifying this may be to our national pride, and though, no doubt, there are records of friendship between the two countries from early days, there seems no reason to suppose that any permanent alliance existed before the time of the Wars of Independence in Scotland, and the contemporary claims of the English kings to the French crown. In these two historical facts we may look for the source of that sympathy which drew the two countries together. But this alliance, springing from a common hatred of England, does not come prominently into notice, as regards our present purpose, until the year 1418, when France, in her hour of greatest danger, appealed to Scotland for help.

It would be impossible to imagine a more complete scene of anarchy than that presented by France under Charles VI. To the confusion arising from the disasters of Poitiers and Agincourt must be added the distracted state of the government. The nobles, headed by the queen and court, taking advantage of the mental infirmities of Charles himself, indulged in every species of unbridled luxury; whilst the wretched peasantry, meanwhile, were ground down by cruel and unjust taxes. The whole country was in a state of utter lawlessness; the population seemed frenzied; so that, to quote the words of the *Chroniques de Saint Denys*, "treading under foot the fear of God and man, they swept over the land with the fury of a tempest; their only thought was of plunder, fire, and bloodshed."

Such was the condition of France when Henry V. of England landed in Normandy, on 1st August 1417, and, meeting with no opposition, marched inland, taking every town on his road. With all speed Charles the Dauphin now tried to raise an army. This was no easy matter; for, though there were marshals and constables of France, there were but few troops to command.

It was in this great strait that Charles turned for assistance to Scotland.

Reduced to the lowest ebb by his own rebellious subjects, Charles sent ambassadors to all the princes in alliance with France to ask for aid, and particularly to Scotland, trusting that from the ancient alliance with that country he might the more readily expect effective assistance. Towards the end of 1418, Charles the Dauphin sent ambassadors to the Scottish court craving the aid of Scotland against King Henry.

A Parliament was assembled; and it was decided by Robert Stewart, Duke of Albany and Regent of Scotland, to send into France a large force under the command of his second son, Sir John Stewart, Earl of Buchan, Archibald Douglas, Earl of Wigtown, and Sir John Stewart of Darneley, who appear to have been selected by the Dauphin himself. The transport vessels were to be furnished by France. The King of Castile, with the Infant of Aragon, allies of the Scots, had promised to fit out forty ships. On the 22nd of July 1419 Henry V. received information of these preparations from the town authorities of Bayonne; and on the 12th of August the Duke of Bedford received orders to intercept the Scots. But the order arrived too late; for, by the 17th of May, Sir William Douglas had already landed in France with 150 men-at-arms and 300 archers. By the 26th of August we find him stationed with his troops at Puiset in Beauce. He had under his command Sir Thomas Kilpatrick, William Fresal, John Tod, Thomas Cunyngham, John Ofur, David Fleming, John of Meldrum, Andry of Meldrum, Alexander de Alexandry, and William Flocart. Each of these captains commanded a body of men-at-arms and archers. Thomas Seton and his brother, each at the head of a company, were conspicuous amongst the most faithful followers of the Dauphin. Thomas received at the hands of Charles the estate of Langeais, and was appointed to accompany him wherever he went. The Earl of Buchan embarked later with a body of troops numbering 6000 men. The Spanish fleet landed this army at La Rochelle, in September 1419.

These troops were thoroughly trained soldiers, who had been hardened in long and bloody wars for national freedom. All were accoutred in the order of Scottish armour and arms, which, by the laws of that period, were plate-mail from head to heel for every man possessed of land yielding an annual rent of £20, with battle-axe, two-handed sword, and iron mace, or spear. Persons of inferior rank, worth only £10 of yearly rent, or £50 in goods, had to provide themselves with helmet and gorget, vambrace, rerebrace, corslet, and greaves.

This invasion, Father Forbes remarks, was truly a great achievement. In those days it was no easy matter for some 6000 or 7000 troops to pass from Scotland to France in carracks and row-galleys, which for sea-worthiness were little better than rafts, and which ran great risk of capture by English cruisers. These difficulties were much increased by the fact that La Rochelle was the only port at which they could attempt to land. Buchan reached France shortly after the murder of the Duke of Burgundy. The Dauphin was unjustly suspected of being accessory to his death. Popular feeling had risen against him; and Henry of England was, in consequence, acknowledged in many cities as heir to the crown.

Our space will not allow us to follow the whole course of the struggle between Charles and Henry, interesting though it would be to trace each step of the first Scottish auxiliaries. That Charles highly prized his northern allies is certain; for shortly afterwards we find him applying for further reinforcements. Accordingly, Sir John Stewart of Darneley landed at La Rochelle in 1421 with some 4000 or 5000 men, and, marching inland, was welcomed by Charles at Poitiers. Soon after this was fought the battle of Baugé, the first great battle in which the Scots took part. Under the command of the Earls of Buchan and Wigtown, they fought valiantly; and it was to them in great part that Charles owed his victory.

The two armies were separated by a rapid river, crossed by a narrow bridge. On the 23rd of March the Scottish general had sent a detachment, commanded by

Sir John Stewart of Darneley and the Sire de Fontaines, to reconnoitre. This troop, coming upon the English unawares, fell back, in time to warn Buchan of the approach of the Duke of Clarence. Happily he had a short time to make ready for an advance, whilst Sir Robert Stewart of Railston and Sir Hugh Kennedy kept the bridge with a small advance corps, over which the Duke of Clarence with his best officers tried to force a passage, having left the great bulk of the army to follow as best they could. The effects of this manœuvre were, by a strange coincidence, the same as at the battle of Stirling, where Wallace defeated Surrey and Cressingham. The Duke of Clarence, conspicuous by the golden crown surmounting his helmet, and by his gorgeous armour, was first attacked vigorously by John Kirkmichael, who broke his lance on him. Then wounded in the face by William Swinton; at last brought to the ground, and killed by a blow of a mace by the Earl of Buchan. The bravest of his knights and men-at-arms fell with him. The Earl of Somerset was taken prisoner by Lawrence Vernor, a Scot; and his brother by Sir John Stewart of Darneley; the Earl of Huntingdon by John Sibbald, a Scotch knight; and the Sire de Fewalt by Henry Cunningham. The rest, furious at the disaster, rushed to the bridge to take revenge; but were killed or taken prisoners, as they arrived, by the Scots. According to Monstrelet, two or three thousand English lay dead on the spot. Bower limits the number who fell to 1617. The honour of having killed the Duke of Clarence has been claimed by various competitors. According to Chastelaire, he was slain by Charles Le Boutellier, a French knight; Father Anselme says that Gilbert de la Fayette killed him *by his own hand*. A Scotch author claims, less absolutely, this honour for John Kirkmichael, Chaplain of Lord Douglas, who was afterwards made Bishop of Orleans by Charles VII. in reward for his good services. "John Kirkmichael," says this author, "broke a spear on the Duke of Clarence." Another Scotsman, Sir John Swinton de Swinton, according to an old tradition, "unhorsed the Duke, and wounded him in front." "The Earl of Buchan," so continues the tradition, "killed the Prince with one blow of his sword." But the merit of the victory belongs to the brave Swinton. The last Swinton de Swinton presented to Sir Walter Scott the point of the weapon with which his ancestor accomplished the deed of prowess. The lance of Swinton is still to be seen in the collection of antiquities at Abbotsford.

As might have been expected, the Scots were, at first, regarded with dislike and contempt by the French people. Owing to their habits of enforced abstemiousness at one time, and the excesses in which they indulged at others, they were denounced to Charles as *sacs à vin et mangeurs de mouton*. Charles paid but little heed to these murmurs; but, after the battle of Baugé, he summoned the accusers before him, and said : "What think you now of these Scots mutton-eaters and wine-bags?" "The malcontents," says the quaint chronicle, "as if they had been struck with a hammer on the head, knew not what to reply."

It was after this first important battle that Charles conferred the greatest honour in the kingdom on Buchan, by making him Constable of France. To this high mark of favour, he added, we are told, a curious present, an astrologer, "Master Germain de Thibonville, doctor of medicine and sovereign astrologer," who seems immediately to have predicted the deaths of Charles VI. and Henry V. On Sir John Stewart of Darneley was bestowed the seigneurie of Concressaut in Berry. Laurence Vernor received the lands of Montreuil-Bonnin in ransom for his prisoner, the Earl of Somerset. These and various rewards, bestowed on others of the officers, were but the first of a series of what we may term the magnificent gifts and honours lavished on the Scots by successive French kings. Verily, if our countrymen were faithful and true in their services to the foreign masters they had voluntarily chosen, they met with constant gratitude and substantial proofs of consideration in return.

Henry V., after a temporary absence in England, returned to France at this period, forcing his prisoner, James I. of Scotland, to accompany him. He hoped, no doubt, that the near presence of their lawful king would be an inducement to the Scots to desert the cause of France. The result was very different. Even when a message was delivered from James himself to Buchan, commanding him to leave Charles's service, Buchan merely replied, that, as long as his sovereign was a prisoner in the hands of strangers, he did not consider that he was bound to obey him. This answer highly incensed Henry; and it was observed that from this time he affected to look on the Scots as rebels, and showed his hatred by severe measures taken on more than one occasion with the Scotch prisoners.

In the autumn of 1422, both Henry of England and Charles VI. of France died. The Duke of Bedford took measures at once to have the infant Henry VI. proclaimed King of France; and Charles's prospects of succeeding to his father's kingdom seemed as dark as ever. He lost no time in applying for fresh troops from Scotland. They reached France the following year, 1423; and, a few months later, was fought the battle of Cravant, disastrous to the French and Scots. The latter fought bravely to the end, though deserted by their leaders and the other mercenary troops. Three thousand Scots were left dead on the field; and, among them, we note the names of Sir Thomas Seton, Sir John Halibourton, Sir William Hamilton, and Sir William Conigham.

After this defeat, Charles sent the Earl of Buchan and other noblemen to Scotland, with a large number of ships. The Scottish envoys induced Archibald, second Earl of Douglas, to engage in the French service; and accordingly he reached France, after many perils, early in

1424, at the head of 10,000 men-at-arms. He joined the Court at Bourges, and Charles immediately appointed him lieutenant-general of his armies, and bestowed on him the duchy of Touraine for himself and his male heirs for ever. Douglas, however, was not long to enjoy his new dignities. He lost his life in the great battle which took place under the walls of Verneuil : a day of defeat and loss to the French, and of great slaughter to their Scotch adherents, to whom no quarter was given by the English.

This engagement is of especial interest to us, as it was after it that Charles gave the strongest proof of his complete trust in the Scots, by assigning to them the care of his royal person.

That there was even in the previous century a body of Scots archers attached to the King's service, called Les Gardes de la Manche, seems to be certain ; but we know nothing of their origin, and Father Forbes considers that we may place at this date, 1425, the first formation of the famous Scots Guard ; although they were not definitely organised till 1445.

Among the Scots slain at Verneuil were John Stewart, Earl of Buchan, son-in-law to the great Douglas, Sir Walter de Bekirtoune, Sir William de Setoune, Sir Alexander Meldrym, and other knights of fame. After some years had passed, a Frenchman who had fought at Verneuil and had afterwards become a hermit visited the field of battle. He had it blessed, and caused a chapel to be erected, after collecting the bones of the slain. In 1426 the States of Dauphiné founded a perpetual service in remembrance of the battle, in the Abbey of St. Antoine de Viennois. This service was known by the name of the Mass of Verneuil.

During the next three years we read of no fresh reinforcements from Scotland. But in 1428 Charles sent the Archbishop of Rheims and Sir John Stewart of Darneley to James I., to implore fresh assistance, and to beg the hand of the Princess Margaret for the Dauphin Louis. Both these proposals were favourably received, and King James promised to furnish his ally with 6000 men-at-arms, and engaged to send his daughter to France in the following spring.

The date of 1428 marks the darkest period of the reign of Charles VII.; and we may well ask what would have been the fate of France had not an unlooked for and providential occurrence turned the tide of events.

One of the most interesting chapters of Father Forbes's book is that in which he treats of the glorious share of the Scotch soldiers in the defence of Orleans and of their connection with Joan of Arc. At the time of the siege the see of Orleans was filled by John Kirkmichael, who, more fortunate than so many of his countrymen, had escaped at Verneuil and had been raised to the bishopric by Charles, in recognition of the services rendered to France by the Scots. It is natural to suppose that he encouraged many of his own nation to flock to Orleans; and we are told that previous to the siege the Scots, with the bishop at their head, fortified the town. During the siege the Scots distinguished themselves by their gallantry. Among them we find special mention of Sir John Stewart, Sir William Douglas of Drumlanrig, Sir William Douglas de Kyross, and Sir Hugh de Kennedy. The two Douglases, who were brothers, both curiously bearing the same Christian name, were killed in repelling an assault of the enemy, and were buried in front of the high altar in the church of Sainte Croix. Father Forbes gives us a graphic account of the battle of Rouvray St. Denis, fought at some distance from the walls of Orleans: an engagement fatal to the French, and in which the Scots and men of Orleans suffered great losses. Among the slain were John and William Stewart; one brother having lost his life in attempting to save the other on the field of battle. They were buried in the cathedral church of Orleans, in the Chapel of Notre Dame Blanche. John Stewart, aware of the dangers that surrounded him, had made his will, and left money for a mass to be said in this chapel every day. His wife, who had been with him throughout the siege, followed him to the grave before the year was out.

On hearing of the defeat of Rouvray, Charles, considering that he had now no hopes of preserving his kingdom, was on the point of leaving it. One morning, when indulging in these sad reflections, he entered his oratory, "and there," says a contemporary writer, "he made a humble request and prayer to our Lord within his heart, without using a word, and begged that, if he really were the rightful heir and descendant of the noble House of France, and if the kingdom were his by right, He would be pleased to guard and defend him, or at the worst permit him to escape without death or imprisonment, and to fly to Spain, or to the land of the Scots, who had, from time immemorial, been brothers in arms and allies of the kings of France."

But better days were in store for Charles and France; and the change was wrought by one who, though a weak woman, was endowed with heroism superior even to that of the many brave men who surrounded Charles.

Joan of Arc, from the first, seems to have looked to the Scots as especially likely to aid her in her work; and we find her acting in concert with them on several important occasions. It was accompanied by Scotch troops, with Sir Patrick

O'Gilvy at their head, that she made her way into the beleaguered city, and after one short week raised the siege which had lasted seven months. In gratitude for their deliverance, the inhabitants of Orleans, with Joan of Arc and Bishop Kirkmichael at their head, went from church to church to thank God. This was the origin of a procession which continued to take place for centuries in remembrance of the Maid of Orleans: a mark of veneration to her who, in its moment of greatest danger, saved her country. When Charles at last yielded to Joan's earnest persuasions, and consented to be crowned at Rheims, many of the Scots officers accompanied him, and attended the ceremony. Among them were Sir Patrick O'Gilvy, Sir Gilbert de la Haye, and Sir Christin de la Chambre, with the archers of the Guard. John Kirkmichael, Bishop of Orleans and peer of France, was one of the consecrating prelates. Joan's mission was now nearly ended; but it is interesting to see that, shortly before she was taken prisoner, she was again in action with the Scots troops. "Unwilling to remain a witness of the King's futile efforts to recover his crown, Joan determined to join those who were willing to fight. One day, therefore, without wishing adieu to the King, she set out, pretending to be going 'to some sport,' and on the 16th of April 1430 arrived at Lagny-sur-

The Scots Guards in France 133

Marne. 'There she knew to be men who made good war against the English.' They were Scotch troops, commanded by Sir Hugh Kennedy, who had already fought by her side at Orleans and Patay. After defeating a body of English troops in August 1429, he had occupied Lagny, and made it a stronghold. The English, to the number of 200 or 400, were devastating the country all around. They were on their return with their booty when Joan received information of their whereabouts. Taking a body of cavalry, about equal in number, she set out and cut them off. The English dismounted, and took up position behind a hedge; but Joan and her troop assailed them on foot and horseback, and cut them to pieces. A few days after this, Joan was taken prisoner before Compiegne, and transferred to Arras. At Arras a Scotchman showed her a portrait of herself which he bore on his person, a symbol of the veneration which her faithful companions had vowed to her. A Scotchman, perhaps the same, followed the Maid of Orleans during the whole of her wonderful career. After being present at her death, he returned to his native country, and became a monk in the Abbey of Dunfermline. At the request of his abbot, he continued Fordun's *Scoti Chronicon*, and in it bore witness to the 'marvellous Maid who brought about the recovery of the kingdom of France,

... whom I saw and knew, and in whose company I was present, during her endeavours for the said recovery, up to her life's end.'"

By putting to death Joan of Arc, remarks Father Forbes, the Duke of Bedford terminated the English ascendency in France. John Theissart, Notary of King Henry the VI., exclaimed after witnessing her execution—"We are all lost men; for a saintly woman has perished." From that day the nationality of France revived.

In the spring of 1436, the Princess Margaret of Scotland reached France, and joining the King at Tours, was there married to the Dauphin Louis: an unhappy alliance, and one ending in the early and tragic death of the bride.

The Scots Guards followed Charles in his final encounters with the English till the truce was signed, and France had an interval of peace after her long struggle. Charles turned these moments of comparative tranquillity to good account by devoting himself to the important work of forming his army; and it is from this period, 1445, which saw the first permanent and regular organisation of the French armies, that we date the definite establishment of the two famous Scotch companies known as Les Gendarmes Ecossais (Scots Men-at-Arms) and La Compagnie Ecossaise de la Garde du Corps du Roi (the Scots Royal Life Guards).

Speaking of these honours bestowed on the Scots, Louis XII. solemnly declares that "the institution of the Scots Men-at-Arms and Scots Life Guards was an acknowledgment of the service the Scots rendered to Charles the Seventh in reducing France to his obedience, and of the great loyalty and virtue which he found in them."

Soon after this, the loyalty of the Scotch regiments was put to the test. Louis, a worthless son, as well as a bad husband, intrigued against his father, and endeavoured to bribe the Scots; but his efforts were vain; and, the treachery being discovered, Louis was banished from the King's presence.

On the 24th of May 1449 one of the English captains openly broke the truce by taking possession of Fougeres in Brittany. Charles in consequence marched into Normandy, and Verneuil, Nantes, and many other cities surrendered to him. At the siege of Rouen, the Scots, commanded by Robert Cunningham, distinguished themselves; and after his victory Charles entered the city in state accompanied by the Scots Guards "sumptuously equipped; Archers and Crossbowmen about 120, more gorgeously clad than the rest. They wore jackets without sleeves, red, white, and green, covered with gold embroidery, with plumes on their helms of the same colours, and with their swords and leg harness richly mounted in silver."

The Scots took part likewise in the sieges of Bayeux and Caen.

But here we must pause to consider the one act of treachery recorded of the Scots Guards. Bribed by the English, Robert, or Robin Campbell, William Cunninghame, Robert Johnston, and James Haliburton, became involved in a plot to deliver up to the enemy the Count Dunois, Lord de Villequier, and two others. The meditated crime was discovered, and the accused were brought to trial. Robert Campbell was declared guilty of high treason, and was sentenced to immediate death. The other prisoners were remanded pending further inquiries. Meanwhile Robert Cunningham seems to have been unjustly suspected of being an accomplice, and he also had to stand his trial. He belonged to a good Scotch family, and King James exerted himself on his behalf, and wrote to the King of France. His letter has been preserved, and we gather from it that James considers the arrest as due to the wicked and calumnious accusations of jealous enemies. At the same time a petition was addressed to Charles by twelve Scotch noblemen, in which they set forth the services rendered by Cunningham both to Scotland and to France, and conclude with a challenge in the name of the Scotch nobility, all the signers undertaking to maintain his honour in personal combat. It certainly seems probable that Cunningham was falsely accused, as a contemporary French chronicler states that during the whole war in Normandy he behaved most nobly and honourably; and later on we find him entrusted with the command of the Scots Guards by Louis XI., a sure proof that that suspicious monarch considered him loyal.

Normandy and Guienne having now returned to their allegiance, only the cities of Calais and Guines remained in the possession of the English. Charles, however, lived but a short time to enjoy his hardly won victory. He expired on 22nd July 1461, his death causing great grief to his faithful Scots, whose lamentations are thus quaintly described by Martial of Paris :—

> Les Gens et serviteurs pleuroient
> A chaudes larmes fondamment,
> Et les Escossoys hault crioient
> Par forme de gémissement.

It might have been expected that Louis XI., on his accession, would have dispensed with the services of the Scots Guards, remembering how they had resisted his offers and bribes at an earlier date. But no doubt he saw in this very incorruptibility his own greatest safeguard; and that he did not trust in vain is proved by the fact that the Scots saved his life on more than one occasion. They fought bravely by his side in the struggles with the revolted nobles, and in the war with Burgundy. At Montlhéry several Scotch officers were killed; and after the battle the remainder of the Guards, "considering the danger that the King was in, and the great loss that they had sustained, and finding that the Burgundians were still pursuing those squadrons they had already broken, took His Majesty, who had been in arms all day without eating and drinking, and was much fatigued and dispirited, and carried him safe to the castle."

When Louis, following his usual crooked policy, strove to raise the Liégeois against the Duke of Burgundy to aid his own cause, Robert Cunningham was despatched to confer with them; the king himself repairing to Peronne with his guard to meet the Duke. Throughout that time of danger to Louis, when Charles, justly incensed by his guest's treachery, thought of putting him to death, the Guards showed their fidelity; and Commines does not fail to note their gallant behaviour. The perils from which he so narrowly escaped caused Louis to think of increasing the number of his guard. Accordingly in 1474 he established a new company of a hundred guardsmen, to which none were admitted save those who could furnish proofs of good descent. We find at this time among Louis's counsellors the Bishop of Aberdeen, Sir William Monipeny, and Patrick

Flockart who had commanded the Life Guards under Charles VII. Sir William Monipeny and his son rose to great favour under Louis, and their services were rewarded by the lands of Villa and Aubin. Alexander Monipeny was likewise appointed steward of the Royal Palace.

At one moment, yielding to Louis's solicitations, James III. of Scotland proposed going over to France at the head of 6000 men to aid the French King in crushing the power of Burgundy; but the Estates interfered to prevent the expedition, showing the King that "he had enough to do at home, and commenting on the questionable dealings of King Louis with regard to the countship of Saintonge," which was to have been made over to Scotland on his marriage with the Princess Margaret. Thus the idea was abandoned. In his declining years Louis seems to have relied more and more on his Scots Guards, and it was to them he entrusted his son on his death-bed.

The reign of Charles VIII. was a stirring time for our Scots. Immediately on coming to the throne the King sent Bernard Stewart of Aubigny to Scotland, to conclude a fresh treaty confirming the alliance between the two countries. The treaty was signed in Edinburgh by James III., 1483. Two years later, Stewart was, by the command of Charles, engaged, with many Scotch recruits, on the side of the Earl of Richmond at the battle of Bosworth. After the accession of Richmond to the throne as Henry VII., and the consequent peace between the two countries, Charles turned his thoughts to the fulfilment of his visionary schemes on Italy. During the long wars that lasted throughout his reign and those of his two successors, Louis XII. and Francis I., we find the Scotch regiments actively engaged in upholding the honour of France. On 8th September 1494 Charles entered Italy, and, after a progress which reads more like a festive procession than the advance of a foreign army, entered Florence on 18th November at the head of his troops. He was surrounded by his Scots Guards, whom a contemporary writer thus describes:—

Nearest the King march twenty-five Scots archers, denominated Life-guardsmen, arrayed in white jerkins embroidered with gold from top to bottom, and wearing a crown on the breast. Now the above-mentioned archers are under the orders of my Lord Stewart of Aubigny, and are quartered nearest the King's chambers. My Lord Stewart of Aubigny has under his orders all the other Scots-guardsmen, as well as 100 men-at-arms not entered in the guard Muster Roll ; and the aforesaid Scots, as soon as it is dark, and when the officer has retired with his archers, mount guard, while the captain of the 100 guardsmen (not the officer in command of the twenty-five Life-guardsmen) goes to fetch the keys.

When the King left Florence and entered Rome on 31st December, his Guards were again the object of much attention. There, as on other occasions, they guarded not only the first door, but all the doors giving access to the King's lodgings.

It would take us too long to follow the whole campaign in Italy and Spain, and we must content ourselves by mentioning the chief actions in which our countrymen distinguished themselves. At Seminara, Bernard Stewart, at the head of the Scots Men-at-Arms, gained a complete victory over the Spaniards under Gonzalvo de Cordova; but, suffering from fever, he was unable to follow up his victory. For a whole year, though ill, and lacking both money and supplies, he defended Calabria against Gonzalvo; but at length, overpowered by the superior number of his foes, and deserted by his sovereign, he signed a capitulation which allowed him to return to France with his few remaining troops. On reaching the French court Stewart was rewarded for his services by the collar of the Order of St. Michel.

Soon afterwards, in the prime of life, Charles died suddenly: an event which caused throughout his kingdom general sorrow, in which the Scots in particular joined so heartily that, as we are told by more than one historian, an archer and a butler of the Guard died of grief. Louis XII.

was as anxious to assert his claims to the crown of Sicily as his predecessor had been; and in 1499 he invaded Italy with an army of 20,000 men, half of whom he placed under the command of Stewart of Aubigny, who "continued to serve France as zealously as the brave, honourable, prudent knight had done since the reign of Charles VIII." After subduing Lombardy and taking Genoa, Stewart was ordered to invade the kingdom of Naples. Success at first crowned his efforts, but the Spaniards, having obtained large reinforcements, marched to meet the invaders, and the two armies met in conflict, 24th April 1503, between Gioia and Seminara. After a hard struggle the victory remained with the Spaniards. Though far outnumbered by their foes, the Scots refused to yield or fly. Three hundred and six men-at-arms, and sixty archers, met their death. Their gallant standard-bearer, Turnbull, was found dead on the field, grasping his lance with his hand, while he held his much loved banner with his teeth. Six of his own clan lay dead beside him. It was noticed that, wherever a Scotch corpse was discovered, one or two Spaniards were stretched near. Stewart, reduced almost to despair by this disastrous defeat, tried in vain to rally the French fugitives, but they did not recognise him, and continued to fly. Some wounded officers, who alone remained on the field, endeavoured to persuade him to accompany them. "No!" cried the brave veteran, "rather let me die by the hands of the enemy than return to my friends like a vanquished fugitive." They, however, at length prevailed on him to retire to the citadel of Angistola, to which Gonzalvo laid siege ; and at the end of a month, having no further ammunition or provisions, Stewart was obliged to capitulate.

After these reverses, Aubigny returned to France, and was sent by Louis as ambassador to Scotland, where James IV. received him with honour. This was his second embassy to his own land ; and yet once again he was to represent France at the court of his own natural sovereign. Anxious, no doubt, to secure James as his ally in his action against Venice, Louis in 1508 despatched Stewart to the Scotch court with a train of eighty horse. In providing him thus honourably, the King seems to have been actuated by James's wishes, who was not only personally attached to Stewart, but had a great respect for his reputation as a warrior. Stewart was received with every mark of attention in Scotland : tournaments were held in his honour, and verses composed by a contemporary poet to celebrate his arrival. But he was already in very feeble health, and these well-deserved honours served but to console his last days. Never again was he to see France, the country of his adoption. Worn out by his long and arduous career, he died at Corstorphine early in June, after directing that his heart should be sent to the shrine of St. Ninian in Galloway. He was buried, as appears by his will, in the Church of the Blackfriars in Edinburgh. Brantôme tells us that he was known as the "Chevalier sans reproche"; and Dunbar, who had so joyfully greeted his arrival shortly before, gives us the following touching lines on his death.

> Pray now for him, all that him loveit heir!
> And for his saull mak intercessioun
> Unto the Lord, that hes him bocht so deir,
> To gif him mercie and remissioun;
> And namelie We of Scottis natioun,
> In till his lyff quhom most he did affy,
> Foryett we nevir in to our Orisoun
> To pray for him, the Flour of Chevalrie.

We have lingered with pleasure over the details that have come down to us of Bernard Stewart, as he seems to stand forth as a representative type of what surely must have been the career and characteristics of many of his countrymen, of whom, unfortunately for us, history has left no record. While their aged commander was peacefully ending his life far away, his gallant soldiers were winning fresh laurels in Lombardy. Louis had placed Robert Stewart at their head; and after the campaign raised him to the dignity of marshal. Stewart seems to have had great influence with the King. It was owing, we are told, to his solicitations that Louis, to show his favour to the Scots who had made their habitation in France, issued the decree exempting them from requiring letters of naturalisation, and giving them the right of devising property and inheriting and holding benefices as if they were Frenchmen. The King gave another proof of his trust in the Scots, just before his death, by making Marshal Stewart, and his lieutenant, John Stewart, swear to execute his last will. The marshal swore that he and his hundred archers would fulfil this promise at the risk of their lives. One of the dignitaries of the court of France at this date also leaves the following testimony to the fidelity of the Guard. "For so long a time as they have served in France, never hath there been one of them found that hath committed any fault against the kings or their state, and they can make use of them as of their own subjects."

Throughout the reign of Francis I. the Scots held high position in France, and were by his side at the victory of Marignano, and again on the fatal day of Pavia, where their brave conduct could not prevent their royal master from being taken prisoner. In happier days, the Scots Men-at-arms distinguished themselves at the battle of Landrecies; and the following year they greatly contributed to the victory of Cerisola, where, led by the Duke of Enghien, they twice broke the Spanish ranks. This was Francis's last battle; he died in 1547, after signing the peace of Ardres.

The middle of the sixteenth century is the period at which we first perceive symptoms of a decline in the friendship between France and Scotland. The death of Cardinal Beaton was the first blow received by this alliance; and although, for a time, the marriage (eagerly promoted by France) between Mary of Scotland and the Dauphin seemed a fresh link to bind the two nations more closely together, there were elements at work which were eventually to destroy the sympathy that had existed so long. The chief thought of Henry II. at this time appears to have been to incorporate Scotland with France; a proposition naturally resented by his allies. In addition to this, the conduct of the French troops in Scotland, and the exactions of French agents in that country, were occasioning a bitter feeling of antagonism among the people. Thus the breach gradually widened; but this general feeling of discontent does not seem to have affected the existence or influenced the conduct of the French regiments. Indeed, in addition to the Guards and Men-at-arms, we find mention at about this time of several fresh companies, which joined the French service, and assisted in the war with

Charles V. Among their commanders are the names of Reyman Cockburn, John Clavers, Cunningham, Mons, and Doddes.

It is a curious fact that Henry, who relied so much upon his Scotch auxiliaries, and was served by them with unfaltering fidelity, was yet to lose his life by the hand of one of their countrymen. At the fatal tournament at which the King was to receive his death-wound, Gabriel Montgomery, son of the captain of the Guard, was his third antagonist. Henry, after running two courses, the first with the Duke of Savoy, and the second with the Duke of Guise, and having acquitted himself with his usual prowess, engaged with Montgomery, and in the first encounter received so violent a shock as almost to lose his saddle. It was now the turn of one of the French officers to enter the lists with the King; but Henry interposed his royal authority, and commanded Montgomery to make a fresh trial in the place of Monsieur de Villeville. Montgomery reluctantly obeyed, and on the second occasion was even more unfortunate than on the first. His broken lance struck the King on the head; and a splinter, entering above the eye, inflicted so severe a wound that he remained almost without consciousness. He was conveyed to his chamber at the Tournelles near at hand, and there, after lingering ten days, died. No proceedings were taken against Montgomery; but we are not surprised to find that he had no wish to remain at court after the terrible event of which he was the innocent cause. He accordingly retired to his property in Normandy. He afterwards visited England, and there embraced Calvinism, and on his return to France became one of the commanders of the Protestant party. After several years he was taken prisoner at the siege of Domfront, and, being carried to Paris, was executed in the Place de Grève May, 1574.

Brightly as the reign of Francis II. seemed to dawn on the prospects of a closer union between the two countries, these hopes were so soon blighted by the King's early death, that these few months have left but scanty records which can lend an additional interest to the history of the Scots Guards in France.

During the first ten years after the accession of Charles IX. to the throne, France was in a state of such complete anarchy, and the historians of the period were so entirely occupied with the dangers that threatened the country, that we must not expect many incidents relating to the Scots. It is satisfactory, however, to perceive among the names of Charles's loyal followers those of John Gordon, Lord of Glenluce, Peter Aliday, Maxville de Lovat, and Claude Stewart. But their influence was not sufficiently powerful to prevent the Royal

Council from proposing at this time to disband the companies of Scotch cavalry, despite the great esteem in which they were held by the French nobles, and the high praise which their services had won in the late war. The Protestant leaning shown by many of the Scots, especially by James, Earl of Arran, then commander of the Men-at-arms, had doubtless much to do with this proposed change. It shortly after took effect, and the body of the Men-at-arms ceased to exist.

Under Henry III. many Scotch Catholics flocked to France; and we find Queen Mary commending them to the favour of Cardinal de Lorraine, and Henry himself urging them to take refuge in his kingdom. The King, whilst apologising to Lord Seton for not re-establishing the company of the Men-at-arms, promises to maintain the Scots Guards in all their privileges, and mentions them in terms of high esteem and praise.

The Scots Guards were the first to salute Henry of Navarre as their sovereign; and throughout his reign their ancient glory revived. The alliance with Scotland was also strengthened; and it was with the aid of the troops sent by James VI. that Henry was able to subdue the revolted nobles, and to secure his hold on the French throne. He conferred even higher privileges on the Guard than those granted by any previous monarch, and continued to all the Scots in France "the graces and privileges whereof they have rendered themselves worthy, through the affection and fidelity which they have borne this crown." Henry also took steps to reorganise the company of Men-at-arms. He desired to make the Duke of Lennox their commander, and entered into negotiations with James VI. for that purpose; but for a time the project fell into abeyance. Henry had a faithful memory for old friends; and when Lord Colville, who had served under him, revisited France in his old age, the King received him with every mark of affection. The courtiers meanwhile, as we are told, looked on with amazement at the old-fashioned equipment of the good old man.

The time had now gone by when France and Scotland could claim the same interests, and consider England as a common foe. James VI. of Scotland now filled the English throne, and the two nations were one. The French felt that the ancient alliance could no longer be continued; and realising, and, perhaps, resenting the new condition of things, began to show less consideration towards the Scotch regiments.

Soon after the accession of Louis XIII., the Guards had reason to complain of certain points of forfeiture of rank and breach of privilege. Their captain, De Nerestan, himself a Frenchman, showed undue favour to his own countrymen; and the company, which should have been wholly Scotch, was now two-thirds French. In consequence of these and other grievances against their commander, the Scots, finding they could get no redress, sent a petition to James VI. praying him to intercede at the French court on their behalf. But this step so enraged De Nerestan and the chief French ministers that even James's endeavours were fruitless; and when Lord Colvill of Culross, to whom the King had entrusted the mission, came to Paris, "a great minister" plainly told him "that France could no longer consider them as they were, viz. Scottes, but English, and therefore were determined to extinguish them." Unluckily at this moment an incident occurred which did not tend to calm the hostile feeling towards the Scots. One of the Guard, a Douglas, was murdered, from motives of jealousy, by a Frenchman. His brother sought to be revenged, and, in company of a young man named Drummond, assaulted and almost killed the author of the crime, after which they fled the country. A Scotch gentleman named Robert Douglas had witnessed the scene, although taking no part in the affair. It seems that he had previously incurred the displeasure of the Government by aiding to write a statement put forward by the Guards pointing out their grievances. The authorities therefore determined to make an example of him, and, this being considered a good opportunity, he was thrust into prison on accusation of having taken part in the affray. Notwithstanding the exertions of the English ambassador, and of several great French noblemen, Douglas was condemned and executed. Another Scotchman was about the same time accused of treason and beheaded, though declared innocent in the memorial addressed to the King and Council by James VI. After these events, James wrote to King Louis insisting on the restoration of the Guards to their original number and privileges, and, should his request be refused, discharging them from continuing to be embodied under the name of the Scots Company. The Guards, however, were maintained, and, shortly after, steps were taken to bring about the restoration of the Men-at-arms. This is proved by a petition to James, dated Edinburgh, 1623, and signed by the Lords of the Privy Council. In the same year, Lord Gordon, Earl of Enzie, was sent to France to press the matter; and shortly before the death of Louis, his letters patent ordering the re-establishment of the Men-at-arms were delivered in London. The Duke of Gordon was made commander; but, as he died soon after, his nephew, Lord Gordon, succeeded him. It was thus that this post of honour, which had been filled for generations by the families of Lennox and Aubigny, passed to that of Gordon, with whom it remained till the final dispersion of the regiment. In the month of July 1645, Lord Gordon made the first muster of his company at Leith, in presence of French officers sent over by Louis XIV. for the occasion ; the latter were honourably entertained, and returned to France much gratified by their reception. In the year 1627, when the war broke out between France and Great Britain, the Men-at-arms were suppressed. But upon peace being proclaimed, three years later, the body was again reorganised, and, with Lord Gordon at their head, took an active part in the war with Germany. He and his soldiers showed so much gallantry that they were always employed in the most hazardous enterprises. In 1635, Charles I. desired to have Lord Gordon's assistance in his own cause ; but Gordon felt that he could not with honour leave the army of the French King, who had resolved to take part in the Thirty Years' War. There were at this moment in the French service, besides the Scots Men-at-arms and the Guards, four other Scotch regiments:— Les Gardes Ecossaises, organised by the Earl of Irvine ; Sir John Hepburn's company ; and the regiments of Colonel Douglas and Colonel Forbes, the former numbering 1000 men. These formed part of nineteen foreign regiments raised by Richelieu ; and the French army was in such an efficient state, that it soon proved that it was more than a match for the Spanish troops which had been so long the pride of the House of Asturia. A few negotiations, preserved in the records of the Privy Council of Scotland, are apparently the last attempts that were made to renew the ancient league and restore the privileges of the Scots in France. In 1642, William, Earl of Lothian, was sent to France for the purpose. Louis XIV. declared that he would renew the league only on the condition that the "Scots directlie or indirectlie enter not in armes in England, whether under the pretext of serving the King of Great Britain or under the pretext of serving religioun, without expresse commissioun from the King their master."

Soon afterwards, the first English revolution caused numbers of Scotch Royalists to emigrate to France. Their prospects were indeed a contrast to those of their countrymen in former times. Instead of being looked for anxiously by their allies, as necessary to their plans of conquest, and seeking on their own part to promote their fortune by voluntarily embracing a foreign service, they were now merely poor fugitives seeking a place of safety. But Louis XIV. had not forgotten the many services rendered to his kingdom by the Scots; and he showed a kindly sympathy with them, and, moreover, continued to them the rights and privileges conferred by so many of his predecessors. He also maintained the company of Men-at-arms and the Guards—the only two corps in the French army which had survived the troubles of the sixteenth century. Owing to their seniority to all other regiments, they took precedence of the whole army in time of war. To the Guards also belonged the honour of being placed next the Sovereign on state occasions, and the still greater dignity of bearing the body of the King at royal funerals. It is not surprising that these high privileges should have often aroused feelings of jealousy among the French, and we have accounts of various endeavours on their part to contest the rights of the Scots. These efforts, however, would appear generally to have been made in vain. In consequence of these favours, it was considered a high honour to enter the company of Guards or Men-at-arms. But their title of Scotch regiments was soon to be but a name. From the end of the seventeenth century, the Guards were recruited chiefly from noble French families; and, though occasionally the descendants of the first Scotch officers were admitted, these cases occur more and more rarely. Thus this famous body, which had been an ornament to our nation for two centuries, and had boasted of having two of our sovereigns as commanders, was gradually transformed into a French regiment. The company of the Men-at-arms shared the fate of the Guards. The French, however, who composed it scrupulously kept up the original customs: only men of the standard height could enter the regiment, and the officer on duty, after the palace gates were closed, replied when challenged, "I am here," in Gaelic. The Guards were at the head of the French army during all the great battles which marked the reign of Louis XIV., and particularly distinguished themselves at Malplaquet. There, commanded by Prince James Stewart, they charged the enemy with such valour as to pierce in succession the first, second, and third lines. The Prince exposed himself with great coolness, and was wounded at the same time as Stewart of Aubigny, who was then commanding the Royal regiment. The last action in which the Guards took part was the battle of Lawfeld in 1747.

Of the thousands of Jacobites who followed their King to France, but few were admitted into the corps embodied by their ancestors; but the unsuccessful candidates were not the less mindful to maintain the honour of their nation, and took a glorious part in the perils and victories of the French army. In consequence of the emigration of so many Royalists, many new Scotch regiments were formed, such as the Hamilton, Campbell, Royal Ecossais, Ogilvy, Douglas, and Albany. Among the brave men who, preferring honour to personal advancement, and refusing to forsake a fallen cause, followed James to France, we must call special attention to the gentlemen who had served under Claverhouse. After the fatal day of Killiecrankie, one hundred and fifty of these gallant soldiers passed into France, and for some time formed the King's guard at the palace of St. Germain. Perceiving, however, that their presence served but to increase the expenses of the royal household, they resolved, although all of good birth, to volunteer as privates in the French army. Having obtained James's consent, these brave men mustered in order to be reviewed for the last time by their exiled monarch. We cannot imagine anything more touching than the scene which took place. The King, deeply affected by the gallantry and unselfishness of his faithful subjects, did not attempt to hide his emotion; and, after thanking each one by name, and bowing most graciously, he burst into tears. The whole body of men knelt and bowed low to the unfortunate monarch, and then simultaneously gave him the royal salute. The historian of these gallant men tells us that during their service in the French cause they were always the first in battle and the last to retreat; and that, though they were often in want of the first necessaries of life, they were never heard to complain, save of the misfortunes of their King. Who does not recall Aytoun's stirring lines in which he relates the story of one of the exploits of this chosen band? The scene, even yet after two hundred years, bears testimony to their prowess by its name—the Island of the Scots. After the battle of Lawfeld, we have no records to enable us to trace clearly the career of the Guards to its close. The state of France was becoming gradually more and more disturbed, and we cannot but suppose that the storm of revolutionary feeling so soon to sweep over the country must have carried away with it the chosen bodyguard of the French Kings. Their previous history tells us that, had the Scots Guards still survived in their national character, they would have been, as ever, faithful to the end, and the Swiss Guards would not have been alone in their fidelity to a fallen monarch. After many years, when France, slowly recovering from the desolation of the reign of terror, once more welcomed a rightful sovereign in the person of Louis XVIII., the Guards were reorganised, and for a few years we see them filling their own place in royal pageants, and exercising their former privileges. They had the mournful honour of bearing the remains of Louis XVI. and Marie Antoinette to St. Denis, and again they accompanied Louis XVIII. to the grave.

But all too soon came the revolution of 1830; and Charles X., forced to fly his kingdom, took refuge in Scotland, linked for so long with the throne of France. With the close of the French Monarchy ends the history of the Scots Guards. All who have followed its records will acknowledge a debt of gratitude to Father Forbes-Leith for presenting us with this hitherto unwritten chapter of national history.

VI

THE LENNOX

SCOTLAND is greatly indebted to Mr. Fraser[1] for the many valuable documents he has brought to light, which not only illustrate the domestic history of so many of our great families, but throw a new light on matters of deep national interest.

In studying such a work as the volume before us, and in striving to place before our readers a few gleanings from its pages, we are puzzled by the very abundance of our materials. The history of the Lennox family is interwoven with that of Scotland from early times, and the members of that family seem to have taken an active part in the concerns of the kingdom—whether for good or evil, we must leave the readers of their history to decide. In turning aside from the general history of such a family, and concentrating our attention on that of one generation only, we are actuated by the feeling that particular interest attaches to the

[1] See *The Lennox*. By William Fraser. Edinburgh: 1874.

persons concerned. Matthew, twelfth Earl of Lennox, from the position he occupied in the annals of his country, and as Darnley's father, claims a special interest—and this of a painful kind, for we can claim no sympathy with his character—and in endeavouring to form some idea of his life and that of his Countess, Margaret Douglas, we obtain curious glimpses of the history of the turbulent times in which they lived, and the story of his parents' chequered life enables us to form a better estimate of their unhappy son's youth and surroundings.

Matthew, twelfth Earl of Lennox and fourth Lord Darnley, was born in Dumbarton Castle, on the Feast of St. Matthew, 21st September 1516, shortly after the siege of the castle by the Duke of Albany. We hear but little of his early days, save that when he was three years old his father entered into a contract of marriage for him with Christian Montgomerie, daughter of the Master of Eglinton. This early planned marriage never took place—the bridegroom-elect was destined to marry a more illustrious bride. In consequence of his father's violent death, which occurred in the fatal feud between him and the Hamiltons, Matthew and his young brothers, according to one account, appear to have been sent, when quite young, into France, to be placed in safety under the care of their uncle, the Lord of Aubigny, and to be brought up as

Frenchmen. But Mr. Fraser quotes documents which prove that Lennox only went to France about the year 1532, when he was a youth of sixteen.[1]

The years he spent in France may be reckoned the fairest of his life, and in considering his future career we are tempted to regret that he did not find an honoured grave in that country, instead of returning to his native land, whose honour he was so often to betray. The Earl of Lennox was appointed to a command in the Scots Guard, and distinguished himself in the war between France and Spain; he was greatly admired by the French for his valour and skill in martial deeds, and his great height and beauty of person enhanced the interest he excited. At length, when the Earl had reached the age of twenty-six, events took place which invited his return to Scotland. James V. dying in 1542, the Earl of Arran was appointed Regent during the minority of the infant Queen. This nobleman and Lennox each claimed to be the nearest to the royal succession in the event of the Queen's death. It is a curious fact, which we have on the authority of John Knox, that James V. had appointed Matthew heir to the kingdom after the death of his infant sons, but

[1] The history of the French branch of the Lennox family is full of interest, and the favours shown to its members by the French sovereigns are honourable alike to them and to those who deserved so well of their chosen masters.

this ambitious dream was of course dispelled on the birth of Mary Stewart. It is said that Cardinal Beaton at this juncture urged upon Lennox that he should return, pointing out to him that Arran's legitimacy was questioned, and that the late King had appointed him next in the succession after the Princess Mary. Some motive of the kind, probably, prompted Lennox's movements, and accordingly he landed at Dumbarton on 31st March 1543. Another secret hope seems to have led Lennox to take this step: he aspired to the hand of the Queen Dowager, Mary of Lorraine, hoping at the same time to take Arran's place as Regent of the realm. James, Earl of Bothwell, returned from exile at the same time, and he was equally anxious to win favour in the eyes of the Queen Dowager. Lindsay of Pitscottie gives a quaint description of the rival noblemen, and their efforts to gain Mary's good graces; how they "daily frequented the court, striving in magnificence of apparel and in all courtly games the one to exceed the other, especially in the Queen's sight." Lennox would seem to have carried the day by his superior attractions of person and skill, but neither nobleman received more than fair words in return for his devotion; and after a time Lord Bothwell, "having spent much" in these vain efforts to obtain the royal favour, was obliged to retire from court.

Lennox now found himself disappointed in the hopes he had entertained. At first ranging himself on the side of the Queen, he supported her against Arran and his faction, but finding before long that Arran had been reconciled to Cardinal Beaton and the Queen's party, and that his own expectations of becoming Regent were frustrated, he retired to Dumbarton, making no secret of his resentment and desire for vengeance. At this point Henry VIII., hoping that if he could secure the aid of one of the princes of the blood, he should the better succeed in his designs against Scotland, made overtures to Lennox, proposing to give him in marriage his niece, the Lady Margaret Douglas. Sir Hugh Campbell, Sheriff of Ayr, was the agent employed by Sadler to try and withdraw Lennox from his allegiance, and he reports that if Lennox receives money from France he will surely remain steadfast to the Queen and the Cardinal, but failing this, it would be easy to gain him to the English interest. Sadler himself adds these words in his report to Henry: " And though the Sheriff thinketh that the said Lennox would be content to marry the said Lady Margaret Douglas, yet, whether he would have her so, as for her he would leave France (French interest) and adhere firmly to your Majesty he is in great doubt." After the coronation of the youthful Queen Mary, Sadler is able to report more decisively on Lennox's intentions; and in a letter undated, but which was probably written the month following the coronation, he tells his royal master that he has just been visited by a servant of the Earl, who informed him that his master had left the Governor and Cardinal's party, and having " been hitherto a good Frenchman, he is now a good Englishman, and will bear his heart and service to your Majesty; and very shortly intendeth to despatch a servant of his to your Highness and to the said Lady Margaret, with his full mind in all behalf." However, Lennox would seem even yet to have been uncertain as to his course of action. In October 1543, while still in Dumbarton, he received considerable sums of money from the King of France, with instructions to distribute it according to the advice of the Queen Mother and the Cardinal. Determining to reap the benefit of the French money, and at the same time to marry the King of England's niece, Lennox gave a portion of the gold to the Queen, dividing the remainder among his own friends. Indignant at Lennox's conduct, the Cardinal and Arran proposed sending an army to Glasgow to seize upon the gold, but Lennox proceeded to Leith and intimated that he was ready to meet the Queen's forces in battle; a delay was created, and no fighting took place, but instead a treaty was signed at Leith to the advantage of the Queen's cause. Lennox soon after this despatched a message to France to apologise to the French King for his conduct, and to make protestations of his desire to be recalled to France, and to the society of his friends there; but added that, being embarked in an enterprise that had His Majesty's especial sanction, and of the success of which (supposing the King did not withdraw his assistance), there was good hope, he could not now desert the Queen and his friends, and leave them to the mercy of his enemy the Regent.

On 13th January 1543-44 an agreement was signed at Greenside Chapel, between Commissioners of the Earl of Arran, Governor of Scotland, on the one side; and on the other, by Commissioners of the Earls of Angus and Lennox, for mutual obedience to the Queen, and for brave and true resistance to the old national enemy England. But despite this solemn protestation, we very soon find Lennox and Angus again engaged in warfare against the Cardinal and Arran, and far from resisting their English enemy, they are content to seek his aid against their sovereign and country. In March of the same year, Arran laid siege, with 12,000 men, to Glasgow Castle, which was garrisoned by some of Lennox's friends. After ten days, the latter were obliged to surrender, which they did under promises of reward from

Arran. These promises were cruelly violated, the keepers of the Castle, John and William Stuart, being thrown into prison, and the rest of the garrison hanged. Enraged at these proceedings, the Earls of Angus, Lennox, and others of the Anglo-Scottish faction, implored the aid of Henry in opposing the Governor and Cardinal. Accordingly, Henry directed his Commissioners, Lord Wharton and Sir Robert Bowes, to meet the Commissioners of the rebel Lords, to determine the conditions upon which the English King would agree to send an army into Scotland. Meanwhile Lennox sailed from Dumbarton to England. In May, Glencairn having joined Lennox at Carlisle, the two Earls joined in an agreement with Henry VIII. of a most treasonable character to their native country. By it they acknowledged Henry as protector of the kingdom of Scotland, and promised to do their best to put him in possession of some of the strongest fortresses in Scotland, especially the Castles of Dumbarton, of Rothesay, and the Isle of Bute. They likewise bound themselves to promote the marriage of their infant Queen with Prince Edward of England, to place Mary under Henry's care, and to serve him against France and all countries, not excepting Scotland, and to further the cause of the Reformation. The King on his part, to encourage his promising adherents, engaged to continue Lennox as his pensioner, to give him his niece, the Lady Margaret Douglas, in marriage, and to make him Governor of Scotland if his schemes should be successful. He also promised to grant an annual pension of 1000 crowns to the Earl of Glencairn. Lennox had now taken the final step, and henceforth, for many years, we find him foremost in the ranks of his country's enemies. The great marriage to which he aspired, and which was to be the promised reward of his treachery, was now to take place, and it will be well to become acquainted with the chief facts connected with the youth of the illustrious bride.

Margaret Douglas was the daughter of Margaret Tudor, Queen to James IV. of Scotland, by her second marriage with the Earl of Angus; and even from her cradle sorrow and misfortune would seem to have been her portion. Her mother, forced to fly from Scotland by the Regent Albany, was compelled to take refuge in the Castle of Harbottle, one of the Border fortresses, then held by Lord Dacre for Henry VIII.; and there, on 7th-8th October 1515, the Lady Margaret was born, and dreary must have been her surroundings. In consequence of the war between England and Scotland, Dacre refused admission to the Queen's Scotch ladies, and it is not probable that a Border fortress of that day contained many of the comforts necessary to the hapless royal lady and her infant.

Poor Lord Dacre seems to have been much oppressed by his royal guests, and in his report to Henry does not conceal the "unusual cumber" which the arrival of the Queen caused in his martial household. Lord Dacre did not, however, neglect his duties to the infant princess. She was baptized the day after her birth, and, as Lord Dacre informs her royal uncle, "everything was done pertaining to her honour, and yet only with such convenience as could or might be had in this barren and wild district, the suddenness of the occasion ordained by God's providence being considered." Cardinal Wolsey had promised to stand godfather to the royal child, and was evidently represented by proxy, as in future years the Lady Margaret claimed his assistance as her godfather. From some contemporary verses, we gather that Henry had desired that in the event of his sister's child being a daughter, she should be called Margaret, and this royal wish was accordingly complied with. When she was three days old, Margaret's youthful father, the Earl of Angus, arrived at Harbottle with his relatives and followers, and was only admitted by Dacre on the condition that he and those who accompanied him should sign the first treaty which was to make them traitors to their country: an act which was not only an indelible stain on the honour of Angus, but laid the seeds of his daughter's troubles in time to come. Angus was proud of the birth of the child, who formed an important tie between him and her powerful uncle, and, whatever his faults, was an affectionate father, to whom Margaret clung during the stormy days of her youth, for little notice was taken of her by her royal mother. After a month had elapsed, Angus escorted his wife and daughter to Morpeth Castle, Lord Dacre's seat, where the latter remained until the following spring, and then proceeded to London at the invitation of Henry, Angus himself preferring to remain in Scotland.

Tottenham Cross was the spot at which all distinguished visitors from the North were welcomed to the capital, and, accordingly, Queen Margaret and the infant princess were there greeted by King Henry, who received them with all honour. The little Margaret was greeted at Greenwich Palace by a companion more suitable to her tender years, the Princess Mary, destined to be her warm friend through life. Mary, Queen Dowager of France, and Duchess of Suffolk, also took an especial and tender interest in her little niece. Her terrible uncle took a great fancy to her likewise, and is said to have loved her equally with his daughter Mary; and it was well for her in the days to come that he cherished some affectionate feeling for his "niece Marget," as he was wont to call her in her babyhood. After twelve months spent at Henry's court, Margaret received a hint from her royal brother that it was time she returned home, and from this time little Margaret's troubles began. Angus met her and her mother at Berwick, and accompanied them into Scotland; but he and the Queen soon separated, violent quarrels took place between them, and agreement seemed impossible. At last, when Margaret was three years old, Angus withdrew her from her mother's care, and took her to his castle of Tantallon, where he formed a household for her, suitable to her rank, appointing the wife of his brother Sir George Douglas as her governess or first lady. For several years Angus kept possession of his little daughter. When he was forced, at the second return of the Regent Arran to Scotland, to take refuge in England, she accompanied him; and when, in 1521, he passed over to France, it seems probable that she followed him and remained with him during his embassy in that country. When the Regent Albany finally withdrew to France, and Angus, returning to Scotland, established himself as Regent, he had Margaret brought home to him. She was then ten years old, and for three years the poor child enjoyed a comparatively peaceful time. But even these years were embittered by dissensions between her parents, and by the desire of the Queen to obtain a divorce from her father. When, in 1528, the revolution took place which gave the government into the hands of the young James V. and the Queen, Margaret again followed the fortunes of her father, and for months became a wanderer, passing from one stronghold to another, wherever Angus could find a safe shelter for her, until at last her aunt, the Duchess of Suffolk, moved by the thought of her position, exerted herself on Margaret's behalf, and invited her to live with her. After a short time Henry appointed Margaret to reside with the Princess Mary, who was then still enjoying her splendid establishment at Beauly. Here the cousins renewed the friendship begun in infancy, and formed a close and affectionate intimacy which ended only with Mary's life. If our space permitted us to linger, it would be interesting to trace Margaret's life through the years which followed; but for a full account of her chequered career, with its transient gleams of prosperity, we must refer our readers to Miss Strickland's admirable memoir of our heroine, and content ourselves with a brief statement of the most important events.

For a time Henry showed much affection for his niece, and invited her father to his court, making him (apparently at Margaret's request) large presents of money. During the brief period of Anne Boleyn's triumph, Margaret gained a new friend, and on the birth of the Princess Elizabeth was appointed to be her first lady of honour. It was during this period that Margaret formed the attachment, fated to end so sadly, with Lord Thomas Howard, son of the Duke of Norfolk, and it is evident that Anne's influence at this time induced Henry to look favourably on the lovers. But with the Queen's disgrace came that of Margaret and Lord Thomas, and they were both, according to Henry's amiable custom, sent to the Tower. In vain did the unhappy lovers plead that the King had himself encouraged their affection: the tide of royal favour had turned, and Parliament, hastening to meet Henry's wishes, proceeded to impeach the Lord Thomas for treason for daring to aspire to the hand of the King's niece. Meanwhile, we are not surprised to learn that Margaret fell ill of grief and terror in her dreary prison; and for once it is pleasing to know that her royal mother exerted herself on her behalf. Queen Margaret received the news of her daughter's imprisonment at Perth. The Queen, full of anxiety and indignation, thereupon wrote to her royal brother and in no measured terms of reproach. After receiving this missive and several others from his sister, Henry relaxed so far as to permit his unhappy niece to be removed from the Tower and placed in a comparatively mild captivity at Sion House. Here she remained for some time, whilst poor

Lord Thomas was still incarcerated in the Tower. Less faithful than her lover, Margaret would seem to have repented her encouragement of his suit, and we find her interceding for forgiveness from her uncle through the medium of Cromwell, and desiring in all things to do his good pleasure. At length, on the birth of Edward VI., Margaret was released from her long imprisonment. Lord Thomas, less fortunate, died in the Tower from fever added to his mental sufferings.

Soon after this, Margaret lost her mother, who, little as she seems to have cared for her daughter during life, strove to make amends to her on her death-bed. She died acknowledging Angus to be her rightful surviving husband, and declaring her penitence for her neglect of Margaret, and confessing that all her personal effects ought to belong to her, on whom she had never expended anything.

Sundry marriages were proposed for Margaret, and, indeed, she incurred Henry's displeasure by encouraging the suit of another scion of the house of Norfolk, Lord Charles Howard, and was, in consequence, again banished for a time from the court; but at the age of twenty-eight Margaret still remained unmarried. We have now reached the moment when Henry, engaged in his schemes against Scotland, thought well to offer his niece's hand as a bribe to Lennox; and we have seen that, after some hesitation, the latter accepted the honour proposed to him. The circumstances would not seem to promise much happiness to the two persons chiefly concerned; but, as far as his own happiness went, Lennox never engaged in a more fortunate venture, and Margaret, on her side, was ever a most attached wife. The marriage took place on 6th July 1544, at St. James's Palace. The bride, although no longer in the bloom of youth, is described by Buchanan as a princess of unusual comeliness and beauty; and the bridegroom, as we know, was her equal in personal attraction. By the marriage settlement, Lennox promised to endow Margaret with part of his Scotch possessions; and the King, on his side, confirmed the treaty entered into at Carlisle, also granting Lennox land to the value of 1700 merks sterling per annum. Moreover, on his marriage day, Lennox obtained from the King letters of naturalisation, thus drawing even closer the bonds which held him pledged to the English interest. Henry graced the marriage feast with his presence, and, during the banquet, made a speech referring specially to the proximity of Lady Margaret to the throne, declaring that should his own heirs fail he should be glad if her heirs succeeded: a prophetic speech, little as Henry himself intended it, and, in fact, those best acquainted with the King considered such a speech to bode little good to the bride. At this time Margaret's claims to the position of third princess of the royal blood were very evenly balanced. Against her was her mother's divorce from Angus, and subsequent marriage; while in her favour there was the Queen's dying declaration that Angus was her only true surviving husband.

The newly-married pair did not enjoy each other's society long. Shortly after the wedding, Lennox, taking leave of his bride, set out on his dishonourable expedition to Scotland, with the intention of molesting the Border, and with the hope of securing Dumbarton Castle for Henry. Lennox had left this stronghold under the charge of one of his retainers, Stirling of Glorat, and did not doubt that he would meet with resistance to his intentions. The event proved far otherwise. Stirling admitted Lennox into the castle and acknowledged him as his master, but, more loyal to his country than Lennox, utterly refused to deliver the castle to the English. Lennox, finding that there was a plot among the garrison to give him over to the Scottish Government, made good his escape with less dignity than befitted his reputation for valour, and, after some successful raids upon the mainland, returned to England. Meanwhile the Scottish Parliament, assembled at Linlithgow, pronounced Lennox a traitor and declared him to have forfeited his lands and vassals. The King of France, on hearing of Lennox's desertion of the Scoto-French interests, showed his displeasure, surely unfairly, by casting his brother, John Stewart of Aubigny, into prison, and depriving him of his offices and dignities. This arbitrary proceeding may have been suggested to Francis by the Scottish Government, as there is a memorandum extant, signed by Arran, and addressed to the Scotch ambassador in Paris, in which he is desired to counsel the French King to beware of advancing any of the house of Lennox in consequence of the treacherous conduct of the head of the Scottish branch.

Margaret would seem to have lived, for some time after her marriage, at Stepney Palace, and here her eldest son, who died in infancy, was born. But as her husband's constant expeditions in the Border countries required a more northern residence, she and the Earl settled at Temple Newsham, in Yorkshire, until lately the property of Lord D'Arcy and Meynel, who was executed for his share in the Pilgrimage of Grace. Here, on 7th December 1545, Margaret gave birth to her second son, who was destined to bring so much sorrow to her maternal heart, and whose unhappy fate invests him with an interest not otherwise belonging to his weak and wayward character. The room in which Darnley was born was long pointed out as the " King's Bedchamber," and we are told that the bed was emblazoned with the famous mottoes of the family—"Avant Darnley" and "Jamais Darrière"—fatal words, which were ultimately to prove his ruin. Young Darnley never saw his great uncle; and the latter, in consequence of a fresh quarrel with Margaret, shortly before his death did his best to exclude him from the succession to the throne. Henry's death at this moment was perhaps fortunate for Margaret, as it is not unlikely that her tyrant uncle would have sent her again to the Tower. Her worthy husband, meantime, continued to assist in the expeditions across the Border. He entered Scotland with Somerset, and was present at the battle of Pinkie Cleugh. His memory is, we fear, justly charged with cruelty to his fellow-countrymen on more than one occasion, and his after life was clouded by remorse, and it is to this sentiment that his strange unwillingness to be left alone is attributed. The English Government rewarded Lennox's fidelity by grants of land; some of the property of the disgraced Percys was awarded to him, and he was made keeper of Wressil Castle. He also received a grant of the Percy mansion at Hackney, and this house Lady Margaret retained until her death. At the period at which we now write, however, Margaret resided almost entirely at Temple Newsham, devoting herself to the education of her son Darnley. She desired earnestly to bring him up in the Catholic faith, of which she was herself a faithful member, and selected for his tutor a learned Scotch Catholic priest John Elder. Under his care the young Darnley made rapid progress with his studies. Music and other graceful accomplishments were added to his more solid acquirements, and when Darnley grew up he was assuredly one of the most highly educated princes of his day. His signature, of which Mr. Fraser gives more than one example, is a beautiful specimen of penmanship, and we are not surprised at Elder's pride in his pupil's success in this and in the more difficult arts of composition and translation. We may presume that Darnley shared his studies with some of his numerous brothers and sisters, but of these younger members of the family little is known. Charles, Lady Margaret's third son, the only one destined to live to the years of manhood, is familiar to us chiefly as the father of the hapless Arabella Stuart.

In the autumn of 1551 Lady Margaret broke the monotony of her life in the north by a journey to London, on the occasion of the visit of the Queen Dowager of Scotland to the court of Edward VI. The attentions she received from Mary of Lorraine were no doubt gratifying to Margaret, and she made such good use of this favourable opportunity as to obtain leave from Mary to visit

Scotland. The English Government, after some hesitation, confirmed this permission, and Margaret proceeded to Tantallon to visit her aged father, who, feeling death approach, earnestly desired to see her. Soon after her return home, the death of Edward VI. occurred: an event destined to bring great changes, for a time, in Margaret's life. As the cousin and early companion of the new Queen, Margaret was in high favour at court, and the old friendship between the royal ladies was tenderly renewed. On the occasion of Mary's marriage with Philip of Spain, Margaret held the position of first lady and custodian of the royal purse. In connection with this office an amusing trait is recorded. When the moment came at which the bridegroom presents the bride with the offering of money, Philip gave three handfuls of gold and silver as an earnest of the riches in store for his wife. Margaret immediately opened the purse and secured the money within it. The Queen was observed to smile at this incident, no doubt recalling the days she and her cousin had passed in which money was often wanting. It is supposed that the young Darnley was likewise present on the occasion of the Queen's wedding festivities. Poor Lady Margaret! if this brief time of favour and friendship gladdened her heart, dark days were in store for her at no distant date.

At Mary's death, Margaret may possibly have

felt disappointed that her cousin had taken no
steps to establish her claim to the throne. However this may have been, she and her husband lost
no time in presenting their homages to Queen
Elizabeth, and were graciously received by her.
It was on this occasion that Elizabeth, after listening
with sympathy to Margaret's description of her
husband's malady, expressed her opinion that his
affectionate wife should never leave him—a piece
of advice not likely to be forgotten; and we
accordingly find Margaret reminding the Queen of
it when she and her husband found themselves
shut up in separate prisons for months together.
The first cloud in Elizabeth's favourable sentiments
towards the Lennoxes arose from the same cause
which was eventually to bring down on the unlucky Margaret the full force of her cousin's
resentment. Great changes had taken place at the
court of France, and the young Queen of Scotland
was now seated upon the French throne. Soon
after the accession of Francis and Mary, Margaret
determined to make an effort to heal the breach
between her family and the Queen, trusting to
Mary's youth and gentle disposition to forgive the
past: the more so, as Mary had never been
personally offended by the Lennoxes. She therefore despatched her son's tutor, Elder, to Mary,
with affectionate letters of congratulation. These
missives were evidently graciously received, as,

somewhat later, Margaret sent another envoy to her royal niece, in whom it is surmised that we may recognise Darnley himself. This mysterious visitor was warmly greeted by Francis and Mary, and entertained at Chambord, where the court was spending Christmas. This reception must have rejoiced Margaret, but Queen Elizabeth probably looked upon these interchanges of courtesy with very different eyes. As yet, however, she took no active steps to mark her displeasure, and, shortly after the death of Francis, Darnley seems to have again visited Queen Mary, bearing letters from his mother. These he delivered to his widowed cousin at Orleans. It is even asserted by one Scottish historian that the marriage with Darnley was arranged at this time between Lady Margaret and Mary. Added to these grave misdemeanours in Elizabeth's eyes, exaggerated reports of speeches made by Margaret were conveyed to her by spies placed at Settrington. Even in her private apartments the poor lady's words were watched. At length, upon receiving the news of the safe landing of Mary in Scotland, Margaret was overheard to express her deep thankfulness for her niece's safety, and this seems to have irritated Elizabeth more than any of her previous delinquencies. Margaret aggravated her offence by sending a messenger into Scotland to congratulate Mary on her return to her kingdom. It would have been impossible, even for Elizabeth, to punish Margaret for expressing favourable sentiments regarding her own niece; but to send an envoy into Scotland, to a power lately at war with England, was considered sufficient ground for accusation. Margaret therefore was summoned to London by her imperious cousin, together with her husband, family, and servants. On reaching town, some of the party were incarcerated in the Gate House prison, the Lennoxes and their children being allowed to take up their abode at Westminster Palace. Lord Darnley, however, showed his sense by leaving the palace and concealing himself in the city. Vain search was made for him, and, as he eluded pursuit, his parents were made to suffer for his disappearance. At first Margaret was forbidden to leave her residence, and Lennox was committed to the charge of the Master of the Rolls; but this being too mild a punishment, he was sent a close prisoner to the Tower. His wife was removed to Sheen, together with Lord Charles and another of the younger children, and here they remained for many months. The poor lady made constant appeals to the Queen through Cecil, that she and her husband might be united, reminding him of her lord's illness and constitutional melancholy, which, as the Queen herself had said, rendered solitude dangerous to him. But months passed before Lennox was restored to his faithful wife, and permitted to share her less rigorous imprisonment. During these months they had both been harassed by the various accusations made against them. Margaret in particular must have been puzzled by the reports of her own speeches furnished to Cecil by his spies: little can she have thought that words spoken in her own room, and probably as quickly forgotten, would be brought against her in this manner. The old charges against her legitimacy were again also brought forward, and for her son's sake Margaret must have felt this bitterly; but Elizabeth dared not press a question in which her own claims must have suffered. After a year or more of captivity, Lennox and his countess were set free, and the latter apparently returned to Settrington. After Elizabeth's serious illness in 1564, during which Margaret's claims to the royal succession were freely discussed in Parliament, the Queen showed more favour to her cousins, and gave permission to Lennox to visit Scotland. For a short time Margaret was even permitted to appear at Elizabeth's court, together with her son, Lord Darnley, and according to her own account he made a favourable impression. Darnley carried the sword before the Queen at all state pageants, this being the privilege of the prince nearest the throne; and he was present at the creation of Lord Robert Dudley as Earl of Leicester. On this occasion Elizabeth tried to draw the Scottish ambassador into an acknowledgment as to his preference for Darnley over Leicester as a bridegroom for his mistress. But Melville, too wary to commit himself, pretended to disparage Darnley to the Queen, and thus prevent her perceiving that he had any leaning to the match, although, as he himself tells us, he had a secret charge to deal with his mother, the Countess of Lennox, to purchase leave for him to visit Scotland. Poor Lady Margaret was wholly unable to purchase anything of the kind, and the money seems to have been provided by Mary herself, and thus, early in the spring of 1564-65, Elizabeth granted permission for Darnley to join his father in Scotland. Lennox had before this obtained a pardon from Queen Mary, and leave to return to his native country; but there had been delays, caused partly by the fears of Knox and his party that the return of Lennox and Darnley, both Catholics, would be injurious to their cause. At one moment Elizabeth had even begged that Mary should be asked to revoke the permission given to Lennox to return, but Murray and Maitland refused to forward this appeal to their Queen.

Finally, as we have seen, Elizabeth, in the summer of 1566, had allowed Lennox to cross the Border and present himself before Mary, who received him graciously. Before many months were over, the marriage between Mary and Darnley was concluded. Even before the event, Margaret had to suffer for her wishes concerning it. Elizabeth, wreaking her vengeance on Darnley's mother, imprisoned her afresh; and, in spite of Queen Mary's warm intercessions on her behalf, Darnley's wedding day found his mother shut up in the Tower, where she was destined to remain during the brief span of her son's elevation, and where she was to receive the news of his awful fate. The exact spot of Margaret's prison in the Tower is known by the discovery of an inscription in a room in that portion of the building now the residence of the governor. The stone bears the record that on the 20th June 1565, the Lady Margaret Lennox was here imprisoned "for the marriage of her son, my Lord Henry Darnley, with the Queen of Scotland." The names of her five attendants are engraved below. And here we must leave the poor lady for a time and follow the fortunes of her husband. Mary and her father-in-law seem to have been generally on good terms, but his conduct on the occasion of Rizzio's murder must have destroyed her confidence in him. Yet, later on, Mary corresponded in a friendly manner with Lennox, and Mr. Fraser gives us a letter hitherto unpublished, of an especially interesting character. It is written in September 1566, at the time when, owing to Darnley's wayward conduct, fresh misunderstandings had arisen between them. Mary states that the importance of the matters in which they disagreed had forced her to take the advice of her Privy Council, and that they had begged the King to state his grievances, as her Majesty was willing to do all in her power to content him; that Darnley had disavowed that he had any cause of discontent or that he entertained the design alleged against him; but his reply was unsatisfactory, and the Queen was ignorant of his future intentions. When, a few months later, the terrible tragedy of Darnley's death occurred, Lennox was overwhelmed by the blow. In his grief and desire for vengeance, he turned to Elizabeth for help, imploring her aid against the murderers of his son, her near relative and native-born subject. Shortly before Bothwell's marriage with the Queen, Lennox returned to England, and was permitted to join his wife, who was still in a kind of honourable durance. What a meeting it must have been, and what words can describe the misery Margaret had suffered in her long imprisonment, with its many privations, all of which, however, must have faded into insignificance beside the agony she endured when hearing of her son's death. It was on the afternoon of 19th February 1567 that the fatal news was conveyed to the wretched mother, aggravated by a rumour that her husband had shared their son's fate. Her grief was so intense as to touch even Cecil, and he hastened to prove to her that it was impossible that Lennox could have perished, as he was known to have been in Glasgow the night of the murder. Having duly impressed the unhappy Margaret with those suspicions of Mary's guilt which were necessary to their plan of action, Cecil then advised Elizabeth to release Margaret, but the Queen took but tardy measures for this, and Darnley had been dead more than a month before Margaret was taken from the Tower, and placed under the charge of the Ladies Sackville and Dacre. It was in this position that Lennox found her, and the unhappy couple proceeded in their grief and desolation to follow the secret wishes of Cecil and his mistress. Convinced of Mary's guilt, they became her most bitter accusers, and their appearance in deepest mourning at Elizabeth's court, and their lamentations over Darnley's fate, was a welcome sight to Mary's enemies. At length, when news was brought that Mary had taken refuge in England, Lennox and his wife presented themselves before Elizabeth, demanding vengeance on their daughter-in-law.

"The lady's face," says a contemporary, "was all swelled and stained with tears. She and her lord wore the deepest mourning. They knelt before the Queen, and Lady Margaret cried so passionately for vengeance that Queen Elizabeth affected to console her with soothing words, and finished by reproving her, saying that such accusations must not rest against the good name of the Princess without further proof."

When the commission deputed to investigate Darnley's murder opened its proceedings at Westminster, Lennox made a speech demanding vengeance for the death of his son. Having fulfilled their part in the terrible accusations brought against Mary, the Lennoxes were allowed to return to their home in the north. After the violent death of the Regent Moray, the position so long coveted by Lennox became his. Supported by Queen Elizabeth, he became Regent of Scotland, and obtained the guardianship of the King his grandson. The chief events of his regency are facts of general history, and our limits do not allow us to dwell on them; we therefore purpose restricting ourselves to some notice of the siege of Dumbarton, and of Lennox's death at Stirling, as on these points Mr. Fraser gives some fresh and interesting particulars.

Dumbarton Castle, held for Queen Mary by her devoted adherent Lord Fleming, was much coveted by the Regent and his party; and it was Lennox's fortune to secure it through the daring of Captain John Crawfurd, one of his followers. The purpose of the besiegers was assisted by an event that occurred within the fortress. The wife of one of the garrison had been punished for some small theft by order of the governor; her husband, desiring to avenge her, offered to betray the castle to Lennox, and proposed a scheme to him which, though dangerous, seemed to be feasible. Lennox confided the execution of the project to Crawfurd, trusting more in him than in Robertson. On the evening of 1st May (on which day expired the truce between the Queen's party and the Government), Mr. Drummond of Drumquhassel was despatched with some horsemen to prevent any one communicating with the castle. Late at night Crawfurd followed him with the remainder of his men on foot, and after halting for a short time at Dumbuck Hill to address some encouraging words to the troops,

They proceeded in single file to the base of the rock, retaining their places by means of a cord that was held by each of the party, the foremost carrying the scaling ladders. Before reaching the castle they had many ditches and a deep water, bridged only by a single tree, to cross. It was resolved to attempt to effect an entrance into the castle at the highest part of the crag called the 'Beik,' where no sentry was placed, there being no suspicion of danger at that point. A fog which surrounded the upper part of the rock was favourable to the enterprise by screening the assailants from observation. After they had joined the ladders so as to make one of sixty steps, they were yet left twenty steps from a tree above them, to which the guide and Crawfurd with great difficulty had made their way without ladders, taking with them cords which they fastened to the tree, letting them hang down to the ladder that the men, taking hold of the ropes, might draw themselves up to the tree. But on the first attempt there was besides a risk of failure from the difficulty of managing the long ladder required by the height of the ascent, and of fixing it with sufficient firmness in the slippery rock. The weight of those who ascended loosened the hold of the ladder, and several of the party fell to the ground. No harm was, however, sustained; and, fixing the ladder more securely, they got to the projecting ledge, where grew an ash tree, by means of the ropes that were fastened to it.

But here their difficulties were far from ended. They found themselves still a hundred fathoms from the bottom of the wall. The ladder was fixed for a new ascent; but at this stage of the proceedings an accident occurred which might have had serious results. Day was now dawning, and the danger was great of their being discovered by the sentries. The feeling of his peril so affected one of Crawfurd's men that in climbing the ladder he was seized with a kind of fit, and held on so firmly to the ladder that his comrades could neither pass him nor withdraw his hold from it. But Crawfurd was equal to the occasion, and binding the poor man securely to the ladder he had it turned round, and the besiegers proceeded on their way. The three men who first scaled the wall were discovered by the sentinels and the alarm was given. The assailants managed to defend themselves until reinforced by their comrades, who all ascended by the one ladder, and meeting with but feeble resistance the place was soon secured. Fleming made his escape by a postern gate which gave access to the Clyde. Lady Fleming was among Crawfurd's prisoners, but was treated with much courtesy, and was permitted to depart in safety. Another of the prisoners was John Hamilton, Archbishop of St. Andrews, who on being removed to Stirling was there cruelly condemned to death and executed. Crawfurd was rewarded for his valour by a grant of lands and a pension of £200 a year. At ten o'clock of the day on which the siege took place Lennox dined at Dumbarton.

While her lord was advancing in Elizabeth's good graces by the manner in which he conducted himself in Scotland, the Countess, "his good Meg" as he was wont to call her, was residing at Elizabeth's court. Having access to the Queen and her ministers, Margaret exerted herself in her husband's interest, and acted as an intermediary between him and the English Government. Lennox and his faithful wife were not destined to meet again, and the mutual affection between them, which, on Lennox's side, is the one redeeming point in his character, was soon to be severed by death. After governing Scotland for little more than one short year, he met his violent end at Stirling, a few days after holding the Parliament at which the infant King made the well-known speech that so greatly startled his leal subjects. These words, "This Parliament has got ane hole in it," coming from the mouth of an infant, were considered prophetic of evil, and Lennox's death seemed to his contemporaries a fulfilment of the child's words.

The assembly at Stirling was considered by the Queen's party to be a favourable moment for an attack on the Regent, and accordingly a large body of men, with Lord Huntly and other noblemen at their head, left Edinburgh for Stirling on the evening of 3rd September, and reached the latter place at four next morning. The whole town was asleep, and the Parliament, in false security, had posted no sentinels. Making their way to the market-place, Huntly and his men surrounded the residence of the Regent and the chief nobles, and secured Lennox and ten of his friends. So far, success had crowned Huntly's efforts, but now, Lord Mar sallying from the castle with a body of men, and being supported by the citizens, defeated the Queen's men and rescued the prisoners, all save one, and he the most important. Lennox was shot in the fray by Captain George Calder, at the instigation, it is said, of Huntly and Lord Claude Hamilton. Lennox had been made prisoner by Spens of Wormiston, who, having been charged by Kirkaldy of Grange to save the Regent's life at any cost, acted so faithfully to these orders that, perceiving Lennox's danger, he threw himself before him, and the bullet passed through his body before reaching its victim. Spens was mercilessly killed by the Regent's followers when they came up, in spite of Lennox's earnest entreaties that he should be spared. Although mortally wounded, Lennox continued to ride until he reached the castle. His chief thought was for his grandson the King. His answer to the encouraging words of his friends was, "If the babe be well, all is well."

Knowing that he had but a few hours to live, the Regent addressed those around him in the following terms:—

I have now, my lords [he said], to leave you at God's good pleasure, and to go into a world where is rest and peace. Ye know that it was not my ambition but your choice that brought me to the charge I have this while sustained, which I undertook the more willingly that I was persuaded of your assistance in the defence of the infant King, whose protection by nature and duty I could not refuse. And now, being able to do no more, I must commend him to Almighty God, and to your care, entreating you to continue in the defence of his cause (wherein I do assure you in God's name of your victory), and make choice of some worthy person, fearing God, and affectionate to the King, to succeed unto my place. And I must likewise commend unto your favour my servants, who never have received benefit at my hands, and desire you to remember my love to my wife Meg, whom I beseech God to comfort.

He then said farewell to his friends, begging their prayers, and after spending some hours in prayer, he expired at four o'clock in the afternoon. Lennox was buried in the Chapel Royal at Stirling Castle, where a tombstone was afterwards erected to his memory by his sorrowing wife.

The news of Lennox's death reached Margaret in London, and it seems probable that Elizabeth herself broke the awful tidings to her. No record of Margaret's feelings on the occasion have come down to us, but we who have followed her through the twenty-six years of her married life, and have tested her affection for her husband, can guess what she must have suffered. In memory of her love for Lennox, Margaret caused a jewel to be made, which she constantly wore and which still exists. It is a gold heart two and a half inches in diameter, richly enamelled and jewelled, and emblazoned with Scotch mottoes and emblematic figures, significant of the Countess's sentiments or bearing on the history of the family.

It might have been supposed that Margaret in her lonely widowhood would have been permitted to spend her few remaining years in peace, but, when her husband had been dead three years, she again incurred Elizabeth's displeasure. This time, Margaret's disgrace was caused by the share taken by her in her son Charles's marriage with Lady Elizabeth Cavendish. The Queen evinced the highest displeasure at the match, and summoned the bride and bridegroom to her presence, desiring Margaret to accompany them. Accordingly the disconsolate family party travelled to town from the north through the fogs and mud of December, well knowing the kind of welcome that awaited them. When the Lennoxes reached London, they were desired to keep entirely to their own residence, and above all to speak to none save those permitted to listen to them by the Privy Council. But even this seclusion was not deemed sufficient punishment for Margaret. After a few days she was removed to the Tower to undergo her third and last imprisonment in that royal dungeon. Here she spent many weary weeks, and was only released to find a fresh sorrow awaiting her. Her son Charles began to show symptoms of decline, and after a few short months he likewise was taken from her, and the only consolation left to the sorrowing lady was her infant grand-daughter, the little Arabella. Margaret's own days were numbered; she never rallied from the death of her son, and fell into a " languishing decay," from which death was soon to release her. Before closing our narrative, it is pleasing to record

The Lennox

that Margaret, ere this, had become reconciled to her wronged and desolate daughter-in-law, Queen Mary. What it was that wrought this change in Margaret's sentiments we know not, but the fact is certain, and we have interesting proof in an affectionate correspondence between the two ladies. We venture to quote a specimen in a letter of Margaret's to the Queen, written from her residence at Hackney, 10th November 1575.

Margaret Countess of Lennox to Mary Stewart.

It may please your Majesty, I have received your token and mind, both by your letter and other ways much to my comfort, specially perceiving what zealous natural care your Majesty hath of our sweet and peerless jewel in Scotland.[1] I have been no less fearful and careful as your Majesty of him, that the wicked Governor[2] should not have power to do ill to his person, whom God preserve from his enemies. Nothing I neglected, but presently upon the receipt of your Majestie's, the court being far off, I sent one trusty who hath done so much as if I myself had been there, both to understand the past, and for prevention of evil to come. He hath dealt with such as both may and will have regard to our jewel's preservation, and will use a bridle to the wicked when need require.

I beseech your Majesty fear not, but trust in God that all shall be well. The treachery of your traitors is known better than before. I shall always play my part to your Majesty's content, willing God, so as may tend

---

[1] James VI.   [2] Morton.

to both our comforts. And now must I yield to your Majesty my most humble thanks for your good remembrances and bounty to our little daughter [1] here who some day may serve your Highness, Almighty God grant, and to your Majesty long and happy life. Hackney this VIth of November, Your Majesty's most humble and loving Mother and Aunt,   M. L.

Indorsed by Thomas Phelipps: "My Lady's Grace the Countess of Lennox to the Queen of Scots."

Shortly before this letter was written, Margaret had solaced her imprisonment by working a touching present for the Queen, namely, a small square of point lace made of her own hair, now gray, mixed with fine flax threads. That Darnley's own mother, at first Mary's bitter accuser, should have become convinced of her innocence is surely a fact well worthy of attention. More fortunate than her unhappy daughter-in-law, Margaret was permitted to close her days peacefully in her own house at Hackney. In the end death came rather suddenly. On 15th March 1577-78 the Countess was taken violently ill with a complaint to which she was subject, and when after much suffering she experienced relief, it was evident that death was near. She then bade a calm farewell to those around her, expressing her joy at leaving this world; and, after preparing for death and receiving

[1] Arabella Stuart.

all the rites of the Catholic Church, she peacefully expired, at the age of sixty-two. Margaret died, as she had lived, in poverty, and Queen Elizabeth bore the expenses of her funeral. She was interred at Westminster Abbey, by the side of her son Charles. When James VI., in tardy recognition of his filial duty, raised a tomb to his mother's memory, he likewise erected the altar-tomb to his grandmother, and we now know that the remains of the unfortunate Darnley rest beside those of his mother.

Our task is now done, and in concluding the story of Margaret Lennox and her family we would suggest to our readers that the history of their lives represents but a small portion of the interesting facts contained in the "Lennox Book," which all lovers of Scotch history would do well to study.

VII

A SISTER-IN-LAW OF MARY QUEEN OF SCOTS

Elle a été belle, sage, vertueuse, bonne, et douce Princesse.
—BRANTÔME.

AMONG the many brilliant personages of the sixteenth century, Claude, Princess of France and Duchess of Lorraine, plays a modest part ; yet the short story of her life has, we venture to think, a gentle and gracious fragrance of its own,—the fragrance of a pure and earnest nature, which remained unspoilt amid the dangers inseparable from her position at the gayest courts in Europe, and which by its tender charity to the poor merited for her during her married life the title of "true Mother of her people."[1]

Claude, second daughter of Henri II. and Catherine de Médicis, was born at Fontainebleau,

[1] "Si grande était la charité de cette jeune Princesse qu'en tout ce pays de Lorraine elle était tenue pour la vraie Mère du peuple."—A. Sorbin, Òraison Funèbre.

12th November 1546. Another son had been greatly desired, and the court was "toute troublée" at the disappointment; but, with all their great faults, the royal parents were singularly devoted to their children, and the little princess was tenderly welcomed, and for three months (a wonderfully long time for the period) remained with her mother. She was baptized on 9th February by the Cardinal de Guise, Archbishop of Rheims, afterwards the famous Cardinal de Lorraine; and was called Claude, in memory of her grandmother, Claude de France, and in honour of the chief of the house of Guise. For political reasons Henri had asked the Swiss cantons, his "bons compères," to be the sponsors; and four delegates were despatched for the occasion by the thirteen cantons, bearing as token of amity a large gold medallion, on which was engraved a hand holding thirteen cords united by one knot and a cross, with the motto, "If God be with us, who can be against us?" The godmothers were Jeanne d'Albret, future mother of Henri IV., and the admirable Duchesse de Guise, Antoinette de Bourbon.

Not long after the ceremony the little Claude was removed to the royal nurseries at St. Germain-en-Laye, where the Dauphin and Princess Elizabeth were already established under the charge of M. d'Humyères, Governor of the Children of France. M. d'Humyères had held this office in the previous reign, and we find the King in constant and intimate communication with his old governor. Thus, on hearing of the princess's safe arrival, 28th March, Henri writes :—

My cousin, I have seen by your letters of the 29th that my daughter Claude had arrived the preceding day in good health at St. Germain-en-Laye, where our other children were also in good health. You will give me pleasure by sending me news of them as often as you can during the journey that I am about to undertake on leaving this.[1]

Madame d'Humyères, who shared her husband's important charge, had, by her devoted care of the children, acquired the entire confidence of the King and Queen. Two other ladies assisted her, and the most celebrated of the court doctors, Gouvrot and Chrétien, watched daily over the children's health. No doubt news of his family was constantly forwarded to the King during his celebrated progress into Piedmont, and it is pleasing to learn that, at the end of about six months, Henri,

weary of all these festivities, and more desirous of seeing his children again than of prolonging his triumphs, quitted it all, and, starting almost alone, never stopped till he reached St. Germain. This King, who has been described as so cold and taciturn, could not "patienter" a few days longer, but "went off in great devotion to see Messieurs his children and enjoy them all to himself."[2]

---

[1] Henri II. à Mons. d'Humyères, 31 Mars 1547. Bib. Nat., France.
[2] *Claude de Lorraine*, by M. de Magnienville, p. 27.

During the King's absence the little court of St. Germain was augmented by the arrival of two children of the family of Count Galeotto Pica della Mirandola, who had just ceded his principality to France. Three months later a much more important addition was made to the youthful company in the person of the Queen of Scots, already, as we know, affianced to the Dauphin. After her perilous voyage from Scotland, Mary Stuart, accompanied by her Maries, reached this happy haven early in October 1548. Every effort had been made to welcome and honour her. The King settled each detail himself, and had written letter upon letter to M. d'Humyères regarding the arrangement of the palace and the etiquette to be observed:

As regards what you ask me [he writes] concerning the rank which I desire my said daughter, the Queen of Scots, to hold, I wish to say that I intend that she shall walk *before my daughters*, as the marriage between her and my son is quite settled; and even without that she is a crowned queen, and as such I wish her to be served and honoured.[1]

The rooms to be prepared for Mary and his own children are designated by the King as "the saloons and chambers above those of the King, as well as those above the rooms of the Queen, the King of Navarre, and the Constable." In spite of

[1] Henri II. à Mons. d'Humyères.

all these elaborate arrangements for their comfort at St. Germain, the royal children seem to have made frequent moves to Blois, to Amboise, to Carrières, or to Maison whenever the fear of "bad air" caused a flight to the north or south.

In 1549, when the Queen went to Rheims for her coronation, the little court was left at St. Germain. In 1551 we find it established at Blois; and here Lord Northampton (sent by Edward VI. to bear the Garter to King Henri) paid it a visit, of which his official report gives us an agreeable glimpse :—

When he reached Blois, Mandose invited him to visit the King's children. . . . Next morning, horses being sent for him and his company, they rode to the castle, where they were received by the governor with great ceremony; and being brought to the Dauphin's presence, were embraced of him, the Duke of Orleans, and the two young ladies their sisters, as amiably as could be imagined.[1]

A few days later Lord Northampton made a formal demand for the hand of Mary Stuart on behalf of his royal master, to which the little Queen, who was present, and who had already learned to love her future husband, herself returned a hearty negative.[2]

---

[1] The Marquis of Northampton to the Council, 16th June 1551. Nantes. Cal. State Papers.

[2] Northampton to Cecil. State Papers, MS.

It was beautiful to see this little court [writes a contemporary] placed apart and generally established at St. Germain, which was, moreover, a true school of good manners and chivalrous exercises, especially after Monseigneur the Dauphin and these young nobles began to grow up, when they had masters to teach dancing and shooting, without counting their other studies of belles-lettres, music, mathematics, painting, and engineering, and other similar sciences, suitable for such scholars.

There appear to have been, besides, three gentlemen attendant on the Dauphin, who trained the young people "in intellectual attainments, in constant cheerfulness, and honest recreations."[1] The recreations, we are glad to find, played an important part. Either in the beautiful park, or in the spacious halls and corridors of the palace, there were mimic fights and tournaments, scenes acted from the romances of chivalry, and other pastimes. Among the latter, we may conjecture that "the hackneys sent to the Dauphin by Governor Lord Arran" figured frequently—the hackneys being, we suppose, Highland or Shetland ponies. We are inclined to agree with Madame Claude's biographer, who thinks that these children, all destined to wear a crown, managed to amuse themselves very well.

Amid all these duties and pleasures, however, sorrow more than once visited the little circle.

[1] *Vie de Philippe de Stozzi.* Bib. Nat.

When Claude was four years old her young brother, the Duke of Orleans, died. Some years later, in 1549, Princess Elizabeth, always delicate, was very ill of the measles, and in the following spring Claude herself was seriously indisposed—an illness which elicited anxious letters from the King and Queen. The little patient recovered slowly, and had to be sent to Amboise, with her brother and sister, for change of air. The political events of the year 1551 were destined to have a lasting effect on the life of our little princess, by bringing to the French court her future husband, Charles III., Duke of Lorraine. Son of the late Duke Francis and his wife, Christina of Denmark,[1] Charles was a mere child when, as the result of the campaign known as that of " Les trois Evêchés," Henri II. took possession of the Duchy of Lorraine. Christina endeavoured to place her son and his inheritance under Henri's protection; but his plans were fixed, and, while showing her every courtesy, he expressed his determination of taking Charles to be educated under his own eye and of marrying him to his daughter. The young Duke accordingly made his appearance at Fontainebleau,

---

[1] Christina was the daughter of Christian II. of Denmark, niece of Charles V., and widow of Francis Sforza, Duke of Milan. During her widowhood her hand was sought by Henry VIII., but she promptly refused him, and in 1541 married Francis, Duke of Lorraine. A beautiful full-length portrait of this lady by Holbein is in the possession of the Duke of Norfolk.

for his advanced age of *nine* seems to have admitted him at once to actual court life, and we do not hear of him as joining the youthful circle at St. Germain, nor do we learn when or where he first saw his future bride. The impression made by Charles at this time was " all that was favourable," a verdict·which proved true also of his after-life.

Two years later Claude began to take her part in court life, under her mother's wing. In a letter from the Cardinal de Lorraine to the Queen Dowager of Scotland he says :—

The Queen takes with her her two daughters; she will give them no household, having decided to let them sleep in her dressing-closet, or in some room as close to hers as possible. They will have with them only Mme. d'Humyères and their waiting-maids, and the said lady declares that as long as she lives no one but herself shall have authority over her daughters until they are married.[1]

Claude was six years old, and her education was now, it seems, to begin in earnest. Her special companions were her sister Elizabeth and the young Queen of Scots.[2] Mme. Claude's biographer describes very charmingly the friendship which united them, and which was to continue in after

[1] Cardinal de Lorraine to Mary of Guise, 22nd February 1553. Labanoff, vol. i.

[2] Although Mary shared many of the studies and amusements of the royal children of France, she owed the most important part of her education to the watchful care of her admirable grandmother, Antoinette de Bourbon, Duchess Dowager of Guise.

years. Queen Mary appears to have led the way in study and accomplishments, and quaint examples of the zeal with which she assisted her little friends still exist in a copy-book discovered some years ago at the Bibliothèque Nationale.

It is not without cause, my dear sisters [writes Mary], that the Queen ordered us yesterday to do what our governesses tell us ; for Cicero says in the second book of De Legibus, he who knows how to command has once obeyed, and he who obeys simply is worthy of one day commanding.

On another occasion, addressing herself to Elizabeth, who was nearer her own age than little Claude, Mary says :—

When, yesterday evening, my tutor begged you to reprove your sister because she wished to rise to take a drink, you replied that you did not dare do so, as you wished yourself to drink. See then, my sister, what we should be, who are examples to the people. How could we dare reprove them, unless we ourselves are without reproach ?

The princesses had as their master in poetry Ronsard, who writes thus of the daughters of his King :—

>   Qui dessous leur mère croissent
>   Ainsi que trois arbrisseaux
>   Déjà grandes apparaissent
>   Comme trois beaux Lys
>   À la fraîcheur des ruisseaux.

And again, to stimulate their zeal for study:—

> Mais que sert d'être les filles
> D'un grand Roi si vous tenez
> Les muses comme inutile
> Et leurs science gentille
> Dès le berceau n'apprenez.

That Mary Stuart profited by Ronsard's lessons we know well; but although the French princesses did not compose verses, we learn that, in the poet's opinion, Claude was already distinguished by her artistic sense and her taste for drawing and combining colours.

Thus another six years passed until 1558, when the first break was made in the happy circle by the marriage of Mary to the Dauphin. During the great festivities which accompanied it, we catch pleasant glimpses of Princess Claude and her *fiancé*. Thus, on the day of betrothal we see that in the state quadrille Duke Charles and she danced together. On the wedding-day Charles led her out again to dance, dressed in cloth-of-gold covered with jewels; and at the pageant that same evening he entered the royal presence with five other princes in ships with silver masts and sails of silver gauze, and, capturing Princess Claude, carried her off in his vessel.

A year later, and Charles and Claude were the centre figures in equally gorgeous festivities.

France was tired of war, and even of victories, and Claude's marriage, as well as the projected alliance of her sister with Philip II., was to cement the peace with Spain. Charles's mother, Duchess Christina, was the person chosen to intervene between the two Powers. Since her son's removal to France she had lived in voluntary retirement, and was now in Flanders, "desiring passionately," as Claude's biographer says, to see her son once more. This happiness was now offered to her on the condition that she would use her influence with the Spanish Ministers. The negotiations were successful, and at Christina's suggestion the French and Spanish plenipotentiaries met at Câteau-Cambrésis, and by the first days of April 1559 the Duchess was able to write her congratulations to the King of France on the conclusion of peace.

On the 19th of January the contract of marriage between the Duke Charles and Princess Claude had been signed at the Louvre in presence of the King and Queen, the Dauphin, the Children of France, the Cardinal de Lorraine, and many other royal and noble personages. The dowry of the Princess was fixed at 300,000 gold "écus soleil," to be paid in the space of three years. After the Treaty of Câteau-Cambrésis, the town of Stenay was added to her portion. Of the wonderful *trousseau* details are preserved in the papers of L'Aubespine, and, as we can imagine, it was worthy of the bride. Dresses of cloth of gold and silver, of satin and velvet in all colours, jewels, a mantle *à la royale*, and another—seemingly a dressing-gown—of silver cloth, all lined with wolf fur, figure in the list, as well as hangings for rooms in *toile d'or damassé*, and cramoisy velvet, etc., solid silver table and toilet services, house linen, litters, carriages, and horses, with cloth-of-silver harness.

On 22nd January, three days after the contract was signed, the marriage took place. At eight o'clock in the morning the "Court of Parliament," in scarlet robes and furred caps, preceded by pursuivants and followed by the royal notaries, proceeded to the cathedral of Notre Dame. They were soon followed by other civil dignitaries, who all took their place in the choir. The body of the great church was crowded with "nobles, gentlemen, noble ladies, and demoiselles," while the porch and square outside, as well as the streets, were filled to overflowing with well-dressed citizens.

At eleven o'clock the royal procession started from the episcopal palace, and, crossing a long gallery erected for the purpose in full view of the people, advanced to the platform at the cathedral door: here, as at the Dauphin's wedding, the marriage ceremony took place, the Cardinal de Lorraine officiating. The herald scattered money to the people's cry of largesse, and then the procession passed into the church, the King leading the young Duchess. They were followed by the Cardinal de Trivulce, the papal legate, the Cardinals of Lorraine, Bourbon, and Guise, by several archbishops and bishops, five hundred gentlemen of the King's household, and a brilliant crowd of royal personages and nobles.

After the nuptial Mass the court again returned to the episcopal palace till four o'clock, when the brilliant assemblage proceeded through the streets, hung with tapestry and decked with flowers, to the great hall of the palace for the nuptial feast. This was followed by dances and pageants as usual, and for several days Paris kept holiday. The Princes of Lorraine kept open house, a tournament took place in front of the grand residence of the Duke of Guise, and "many other things exquisite or of mark" were done on this joyful occasion.[1]

This is the moment of her history in which Claude's biographer endeavours to describe her personal appearance, and with him we regret that the artists who portray her seem to have been very unsuccessful. Neither the picture preserved at Munich, nor the coin bearing Claude's effigy as

[1] In the gallery of the Arazzi at Florence may be seen a fine piece of tapestry representing one of these festive scenes. A tournament is depicted within a framework of flowers and fruit. On one side we see Princess Claude, on the other Catherine and her court, while Duke Charles occupies the centre on horseback.

Duchess of Lorraine, give us any idea of the Princess with the "ivory complexion and limpid eyes," or again the "visage avec une certaine gaieté," which Brantôme describes. He adds that in beauty she resembled her mother, and in goodness and knowledge her aunt Margaret of Valois.

Soon after their marriage Charles and Claude made a little journey to visit the Duchess Christina. The wish of the latter to see her son does not appear to have been realised till now, when he took his young bride to greet her at Mons. Here Claude was also introduced to her powerful cousin and future brother-in-law, Philip of Spain. In the midst of the peace negotiations which occupied him, Philip treated his guests right royally, and they returned laden with gifts. On their return to the French court, some months were passed in further festivities, which were occasioned by the proclamation of peace and the marriages of Princess Elizabeth and the Duchess de Berri. But France was soon to mourn instead of rejoice. On the 29th of June 1559 the King received his death-wound, and a few days later breathed his last. On our Princess—only now thirteen—the blow of losing so tender a father must have fallen heavily, while the sorrow of leaving her mother in her grief, and the separation from her sisters, must all have added to the usual pain felt on leaving home and country; but the time had come for Charles to return to his dukedom. As soon as the King's funeral was over, the young pair set out to accompany Francis II. to Rheims for his coronation, from whence to proceed to Lorraine. In those days royal progresses were slow, and in this case the journey was prolonged by an indisposition of the young Queen of Spain, which kept the court at Villers-Cotterets. At last, on 15th September, the *cortége* reached Rheims, and the King and Queen, and Elizabeth of Spain, made their state entry.

On the 18th the ceremony took place, of which the Spanish ambassador gives the following graphic little account :—

The coronation of the very Christian King took place yesterday very solemnly [he writes]. The Queen our mistress and the Queen of France, with the Duchesses of Savoy and of Lorraine, were on the platform erected for them, and near them was Monseigneur the Duke of Savoy. To-morrow the King leaves for Saint Marcoul, and from there he is to take the road to Bar-le-Duc.[1]

Political reasons were assigned for this journey of the court to Lorraine ; but the affection which united the young King and Queen to Charles and Claude appears to have been the real motive. At Bar, before separating from his sister and brother-in-law, Francis admitted Charles to the Order of

---
[1] Perrenot de Chantonnay to the Duchess of Parma, 19th September 1559.

the Knights of St. Michael on Michaelmas Day, and formally recognised his suzerainty over the Barrais.

The Duke and Duchess now proceeded to their capital of Nancy, where everything was ready for their solemn entry. It appears, however, that, educated as he had been at the court of France, an absolute monarchy, Charles was not as yet prepared to meet the wishes of his nobles, and to give the usual pledges required of a Duke of Lorraine on his accession—the promise of respecting their privileges and confirming their prerogatives; and for this reason he eluded the formal ceremonial, and brought his Duchess quietly into the town, from whence they shortly went on to the famous Abbey of Rèmiremont. Here he willingly performed a duty also required of him—that of vowing, in the presence of the abbess, and with his hands clasped on the shrine of St. Romaric, to respect for ever the privileges of the canonesses of the monastery. After this ceremony Charles and Claude returned to Nancy, and, confiding the care of the duchy to Duchess Christina, they once more joined the court of France. And it was only after another two years had passed that they entered upon the government of the duchy.

In the autumn of 1560, then, Charles and Claude commenced their new life and duties. The medal struck of Charles in the same year represents him as a handsome man in the prime of life, with high forehead, straight nose, and martial and dignified air. His qualities as a ruler were of a high order, to which the events of his exceptionally long reign bear witness. A fervent Catholic, his efforts were at first chiefly directed to preventing the spread of heresy in his domain; and although free from the spirit of cruelty of his age, and an enemy to violent measures, he established a sort of cordon on the frontiers of Lorraine, forbidding the entry into the duchy of any persons affecting the new opinions, and to meet the danger on its own ground he founded the University of Pont-à-Mousson. "A legislator and administrator, loved and admired by his people, . . . prudent, affable, and, when required, of an unbounded generosity." Such was the man to whom Claude owed fifteen years of peace and happiness. Faithful to his motto, "Par amor aequa fides," Charles seems to have surrounded his wife with constant marks of his affection. The old account-books of the Treasury of Lorraine still bear witness to this by entries such as these—"a golden ornament," or "pieces of precious stuffs that M. le Duc gave to madame" on his return from short absences, or on the births of the children; and again, sums of money given to the bearers of letters from the Duchess to Charles, if he was absent even for a few days.

The household of his wife was established on a footing of great splendour by Charles. Claude had eight ladies of honour—among whom we are glad to find her old friend Mme. d'Humyères—and also eight young *demoiselles d'honneur*. To these were added three *maîtres d'hôtel*, three equerries, and many others, also two chaplains. The Duke's household was on a still greater scale, and in festivities and pastimes the court of Lorraine seems to have closely followed the example of that of France, although in this instance the gay doings were tempered, we may suppose, by the simple and domestic tastes of Charles and Claude.

It is impossible to follow our Duchess in her daily life as we would wish. With her biographer, we lament over those archives at Nancy, "so well classified, yet so niggardly of details." It is provoking to find bare mention of a "brilliant feast," a royal visit, or a journey made by Claude, and to be unable to follow her. Her own letters and the history of her times help us a little, however, and the simple records of her charities—of her gifts to the Church or the poor, her alms each time she goes to church, etc.,—all show us her pious, gentle nature, and help us to understand the influence she exercised around her. "Truly," says Brantôme, "all who had to do with her found nothing but courtesy, gentleness, and goodness."

Claude was hardly established in the palace of Nancy when she received a visit from Count Herbertstein, sent by her uncle the Emperor Ferdinand to congratulate her upon her accession. In return Claude sent a long letter "in her best writing" to the Emperor, still preserved in the archives at Vienna. This letter, dated from Saint Mihiel, 1st January 1560 (old style), is indorsed, "Received, 25th January." Communication was difficult in those days, and the Emperor little knew that his congratulations should more truly have been condolences. On 5th December a great sorrow had befallen France and Lorraine in the early death of Francis II. The illness had been too rapid for Claude to be with her brother; but the sorrow of his loss affected her health, and her mother wrote, anxiously inquiring about her, to the Duchess Dowager of Guise. Grief, and possibly uneasiness as to the future—for who could say whether the young King would be as favourable to Lorraine as his brother had been—were the causes of Claude's indisposition: she was, however, able to accompany her husband early in the following year to Rheims for the new coronation.

Your sister of Lorraine will come to see me at Rheims [writes Catherine to the Queen of Spain]. I know not who told such untruths as to say that I paid no attention to her and to her husband, for as it happens, she has had news oftener of me and of her brother since the death of her [brother] than she had had before. . . . I am her mother, and yours, who will let you always know that there is no one who loves you nearly as much as I do.[1]

Charles IX. was crowned on 15th May 1561. The same ceremonial which had been observed for Francis II. was exactly followed. At the conclusion the Duke and Duchess of Lorraine accompanied the King to Marchais before returning to Lorraine. As soon as they were at home again, they received a visit from the widowed Mary of Scotland. Mary had spent the sad winter at Rheims with her aunt Renée of Lorraine, the Abbess of the convent of St. Pierre-les-Dames. In this abbey was buried the heart of Mary of Guise, also lately deceased, and it was here that the young Queen took refuge "to mourn for the double loss she had sustained in the short space of six months."

Charles and his mother, and many nobles and ladies, met Mary at the frontier. At Nancy Claude welcomed her with affection and honour, and here a great entertainment was prepared for the poor Queen, and all the ordnance of Nancy, great and small, was fired in her honour! "The Queen of Scotland," writes Throckmorton, " was accompanied at Nanci with the Dowager of Lorraine, whom they call there 'Son Altezze,' the Duke and Duchess of Lorraine, M. de Vaudemont,

[1] Catherine de Médicis à la Reine d'Espagne, May 1561.

the Cardinal of Guise, and the Duc d'Aumale." The good Lorrainers were filled with sympathy for one with whom they had formerly rejoiced in her days of happiness, and whom they now admired more than ever in her white mourning.

Claude endeavoured to console and cheer her sister-in-law by every sort of festivity, including Mary's old favourite pastime of hunting; but the spirits of the latter were unequal to these kind entertainments, and she fell sick of the tertian ague. Mary's grandmother, the Dowager Duchess of Guise, hearing she was ill, hastened to Nancy "with goodly speed," to use Bishop Lesly's words, "and caused the Queen to be carried therefrom by easy journeys to Joinville, affirming, by long experience, nothing to be better for the relief of that sickness than easy travel and changing of the air."[1]

Mary and Claude never met again, nor have we been able to discover any of the letters which probably passed between them in the years that followed.[2] This visit to Lorraine brought about the introduction of the art of straw-plaiting into the United Kingdom. Mary, seeing the utility of the work, persuaded a company of Lorrainers to

---

[1] *Hist. of Scotland*, Lesly, pp. 295, 296.

[2] One little memento of the friendship which united Mary and Claude exists in the following note from a list of accounts: "À Jacques l'Anglois, peintre de Madame la Princesse de Lorraine, trente-huit francs pour une peinture de la Reine d'Écosse qu'il a faite du commandement de S.A. étant alors à Paris."

return with her to Scotland, from whence, many years later, they were introduced into England by James VI., and established at Luton in Bedfordshire.

The next year, 1562, was marked by Claude's long-deferred solemn entry into Nancy. Charles had sought in vain to evade giving the pledges which the Lorraine nobles desired; but the question became serious, the nobles declared an intention of refusing subsidies to their Duke, and Charles was therefore forced to yield. He pronounced the usual form of words, but at the same time he had a document drawn up protesting against the kind of violence he had been subjected to. This paper, still preserved at Nancy, was happily never afterwards required by the good Duke.

In the autumn Charles went to assist at the coronation of Maximilian as King of the Romans, which took place at Frankfort on Christmas Eve. In reference to this ceremony, we may quote an old Lorraine proverb, which places such a function with "the coronation of a King of France at Rheims, and the funeral of a Duke of Lorraine at Nancy," as among the finest ceremonies of Europe. Claude remained at home on this occasion, and for the first time acted as Regent. Touching her exercise of these new duties, we have Brantôme's words of approval. He tells us the Duchess had "a good intelligence and wit, which she always showed by wisely and prudently seconding her husband in the government of his lordships and dominions."

On the 8th of November 1563, Claude's first child was born, an event which caused universal rejoicing. Letters of congratulation flowed in, and the archives contain many references to the occasion, and especially to the christening. The King of France and the Ambassador of Spain were the god-parents. "On 7th May the King of France, called Charles, came to Bar with a large court to hold the Marquis, son of Monseigneur of Lorraine, in the holy fonts of baptism. . . . He was called Charles. There was made a great and marvellous feast, during the space of ten or twelve days." The child's title was Marquis du Pont, which—owing to his father's long reign—he bore for forty-five years. This was the first of nine children, and Claude's life was in future divided between her duty to her little ones and the obligations of her position. When her health permitted, she always accompanied her husband to the different ducal residences—Lúneville, Charmes, etc.—or to visit their intimate friends, such as the Count of Vaudemont, or the Guises. At Condé, the residence of the latter, the child marquis was evidently with his parents, as his little desk and stool are mentioned as part of the furniture.

Grave and sorrowful events affecting her family took place during the years following, and we have glimpses of the share taken by Claude in these trials. For instance, when the news of the assassination of the Duke of Guise reached Lorraine, and the deepest feelings of indignation were roused in the country, Claude's sorrowful letter to her mother shows how rightly she had judged of the blow which had fallen on "her house" of Lorraine. "I think," she writes, "that they will *never* forget it," and she begs for justice on the "*unhappy* and wicked ones who have been the cause." Charles and Claude were at Paris during the Massacre of St. Bartholomew, that terrible event wrought by the wicked policy of her mother and brother; and the following passages from an account of the occurrence, written by Claude's sister, Margaret of Valois, show us the suffering of the sisters on that sad night. Margaret, who had been married barely a week to Henry of Navarre, knew nothing of the plan. On the evening of 23rd August she and Claude were sitting with their mother, when Catherine told her to retire. When "as I made my courtesy," Margaret says, "my sister took me by the arm and stopped me; weeping bitterly, she said to me, 'My God! my sister, do not go there.'" Catherine bade her be silent, and repeated the order. Claude again interceded for her sister, saying, "There is no reason for sending her to be sacrificed like that; no doubt if *they* discover anything, *they* will avenge themselves" (evidently Claude had been made to believe in the existence of a plot). The discussion continued; but at last, writes Margaret, "my sister, bursting into tears, bade me good-night without daring to say more, and I went away in fear and trembling."

In 1568 a sorrow of a very different kind had fallen on Claude, in the death of her sister the Queen of Spain. On hearing of this loss, Claude wrote to her mother to console her.

Madame [she writes], having seen by the letter of your Majesty the extreme loss I have sustained by the death of the Queen my sister, which is so great a grief to me that if it was not for the consolation I receive from your Majesty, and your orders, which I endeavour to obey as well as I can, it would be very difficult for me to get through these days, knowing the loss also which it is to his Majesty the King, and to his kingdom, etc.

Among Claude's letters there is another, written in a lighter vein, to her young cousin the Duchess of Guise, which, in its simple, easy style, might have been written to-day. It ends thus:—

There, that is all our little news. I beg of you to write me yours in the same intimate way, and I assure you you will never show your affection to any one who loves you more than I do. Let me hear when you go to Joinville, as we are going to Bar, which is only seven short leagues from there; and now I kiss your hands a hundred thousand times as well as your good husband's, and I pray God to give happiness to a life already so blessed, though not even yet as happy as desires your entirely affectionate good cousin,

CLAUDE DE F.

We have perhaps lingered too long over these scanty records of Claude's short life. The end came quickly, and, four years after her sister's death, Claude died at the early age of twenty-nine. One day of November 1574, couriers were sent in all directions to summon Duke Charles, who was absent. Claude had given birth to twin daughters, and was in great danger. The most celebrated doctors were called to her sick-bed, but she daily grew worse: the illness lasted till February. On the 6th of that month she wrote her last will, a document which bears testimony to her deep religious faith and tender thought of others. A few days later—on 25th February—Claude breathed her last. France and Lorraine mourned her death; and, as Brantôme tells us, her husband so lamented her that, although he survived her for thirty years, he would not remarry, saying "he would never find her equal, although," he adds quaintly, "if he did, he would marry again."

The funeral service was worthy of her whom the people of Lorraine called their "Mother," and Claude was laid to rest in the Collegiate Church of

St. George at Nancy, where her husband also was buried in later years.

In our days a marble slab in the ducal palace at Nancy still commemorates this young Duchess, who, "by the royal splendour of her acts, enhanced the august title of 'Most Christian.'"

VIII

SCOTTISH CATHOLICS UNDER MARY AND JAMES

E have again to thank Father Forbes-Leith for placing before us new and valuable facts relating to our national history. We have had occasion in these pages to draw attention to his two admirable works, *The Life of St. Margaret, Queen of Scotland*, and *The History of the Scots Guards in France*, and the volume now before us will yield to neither in the interest of its contents.[1]

In publishing these "Narratives," Father Forbes-Leith proposes to make more generally known the condition of Scottish Catholics after the period of the Reformation, and, to use the author's own words, "without professing to be a consecutive history, they will enable the reader to form his own judgment from the evidence of contemporary witnesses."

[1] *Narratives of Scottish Catholics under Mary Stuart and James VI.* Edited by W. Forbes-Leith, S.J. Edinburgh, 1885.

The many original documents contained in the volume, and now published for the first time, are of singular value, and among them none more so than the Report by De Gouda, the Papal envoy sent to Queen Mary in 1562, and a long-lost portion of Bishop Leslie's Narrative, discovered among the archives of the Vatican. It is of the contents of these two papers, which form in themselves a rare and interesting chapter of Scottish history, that we propose to give some short account.

At the time of De Gouda's visit to Scotland, Queen Mary had passed through the first few and stormy months of her reign. She had settled her Cabinet and Council, and was preparing to make a progress through the central counties of the kingdom, when word was brought to her that a Jesuit had arrived in Scotland, bearing a secret message from the Pope. So great was the feeling among the Reformers against any intercourse with Rome, that Mary dared not receive the Papal envoy openly; and, owing to the difficulties of her position, and the dangers to which De Gouda was himself exposed, some time elapsed before the interview could take place. De Gouda, in the report of his journey, addressed to his Superior, Father Laynez, the General of the Society, gives an interesting account of his adventures, and in particular of his audience with Queen Mary.

Of Father de Gouda's personal history, we

have no record. The nature of the mission confided to him, however, and the manner in which he carried it out, sufficiently testify to the prudence and zeal which characterised him. At the time when De Gouda was chosen to undertake the perilous task of bearing the Pope's letter to Scotland, he was stationed in Holland. Summoned to Louvain by his Superior, Father Everard, about the Easter time of 1562, he was there informed of the mission to be entrusted to him, and received, through the medium of Cardinal Amulius, the Apostolic Brief which he was to bear to Queen Mary, the Bishops, and some of the Ministers of State in Scotland. De Gouda was unable to start on his journey till the month of June; on the 10th of that month he reached Antwerp, accompanied by Mr. Edmund Hay, a Scotch priest, whose acquaintance he had lately made, and who offered to proceed with him to Scotland. De Gouda and Hay were fortunate in finding a Scottish vessel on the point of sailing from Antwerp, and embarked at once. The suspicions of the crew were aroused by the appearance of the strangers, but in the hurry of departure they escaped question. Before the voyage was over, however, the Protestants on board, whose suspicions increased, questioned Mr. Hay about his companion, but he managed to satisfy them without betraying De Gouda, and the Nuncio escaped discovery. On reaching the Scottish port, Mr. Hay took the Nuncio to the house of a relative of his own, where they had the good fortune to meet one of the Queen's servants, "Mr. Stephen,"[1] who informed Her Majesty of their arrival, and inquired of her when she would receive De Gouda. It was a month before the Queen was able to send a definite answer. Meanwhile De Gouda wrote often to Her Majesty, and finally sent Mr. Hay to her to ask for an audience. The Queen, as we have seen, decided to receive the Nuncio in private, and could not, owing to the prejudices of the Reforming party, allow the Pope's letter to be read, or any message to be delivered publicly before the officers of State. News of the arrival of a Papal Nuncio had meanwhile been rumoured throughout the country, causing horror and alarm among the Protestants. John Knox in his sermons stormed against the Pope, denouncing De Gouda, and urging the nobles and people to take violent measures not only against him, but against the Queen herself for admitting him into her kingdom. De Gouda and Hay were in danger of their lives, and had to remain for a time concealed in the house of Mr. Hay's parents. Here a curious inaccuracy of dates occurs in De Gouda's letter. He speaks of leaving Antwerp on 10th June, of reaching Scotland in nine days, and of spending

[1] Stephen Wilson.

two months concealed in the Hays' house before he visited the Queen, yet, as we shall see, the date assigned for this interview is 24th July. Either De Gouda's memory must have misled him, or some mistake has arisen in the translation of the letter. When at last De Gouda and Hay were summoned to the Queen, they were escorted—not without danger—to Edinburgh, to the house of Her Majesty's Almoner. The Queen, apprised of their arrival, appointed the following day, 24th July, for the audience.

We will give De Gouda's own account of this interview :—

We were ushered along with the Almoner into a private room, at an hour when the courtiers were attending the great preacher's sermon, and could not, therefore, know of our interview. I was admitted first, by myself, and having respectfully saluted the Queen, in the name of the Pope, briefly stated the object of my mission, and delivered his Holiness's letter. She said she understood my Latin but could not well reply in that language. I asked if I might call in my colleague Mr. John Rinaldus, who was a Frenchman, and Mr. Hay, a Scot, who were outside, and who would interpret faithfully. She agreed, and they came in, when the Queen turned at once to Mr. Hay, as a subject of her own, whom she had met before, and spoke in the Scottish language. She began by excusing herself for receiving the Pope's Nuncio with so little ceremony, which she said was owing to the disturbed state of the kingdom. Having read the Apostolic Brief, she hoped the Supreme Pontiff would have regard to her ready will, rather than to anything she had actually done since her return, and much wished that his Holiness could have seen the condition in which she found her kingdom. She herself, and the other adherents of the orthodox religion, had been obliged to do many things which they did not like, in order to preserve the last traces of the Catholic faith and worship in the country. The Pope exhorted her in defending the faith to follow the example of Queen Mary of England, now departed in Christ; but her position and that of her kingdom, and of the nobility, was unhappily very different from that of the English Queen. To the request that Scottish prelates should be sent to the Council of Trent, her reply was that she would consult the Bishops as to the means of accomplishing this, but greatly feared it would be found impracticable. For herself, she would rather forfeit her life than abandon her faith. Such was the substance of her reply to my message, and to the Pope's Brief, and there was no time to add more for fear the courtiers should come back from the sermon. I then asked what I should do with the letters of the Pope addressed to the Bishops and how these could be delivered. Would she send for the Bishops and give the letters to them herself, or should I convey them? She said it was out of the question my delivering them, adding, after a moment, that the attempt would cause a great tumult, and the heretics would stop at no violence in order to prevent it. I said my orders were to deliver them, but she again replied that it was impossible except perhaps in the case of one Bishop. She alluded to the Bishop of Ross, the President of the Council, or of the Parliament, who was then in town, and to whom she sent her secretary the same day, requesting him to see me; but all this may be more conveniently related further on. I then asked her whether she would like me to speak to her brother, the Earl of Mar (who was a natural son of the late king, and the first man in Scotland), and to explain the object of my embassy lest he should suspect me of any designs against himself or any of the great nobles. She said she would inquire whether he would see me, but I heard no more of it, and learnt afterwards that it would never have done for me to have gone near him, since every one is so prejudiced and embittered against the Pontiff. I then asked her for a safe conduct, or security of some sort, while I remained in the kingdom, but was assured by her that no one would attack me publicly. Were I in danger of being privately murdered, she could not prevent it, and did not suppose she could punish it by a legal sentence; but I should be in greater peril than ever if she gave me a safe conduct, because this would indicate under what character I had come, whereas I was safe in my present concealment. She warned me to keep my room, and never to venture out. In concluding our interview, I remarked that I had been anxious to consult her, had time allowed, on the best means of succouring her people so miserably led astray by heretics; but as it did not permit (for it was necessary she should dismiss us before the return of her brother and the other heretics from the church), I would only say that the best thing to do was what had been done by the Emperor and most of the Catholic princes, including her uncle, the most Reverend Cardinal of Lorraine, namely, to establish a college where she could always have pious and learned priests at hand, and where the young men, on whom the hopes of the country depended, could be trained in the Catholic religion. She replied in one word that this might come in time, but was impracticable just then, and immediately dismissed us. [Pp. 66-68.]

In a letter of Randolph to Cecil, dated 1st August, which seems to have escaped Father Forbes-Leith's notice, we find some curious contemporary evidence regarding the Nuncio's interview with the Queen. Randolph tells us that while De Gouda was still in conversation with Her Majesty, Mar returned unexpectedly from the sermon, and entering the room suddenly, almost discovered the Nuncio. Although De Gouda escaped Mar's observation on this occasion, suspicions of his presence in the Palace were aroused, and Randolph himself saw "so strange a visage" that he could not but think he had had a glimpse of the stranger. Randolph also declares that it was only through Mar's influence that the Nuncio was not murdered before he could have access to the Queen, and expresses, with characteristic frankness, his fear lest Mar should have occasion hereafter to repent of this act of mercy.

These reflections of the English Ambassador, and still more the Queen's own words to De Gouda, help us vividly to realise the difficulties in which Mary was placed. Forced to receive the Pope's messenger in secret, and unable to take those ordinary measures for his safety which would have secured him from the fury of the populace, the liberty sought for by the lowest of her subjects was denied to their Queen, and she was daily and hourly made aware of the hatred felt by her people for that faith for which she was ready to give her life.

At the Queen's desire, De Gouda, after his audience, sent her the Apostolic Letters addressed to the Bishops, to whom she undertook to deliver them, as it was judged impossible for him to do this in person. Mary, as we have seen, desired that the Bishop of Ross should confer with the Nuncio; but the Bishop, a timid man, told Her Majesty he could not venture to do so. His message to the Nuncio was still more emphatic: he assured De Gouda that at whatever place, or in whatever dress he should visit him, his visit would cause the sacking and plundering of his (the Bishop's) house within twenty-four hours, and endanger his life and that of his household. De Gouda then endeavoured to open a correspondence with the Bishop, begging him either to write to him or to the Pope himself; but the Bishop was convinced that the Nuncio's papers would be discovered and seized before he could leave the country, and could not be persuaded to write.

De Gouda's hopes of effecting an interview with the Bishop of Dunblane were likewise disappointed. Hearing that this prelate had left Edinburgh to return to his episcopal city, the

Nuncio followed him thither disguised as one of his household, but when he arrived the Bishop dared not see him. His attempts to enter into correspondence with the other Bishops were crowned with little success. Two prelates alone replied to his letters: the Archbishop of St. Andrews and the Bishop of Dunkeld.[1] The latter consented to see De Gouda, but only provided he should go disguised as a banker's clerk, and discuss money matters while in hearing of the Bishop's servants, to divert suspicion. This cold and timid behaviour on the part of the Scottish Bishops was a grief and disappointment to the Nuncio, and his heart was wrung by the condition of the Church throughout Scotland. At this period the monasteries were already all in ruins, and the churches and altars overthrown and profaned. The ministers, who were either apostate monks or ignorant laymen of the lowest class, confined their ministrations to declamations against the Pope and the teaching of the Catholic Church. Some Catholic preachers still remained, but they were few in number, nor were they possessed of those qualifications necessary to cope with the difficulties of the times; and of the few members of religious houses still remaining in the

---

[1] In a subsequent letter, Father De Gouda mentions that he had afterwards received a letter from the Bishop of Aberdeen also, showing his good disposition towards the faith.

country many had no fixed place of residence, and they and the small number of secular priests were often forced to adopt the dress of laymen. After dwelling on the desolation he had witnessed, the Nuncio thus refers to some of those causes which had undoubtedly led to this terrible state of things :—

I must first indicate in brief to what the best and most sensible of the Catholics attribute all these misfortunes. They consider them as owing to the suspension of the ordinary mode of election to Abbacies and other high dignities. These preferments are conferred upon children or other incapable persons, without any care for God's honour and the service of the Church, and very often one such person holds several offices in the same church. For instance, a son of one ot the Bishops has been appointed to the Archdeaconry and two Canonries in his father's cathedral. Besides which, the lives of priests and clerics are not unfrequently such as to cause grave scandal: an evil increased by the supine indifference and negligence of the Bishops themselves. Though we can hardly wonder at this, as they are so miserably oppressed that they cannot venture to discharge their duty, however much they may desire it, on account of the fury or audacity of the heretics. I will not describe the way in which these prelates live, the example they set, or the sort of men they nominate as their successors: only, it is hardly surprising if God's flock is eaten up by wolves while such shepherds as these have charge of it." [P. 76.]

The Nuncio proceeds to suggest to Father Laynez

the measures which appeared most necessary to ensure the well-being of the Queen and the restoration of religion in Scotland: measures which—had the evils of the times and the bitterness of the enemies of the Church not conspired to render them impossible of execution—would have supplied Scotland with holy and learned priests and pastors, and confirmed the people in the faith to which so large a number still secretly adhered. The Nuncio concludes his very interesting letter with a short account of the dangers which beset his departure from this country. Owing to the zeal and energy of Mr. Hay and another friend, Mr. Crichton, De Gouda escaped these perils, and, disguised in sailor's dress, got safely on board a vessel bound for Holland.

We must now turn to another paper, which, although also dealing with Queen Mary's reign, refers to very different matters from those described in the Nuncio's letter. The fragment of Bishop Leslie's *History* now published for the first time, and which we regard as one of the most interesting of the documents contained in Father Forbes-Leith's book, deals with the period between the years 1562 and 1571. Commencing with the description of Queen Mary's expedition to the North, and the disgrace and death of Huntly, the narrative leads us to the moment when Lennox met with his violent death at Stirling, and here unfortunately the MS. abruptly closes. The portion of this history which appears to us to deserve especial attention is that which refers to the downfall of Huntly and his family, and the share taken by Moray in procuring their disgrace. It will be remembered that Leslie was one of those commissioned by Huntly and the Gordons to represent them in the embassy sent to Queen Mary in her widowhood, previous to her return to Scotland; and, owing to his intimacy with the family and his knowledge of the events recorded, his testimony regarding the causes which led to their ruin is of peculiar value.

To understand the position of affairs at the time when Bishop Leslie's narrative opens, it will be necessary to remember that when Queen Mary reached Aberdeen in the autumn of 1562, Lord John Gordon, second son of Lord Huntly, who had been imprisoned for wounding Lord Ogilvie in the streets of Edinburgh, had lately escaped from his prison and joined his father in the north. This affray in which Gordon had taken part was favourable to the designs which Moray undoubtedly cherished against his family. Hatred of Huntly's faith and a dread of his power in the north were not the only reasons which prompted Moray to seek Huntly's disgrace. The Queen had but lately, on the occasion of her brother's marriage, given him an inchoate grant of the earldom of

Moray and of the lands of Abernethy; but the lands belonging to the title were in Huntly's possession, and he refused to part with them. Moray determined to secure them, and to effect his purpose Huntly's ruin must be compassed. In order to further his project, Moray advised the Queen to make an expedition to the north, suggesting that he might receive his earldom from Huntly in her Majesty's presence; and on hearing of Lord John Gordon's escape, he ordered him by public proclamation to appear for his trial before the Queen, at Aberdeen, on 3rd September. Lord Huntly accompanied his son thither on the day fixed, and Lord John submitted himself to the Queen's good pleasure. She, by Moray's advice, ordered him to be shut up in Stirling Castle; but Lord John, warned by his friends that he would be in great danger if he suffered himself to be again imprisoned, thought fit to disobey the Queen's commands, and, together with with some young companions, determined to be avenged on Moray. Assembling an armed force, they attacked Moray at Inverness, whither he had gone with the Queen, and would have taken his life, had not Moray had warning of the attempt and protected himself by doubling the guard.

An ambuscade was also prepared for Moray by the Gordons at Strathspey, but the Queen, hearing tidings of this, summoned the chiefs of the neighbouring clans, and, assembling a powerful force, she and Moray returned by another route to Aberdeen.

While the Queen thus remained at Aberdeen, messengers were sent out to call upon all men of noble birth in Fife, Loudoun, Mearns, and other districts in the vicinity, to protect Her Majesty, or rather Moray, from the attempts of Huntly. The Earl was then summoned to defend his cause before the Council at Aberdeen; but he sent Master Thomas Keir, his secretary, to make his excuses to Her Majesty and the Council for not appearing in court, on the ground that he could not do so in safety, the whole proceedings being carried on according to Moray's directions and in his interest. Lest, however, he should seem to be avoiding his trial through consciousness of guilt, he offered to surrender himself prisoner at Edinburgh, Stirling, or any other fortified place, on condition that no capital sentence should be pronounced against him except with the consent of the whole nobility of Scotland. Moray prevented this message being carried to the Queen, threw the messenger into prison, and compelled him by threat of torture to give evidence against his master and his master's children; he also took from him the Great Seal, which Huntly, who was the Chancellor of Scotland, had entrusted to him. [Pp. 86-87.]

On hearing of the fate that had befallen his first messenger, Huntly sent a second to the Queen, bearing the same message, and Moray again used violence to extort evidence from this man against the Earl and his sons. Meantime the Prior of Coldingham,—another natural brother of the Queen,—accompanied by a small force, left Aberdeen by night and hastened to the Castle of Strathbogie, twenty-four miles distant, hoping to make prisoners of Huntly and his sons; but they, having warning of the expedition, made their escape to the mountains. Coldingham made his way into the castle at the head of his men, and was received by Lady Huntly with outward marks of hospitality and friendship. She was a clever, spirited woman, and took this opportunity of strongly asserting, before Coldingham and the other noblemen, her husband's innocence and his loyalty towards the Queen, and earnestly begged them to advocate his cause with her Majesty; but we do not learn whether they complied with her request.

This was not the only occasion upon which Lady Huntly bore witness to her husband's loyalty to his sovereign. In one of Randolph's letters, written at this period, we find the following anecdote. A certain Captain Hay was sent to Strathbogie, bearing a message from the Queen to Huntly. While he was in the castle, Lady Huntly took the messenger aside, and, leading him to the chapel, there solemnly asserted her husband's innocence of the crimes alleged against him, in these words :—

Good friend, you see here the envy that is borne unto my husband. Could he have forsaken God and his religion, as those who are now about the Queen's grace —and have the whole guiding of her—have done, my husband had never been put at as now he is. God [saith she], and He that is upon this holy altar, whom I believe in, will, I am sure, save us, and let our true-meaning hearts be known; and as I have said unto you, so, I pray you, let it be said unto your mistress. My husband was ever obedient unto her, and so will die her faithful subject.

This message was reported to Mary, but Huntly's enemies had so far prejudiced her mind against him that she refused to believe in it.

Soon after Coldingham's expedition to Strathbogie, Huntly sent his daughter-in-law, Lady Gordon, to the Queen with the same message he had before endeavoured to send her; but when she was two miles from Aberdeen she met a royal messenger, bidding her return at once to her own castle. This order was really sent by Moray, for the Queen had greatly desired to see Lady Gordon; but Moray was aware that should his sister discover the truth regarding Huntly's innocence and his own plots, she would in all probability take Huntly into favour, and place but little trust in himself for the future. Meanwhile Huntly, convinced that no castle walls could protect him from his enemies, gathered together a force of twelve hundred men from among his clansmen and followers, and occupied the neighbouring hills. On hearing this, Moray collected some troops and marched against him. When in sight of Huntly's force, Moray sent a herald to summon the men to lay down their arms, promising that if they did so all might depart in safety, except Huntly and his sons and some of his friends. A good many of Huntly's followers took advantage of this message to forsake his cause. Seeing that he was deserted by these men, and perceiving that the enemy were beginning to surround him, thus rendering escape impossible, Huntly determined to give battle. Before giving the signal for assault, he thus addressed his companions :—

If we were about to fight on equal terms [he said], or if we had the alternative of either fighting or retiring, and chose to engage in battle without the necessity which now compels us, I should exhort you to acquit yourselves well in the field. As it is, we are surrounded by an enemy who is advancing upon us, so that our only hope lies in displaying courage and fortitude; it needs not that I say more. To yield would be disgraceful, and death against the odds opposed to you were most glorious. When I look round and see you all so full of strength and courage, many words are uncalled for. Meet boldly the enemy's attack, and doubt not God will give us strength. It is His cause, and the cause of justice, which we defend against the oppressor of our country and of the true faith. We are few, but God can preserve the lives of His servants whether they be many or few. I hope some of those who now appear in arms against us will prove our friends. But should they all continue to oppose us, we have one friend a match for all —the justice of the cause for which we fight and are ready to die; and if this suffers defeat, nothing will be left worth living for. [P. 89.]

These words, in which we may see the true sentiments which animated Huntly in his opposition to Moray's tyranny, encouraged his soldiers, and they stood the first attack with great spirit, driving back the enemy, and putting many to flight. But the men of Fife, and the light cavalry under Coldingham, charging on the left wing, with the musketeers on the right, Huntly's men were, after severe fighting, overcome by the numbers of the foe, and the few who survived turned and fled. Huntly was made prisoner and put to death on the field by Moray's order, a firelock, it is said, being discharged close into his ear. His son, the Laird of Findlater, and many others, were made prisoners and conveyed to Aberdeen. About 140 noblemen, many of them relatives of Huntly, fell in this battle. The Queen had specially charged Moray to spare Huntly's life, and received the tidings of his death with tears. Her grief increased when Moray condemned the Laird of Findlater to share his father's fate, and we realise how little authority Mary was permitted to exercise, by the fact that she was unable to prevent the sentence from being carried out. Many of Huntly's servants and followers were hanged, and Moray remained in the undisputed possession of absolute power: a position in which he could safely crush the most powerful among the other nobles, against the Queen's wishes, and often without her knowledge.

In the following year, 1563, Huntly's heirs were deprived of their inheritance, and the whole family of Gordon branded as traitors. Regarding the fate of Huntly's eldest son, Lord George Gordon, the following story is told. Sentence of death had been pronounced against him also when Parliament met, but the Queen made such earnest solicitations in his favour that his life was spared. He was, however, imprisoned for several years, and on one occasion his life was in imminent danger. Moray, knowing that the Queen entertained a kindly feeling for him, and fearing she might liberate him,—a step likely to be highly injurious to Moray's own schemes,—sent a letter stamped with the Queen's seal to the keeper of the castle where Lord George was imprisoned, desiring him to execute his prisoner without delay, yet assigning no reason for this command. The keeper, a prudent and kind-hearted man, while informing Lord George of the order he had received, yet thought well to make inquiries before carrying it into effect. At his own risk, therefore, he visited the Queen, praying Her Majesty to pardon him for delaying to execute her command. Mary was much surprised at hearing him refer to an order she had never sent, and on being shown the paper at once perceived the fraud. To secure Lord George against any further attempt she ordered him to be set at liberty.

Although we have confined our attention to two only of the papers contained in the volume we are considering, there are others of almost equal interest which we regret we are unable to notice. In particular we commend to our readers the letter of Father John Hay, describing his expedition to Scotland in 1579. The dangers incurred by Father Hay on his return to his native land, and his account of the state of Scotland at that time, render this letter peculiarly interesting. In concluding this imperfect notice of Father Forbes-Leith's book, we cordially recommend it to our countrymen as a very valuable addition to our knowledge of one of the most interesting periods of Scottish history.

IX

MARY STUART

1542–87

MARY STUART, whose charms and whose misfortunes render her one of the most interesting figures in history, was born at Linlithgow Palace on 8th December 1542, at a moment of deepest gloom in the history of her country. Her royal father, James V., lay dying at Falkland—of a fever, as men said, but more truly of a broken heart caused by the evils of the times, and the fatal issue of the battle of Solway Moss. The state of the kingdom, exposed both to the domestic treachery of the nobles and the rapacity of Henry VIII. of England, seemed well-nigh desperate; and it is not surprising that the birth of a female heir to the throne, instead of the longed-for prince, should have appeared a fresh misfortune, not only to the nation at large, but to her father himself. When the news was brought to the dying monarch, he roused himself from the lethargy in which he lay, to exclaim, in mournful allusion to the Crown of Scotland, "It came wi' a lass and it will gae wi' ane." These were James's last words. Soon afterwards he passed away, and the infant Mary was proclaimed Queen of Scotland : a dignity which brought her unceasing strife and sorrow for forty-five long years.

Tradition tells us that Mary was baptized in the church of St. Michael, Linlithgow, and nine months later the baby Queen was solemnly crowned at Stirling. It was about this time that the first coin bearing Mary's effigy was issued. On it she appears as a round-faced baby wearing a cap of the period, and we cling to the tradition which asserts that with this coin of the baby Queen originates the Scotch name for a halfpenny, a *bawbee*. If our space permitted, it would be pleasant to linger over the description of Mary's infancy and the quaint etiquette which surrounded her in the mourning chambers of her mother ; for Mary of Guise was too true a mother to suffer any separation from her child, and accordingly the royal nurseries were established under her own eye. There exists a charming description of a visit paid to the two Queens by Henry VIII.'s ambassador, Sir Ralph Sadler. This astute gentleman, having paid his respects to the Queen Dowager, begged for a sight of her daughter, and Mary of Guise conducting him herself to the nursery, Sir Ralph paid his homage to the infant Majesty of Scotland, whom he describes to Henry as being " as goodly a child as I have seen of her age, and as like to live with the grace of God." This report was no doubt highly pleasing to the King, whose present policy it was to obtain Mary's hand for his son Prince Edward : a project warmly opposed by all true Scots, who saw in it only a new plan for the subjugation of their country. Henry had, however, supporters among the Scottish noblemen. Among the prisoners taken at Solway Moss and conveyed to England, he had found the tools he sought. Having convinced these gentlemen of the advantages of the proposed marriage (especially to themselves), Henry despatched them to Scotland, where they were received with much contempt, and were styled in derision the " English lords." The Regent Arran, however, favoured them ; and with this powerful ally the Queen's union with Prince Edward might have become a reality had not Henry's own arrogance defeated his plan. He demanded that Mary should be delivered up to him to be educated in England, that all treaties with France should be cancelled, and that Dumbarton and five other principal strongholds of Scotland should be given over to him !

We cannot wonder that such proposals roused the national spirit to the utmost, so that Sadler reports that the people would rather "suffer extremity than come to the obedience and subjection of England." Nay, that "if there be any motion to bring the government of this realm to the King of England, there is not so little a boy but he will hurl stones against it, and the wives will handle their distaffs, and the commons universally will rather die than submit to it." Warned by the feeling throughout the country, Arran deserted Henry's side, and, consenting that Cardinal Beaton should resume the reins of government, consigned the charge of the Queen to that able prelate and the staunch national party.

For the next few years, however, the question of the English alliance continued to trouble the kingdom, while the young Queen grew and prospered, in happy unconsciousness of the grave issues at stake. At length, after the disastrous battle of Pinkie (10th September 1547), even Stirling Castle, where the two Queens now resided, seemed no longer a safe refuge for the royal child from the power of Henry and the treachery of her own subjects; she was consequently removed to the Priory of Inchmaholme, on Lake Menteith. Here—in company with her mother, her faithful nurse Janet Sinclair, and her young namesakes and playmates, the four Maries—the young Queen spent some of the most peaceful hours of her life.

Although Mary was only in her fifth year, she

had already made good progress in her education, and at Inchmaholme pursued her studies under the care of the prior and another learned priest.

French was literally her mother tongue, and she likewise learnt Latin, history, and geography, while her governess, the Lady Fleming, instructed her in the womanly arts of tapestry-work and embroidery: accomplishments which often served to cheer her weary imprisonments in after years. Mary already possessed that charm of manner, the result of a pure and warm heart, which was to gain for her so many devoted friends, while it fascinated even her bitterest enemies; and at Inchmaholme, as elsewhere, she won all hearts. Happy would it have been for Mary, exclaims one of her biographers, if she had inherited no wider kingdom than that small and peaceful island!

Meantime the state of the kingdom continued so unsettled, and the danger to Mary so imminent, that her mother and faithful councillors resolved to send her to France, where she could remain in safety until she was of an age to be married to the Dauphin, a union which Mary's connection with France and the alliance which had so long existed between the two countries rendered peculiarly appropriate. It was, however, no easy matter to arrange for the Queen's safe journey. Henry of England's cruisers were on the alert to prevent the escape of so valuable a prize, and the French admiral had to resort to a subterfuge to throw them off the scent.

Admiral de Villegaignon, with four galleys belonging to the French navy, lay off Leith ready to set sail for France. This all the world knew, and every one was also aware that when he sailed, according to arrangement, the Queen was not on board his vessel. But happily Mary's enemies were not aware that the gallant admiral, as soon as he was out of sight of land, changed his course, and skirting the coast of Sutherland and Caithness, the small French fleet passed through the Pentland Firth and made its way in safety up the Clyde to Dumbarton. Here the two Queens were awaiting it, and Mary was consigned to the care of Monsieur de Brézé, who had been charged with the honour of conveying her to France, whither she was also attended by her Maries and my Lords Erskine and Livingstone, besides other faithful followers. The poor little Queen, separated at six years of age from her mother and country, was seen to weep; but, early trained in those habits of self-control rendered necessary by her sad circumstances, she offered no resistance, and allowed herself to be carried to the galley which the King of France had sumptuously prepared for her voyage. An eye-witness of Mary's departure says that "the young Queen was at that time one of the most perfect creatures the God of Nature ever formed, for her equal was nowhere to be found, nor had the world another child of her fortune or hopes."

The voyage, in spite of the dangers to be apprehended both from English ships, and winds and waves, was safely accomplished, and on 13th August 1548 Mary landed at Roscoff, on the coast of Brittany, where she afterwards erected a small chapel, dedicated to St. Ninian, in thanksgiving for her safety.

Mary's arrival in France marks a new and happy epoch in her existence, in place of the strife and danger which had surrounded her in her own country. A life of freedom and sunshine now opened before her, and the little maiden who had been Queen of the few faithful hearts at Inchmaholme became at once, by her innocence and charm, sovereign of all hearts in her adopted country.

In Brittany Mary was welcomed with the honours due to her rank, and she made a right royal progress to St. Germains, where, the King and Queen being absent, she was received by the royal children of France. Besides the Dauphin, Mary was now greeted by Prince Charles, Prince Henry, and the three Princesses Elizabeth, Claude, and Margaret, all eager to welcome her as a sister. From the first moment of their meeting the Dauphin was taught to look upon Mary as his future wife, and she received with innocent satisfaction the little attentions he paid her. All these royal children were younger than Mary, and for this reason, as well as because of her superior dignity as a crowned Queen, she, by special desire of the King, took precedence of all.

The projected union of the crowns of France and Scotland was very pleasing to the King, and from the first he took an affectionate and fatherly interest in Mary, calling her his " Reinette," or little Queen, and occupying himself with arrangements for her comfort and pleasure. Far different were the sentiments of his consort, Catherine de Medicis, who appears always to have disliked Mary, and in later years this antipathy proved fatal to the interests of the young Queen. Fortunately for Mary, she did not depend on the Queen for her education or guidance during these early years ; for although she, together with the French Princesses, appeared on state occasions at court and shared in the brilliant gaieties of the period, her time was chiefly spent under the affectionate care of her maternal grandmother, Antoinette de Bourbon, Duchesse de Guise.

This lady, whose prudence and piety won for her the admiration of all, took charge of Mary's education ; and to her influence we may trace those strong sentiments of faith and of loyalty to the Holy See which always characterised Mary, as well as the tender consideration for others which the Duchess's example was well calculated to encourage. In Mary these sterling qualities were united with the undaunted personal courage which she inherited both from her Guise and Stuart ancestors. This gift of courage was specially appreciated by Mary's uncles, and the great Duke of Guise once said to her : " My niece, there is one trait in which, above all others, I recognise my own blood in you. You are as brave as my bravest men-at-arms. If women went into battle now, as they did in ancient times, I think you would know how to die well." Little could the Duke foresee how truly his words would be fulfilled. Yet perhaps even in her bright girlhood Mary's countenance was not free from the tinge of melancholy which seemed to overshadow her race ; for it is said that when Mary of Guise showed her to the famous Nostradamus, he gazed long at the fair child, and in answer to her mother's questions as to what he could predict as to her future career, he is said to have replied that he saw blood upon her brow. This anecdote is connected with a visit made to France by Mary of Guise in 1550 : a visit full of happiness to both mother and daughter, which mercifully they could not forsee to be their last meeting on earth.

After the Queen Dowager's return to Scotland, she showed her appreciation of her daughter's progress by consulting her on private matters concerning the government, thus early initiating her in her future duties. An affectionate correspondence took place between them, while Mary's uncles also kept her mother well informed as to the state of her health and the progress of her education. In addition to her knowledge of Latin and French, Mary spoke Italian fluently, and wrote verses admired by such critics as Ronsard and Brantôme. She was well read in ancient and modern literature, and, above all, she was a careful student of Holy Scripture. No womanly accomplishment was disregarded by the young Queen; for, remarkable as were her literary powers, she showed equal proficiency in lighter studies. Music and dancing were favourite diversions, and throughout her life she delighted in riding and was a fearless horse-woman.

As we now approach the moment of Mary's marriage and her entry into public life, it may be well to give some description of her person, and for this purpose we will endeavour to describe her as she is represented in a picture painted at this time, and given by herself to one of her faithful subjects.[1]

In this beautiful portrait Mary wears a dress of rich crimson damask, embroidered with gold and

[1] The Earl of Cassillis—this portrait is now in the possession of the Marquis of Ailsa.

jewels; her only ornament is a string of pearls with an amethyst cross. On her head she bears a little round cap ornamented with precious stones which are raised in front, thus giving a regal character to the head-dress. The Queen's complexion is that of a delicate brunette, the hair of a rich chestnut colour, which well accords with the darkness of her eyes and majestic eyebrows; the hair is parted in wide bands across her forehead, and rolled back above the small, delicately formed ear. It is not difficult to believe that Mary was considered one of the most beautiful women of her time.

The spring of 1558 witnessed Mary's marriage with the Dauphin. She was then in her seventeenth year, and the youthful bridegroom was two years younger. In view of an event of such deep importance to both nations, the King of France invited the Estates of Scotland to send deputies to Paris to witness the ceremony. The proposal met with a cordial acceptance, and the Scottish envoys were received in Paris with every mark of esteem and distinction. In the midst of these pleasing preparations, and when the union of the two kingdoms seemed complete, a transaction occurred which, deplorable in itself, also laid the seeds of future misfortunes. Three days before her marriage, the young Queen was induced to sign three secret documents, the legal significance of which was probably unknown to her. By these thrice-fatal deeds Mary made over the realm of Scotland to the King of France, in the event of her own death without heirs. She assigned to him possession of Scotland until he should have repaid himself the monies advanced by him for her personal expenses or education; and, thirdly, she declared that, although in the future she might sign a declaration concerning the lineal succession to her crown, her real wishes were contained in the two previous declarations. It is difficult to excuse those who advised the young Queen in the execution of these extraordinary documents; and if, as is probable, they were signed by her out of deference to the wishes of her relations, it is an instance of one of the weak points in Mary's character. Loyal and straightforward herself, she was easily deceived, and placed implicit confidence in those connected with her by blood or friendship —a trust which, alas! was often fatally abused.

The Queen's declaration, however, remained a secret for the present, and no cloud appeared to obscure the radiance of the wedding-day. The young royal pair were united by the bride's uncle, the Archbishop of Rouen, in the Cathedral of Notre Dame. Mary's dress is declared by a contemporary chronicler to have been beautiful beyond description, and seems to have consisted of a pure white robe with a royal mantle and train of cut velvet embroidered with pearls. The train was carried by the Queen's maidens, presumably the Scottish Maries. The Estates of Scotland had utterly declined to send over the Regalia for the occasion, but Mary wore a magnificent crown, the gift probably of her uncles or the King, and round her neck hung the famous jewel known as the " Great Harry," a present from Henry VIII. to her grandmother, Margaret Tudor.

In this gorgeous apparel Mary's beauty was dazzling, and it is said that one poor woman exclaimed that she must be an angel! The wedding festivities were endless, and the whole country rejoiced in sympathy with the Dauphin and his wife. Adored by her young husband and surrounded by the affection of her relations and of her people, Mary's destiny seemed a brilliant one indeed ; and who could foresee the dark days which were to come?

A few months after the marriage an event took place of grave importance to Mary. Her cousin, Mary Tudor, died, and the question of the Dauphiness's succession to the throne of England began to agitate men's minds. Elizabeth's claims to the throne were denied by many, and, failing her, Mary was undoubtedly next in the succession. Her claims were warmly supported by the King of France, and by nearly all the Catholics of England and Scotland. By the mere force of circumstances Mary was thus placed in an attitude of hostility to Elizabeth. She was—probably against her own wishes—proclaimed Queen of England by her French relations, who also caused the arms of that country to be engraven on her plate and emblazoned on her armorial bearings. Elizabeth's fear and jealousy were aroused by these demonstrations of rivalry, and the question of the succession proved for ever a barrier between the two Queens, and was, together with Mary's faith, the true cause of Elizabeth's incessant persecution of her rival, as she considered her.

Other changes were at hand. In the course of 1559 Henry of France lost his life at a tournament, and Mary and her young husband ascended the throne. Their reign was brief and uneventful; barely two years from the time of their marriage Francis also died, and Mary was left a childless widow, to commence alone the life of duty and self-sacrifice which the interests of her own country now imposed upon her.

Within a few months of Francis's death the Queen returned to Scotland; but before following her thither we must cast a glance at the position of affairs in that country.

The death of Mary of Guise, which had occurred two years previously, had been a severe blow to the cause of the Church. The government of the country now lay in the hands of the lords most devoted to the doctrines of the so-called Reformers, among whom Mary's illegitimate brother, Lord James Stuart, stood pre-eminent. The after history of this nobleman is well known, but here it will be well to remember that even at this early date Lord James had traced for himself a policy of antagonism to his sister's interests. For some time previously he had been engaged in secret dealings with Elizabeth, nor did he shrink from sharing that Queen's endeavours to intercept Mary on her homeward voyage. It would have been highly satisfactory to him, no doubt, had Mary been safely consigned to Elizabeth's keeping, and himself, in reward for his good services, appointed Regent of Scotland. The day of Lord James's triumph was, however, still distant.

In the month of August 1561 Mary set sail for Scotland. The voyage was, she well knew, a hazardous one; for Elizabeth's vessels were on the look-out for her, as her father's had been thirteen years before, when Mary set out for France. On the present occasion a thick fog favoured the Scottish Queen, under cover of which she made her way safely home. The historian Brantôme, one of the gallant train of Frenchmen who accompanied her, tells us of her grief on leaving France. She passed the night on deck, watching the receding shores of the country in which she had been so happy, and which a sad presentiment told her she should see no more.

The friendly mist which had facilitated the Queen's safe voyage unfortunately also shrouded the shores of Scotland, and threw additional gloom over the melancholy reception prepared for her by her people. On reaching Leith the royal party was obliged to remain on board their vessels until such time as the Queen's lieges were ready to receive their mistress; and then, mounted on horseback, Mary, attended by her suite, made her entry into Edinburgh, dismounting at Holyrood. The influence of Knox and his followers had effectually prevented the usual manifestations of loyal rejoicing suitable to the return of a sovereign to her kingdom ; and the only sign of welcome shown by the citizens of Edinburgh consisted in a concert of no very inviting kind. As night closed in, the Queen was serenaded by five or six hundred of her subjects, who sang psalm tunes under her windows to the accompaniment of a few violins and fiddles. Mary, with her usual sweet courtesy, thanked the musicians ; but her night's rest was not improved by the inharmonious sounds.

Mary might well feel saddened by the gloomy and hostile attitude of her subjects, and the future must have looked very dark ; but she was a brave woman, and set herself undauntedly to the task before her. In so slight a sketch it is, of course, impossible to enter into any detail regarding the Queen's life, social or political, or do more than glance at the chief events among the many that are crowded into the four short years of her reign.

One of Mary's first acts was to issue a proclamation guaranteeing liberty of conscience to her subjects. It might have been supposed that what she so freely granted to others would not have been denied to herself, but the event was far otherwise. Knox thundered against the Queen from the pulpit; the royal chapels were—on more than one occasion—assaulted by the mob; and every opportunity was taken to insult the faith which was Mary's dearest possession. In other respects she soon gained the affection of the majority of her subjects, and her winning manner and kind heart brought her the love of the poor. In her charities she followed in the steps of her great predecessor, St. Margaret, by setting aside a portion of her income for orphan children, and by reviving or continuing the office of "Advocate of the Poor." She would herself preside in court from time to time, to see that the claims of the poor were attended to, and that justice was done to them whatever might be the rank of their opponent. The Queen took a prominent part in all affairs of state; and, in a letter to one of his colleagues, the English ambassador draws a pleasing picture of her seated at her work-table in the council chamber, and brightening by her presence the grave and often stormy debates of her privy council. Among the nobles who composed it are the well-known names of Arran, Huntly, Morton, Bothwell, with Lord James Stuart at their head. In him Mary confided implicitly in the early days of her reign, and most of her misfortunes may be traced to his influence. The Queen created him Earl of Mar some time after her arrival in Scotland, and finally Earl of Moray, ceding to him a large part of the territories belonging to this title forfeited by Lord Huntly, whose disgrace and death are too surely to be laid at Lord James's door. Few things in the history of this period are more pathetic than the so-called rebellion of Huntly and the overthrow of this gallant Catholic nobleman, who should have been Mary's chief support had not the intrigues of her unworthy brother poisoned her mind against him.

The next great political event was the Queen's second marriage. Ever since the death of Francis this question had seriously occupied the courts of Europe, and various suitors had been proposed, among whom it seems probable that Don Carlos, son of Philip II. of Spain, would have been the most acceptable to Mary herself. But it was evident that any foreign alliance would be displeasing to the Scotch, and that of Spain in particular, on account of the excited state of religious feeling in the country. A nobleman of

English or Scottish birth was thus apparently the most desirable husband for the Queen, and Lord Henry Darnley seemed to unite the necessary qualifications. Son of Lord Lennox and Lady Margaret Douglas, he was the Queen's cousin and a Catholic, and the next to herself in the succession to the English throne.

Darnley was young, handsome, and attractive, and he won Mary's heart in spite of his weak and wayward nature, which was soon to work such mischief both to her and to himself. The marriage was solemnised in the Royal Chapel of Holyrood on 29th July 1565. Darnley had been created Duke of Albany, but this did not content him; and the Queen yielded so far to his wishes as to declare that he should bear the title of King, and sign with her all public documents. Even this dignity did not long satisfy Darnley. From the first his foolish vanity made him enemies among the nobles, while his weak and unworthy conduct was a constant source of anxiety to Mary. Other troubles weighed upon her at this time also. Knox and his followers were making fresh efforts, on the score of religion, to disturb the peace of the kingdom, in which they were encouraged and supported by Moray and others of the lords. The Queen herself took the field against the insurgents; and this rebellion, the second in two years, was easily crushed. Moray and his confederates escaped to England, where they found liberty to plan further mischief.

The next plot against the Queen's peace ended in a tragedy well known to all, and the fact that her husband was involved in it gives a peculiar horror to the crime. We have said that Darnley's ambition was not yet satisfied, he aimed at obtaining the crown-matrimonial; and in his discontent Moray and the disaffected nobles saw an apt instrument for the furtherance of their designs. They accordingly persuaded Darnley to enter into a convention with them, in which they pledged themselves to maintain his right to the crown and the supreme power, Darnley on his side promising to uphold their interests and to protect them in case of failure in the execution of their plans. These general resolutions soon took a definite form and purpose, the first fruit of which was the death of an innocent victim in the person of the Queen's Italian secretary, David Rizzio. This able foreigner had won the Queen's favour by his talents and faithfulness. She employed him for her private correspondence, and sought his advice in state matters. He was unpopular with the proud nobles, who could not brook seeing one of Rizzio's inferior birth and position preferred before them; and to Darnley he was specially displeasing, as it was known that he had upheld the Queen's resolution not to grant the dignity Darnley sought.

The confederate lords therefore determined that Rizzio should die, and to cloak their proceedings, they endeavoured to provoke Darnley's jealousy, by spreading reports derogatory to Mary's honour. Darnley seems to have paid little attention to these false accusations, but, inflamed by his own ambitious wishes, he consented to take part in the cowardly plot.

On the evening of the 9th of March 1566, three hundred armed men surrounded Holyrood, some of whom entered the palace while the rest remained outside to guard the approaches to the building. Darnley's apartments were on the ground floor, under those occupied by the Queen, and here he awaited Ruthven and the other accomplices. Darnley then led the way up the private stair, through the Queen's bed-chamber, into the small turret-room where she was at supper with the Countess of Argyll, Lord Robert Stuart, and three of her attendants, among whom was the unfortunate secretary. Here, regardless of the Queen's presence or of her condition,—for she was shortly expecting the birth of her child,—Rizzio was cruelly murdered, and every insult offered to Mary herself, who endeavoured to protect him. That night the Queen was a prisoner in her own palace, and to what extremities the rebels would have proceeded we cannot tell, had not Mary's own courage procured her release and that of the unworthy Darnley, who had by a partial confession obtained her forgiveness.

On the second night after the murder, the royal pair escaped from Holyrood and rode to Dunbar. Here they were safe, but Mary was, as she wrote to one of her uncles, a Queen without a kingdom. Happily this state of affairs was of short duration; her loyal subjects rallied round their sovereign, and ten days later Mary returned in triumph to Edinburgh. Darnley, who had acknowledged only a portion of his own share in the late crime, now turned informer and revealed the names of some of his accomplices. These in their turn laid before the Queen the two bonds with their fatal signatures, and she thus became aware of the extent of Darnley's treachery and ingratitude. We can imagine what such a revelation must have cost Mary, and the utter faithlessness of her husband must have caused her to distrust all around her; but she was, as always, too forgiving. At this moment, when her condition unfitted her for political cares, the peace of the kingdom was her first thought, and a reconciliation was effected for the time between her and her rebellious lords. Edinburgh Castle was considered the safest residence for her at this time : here; therefore, she took up her abode, and on the 19th of July the pealing of cannon announced the birth of an heir to the throne. This event seemed a promise of future peace and prosperity to the kingdom, and for a time all parties united in common rejoicings. Elizabeth herself sent messages of good-will and congratulation, and agreed to be godmother to the infant Prince.

It had been arranged that the baptism should take place at Stirling, but before that event the Queen's life was placed in great danger by a serious illness at Jedburgh, whither she went to hold the Assizes. On this occasion Mary's courage edified all around her. Aware of her danger, she prepared for death with great faith and calmness. Addressing the noblemen who surrounded her, she commended her son to their care, and implored them not to persecute the Catholics. She declared that she died in the Catholic Faith, and that she pardoned all who had injured her, and in especial Darnley.

The latter, whose conduct was becoming more and more heartless and capricious, was not with her during her illness, but on her convalescence he paid her a hasty visit. It was about this time that the designs against this unhappy prince first come before our notice. The chief noblemen whom he had so deeply offended had determined upon his ruin. The first step in these proceedings was to suggest to Mary that she should consent to a divorce or separation from her unworthy husband, and for this purpose a deputation consisting of Moray, Argyll, Maitland, Huntly, and Bothwell waited upon her. To their proposal, however, Mary returned a distinct and dignified refusal. "I will," said she, "that ye do nothing through which any spot may be laid on my honour or conscience; and therefore I pray you rather let the matter be in the state that it is, abiding till God of His goodness put remedy thereto."

Thus balked in their wishes, Maitland and his accomplices set themselves to plan a deadlier method of revenge.

In the meantime, the Court assembled at Stirling for the baptism of Prince James, which was performed on 17th December with great magnificence. Mary bore her part in the festivities with her usual grace and amiability, but she was sad at heart, for Darnley had—from a feeling of pique and jealousy—utterly refused to be present on this happy occasion. He foresaw that he would not be treated by Elizabeth's envoys with the deference and honours he desired. He therefore withdrew to Glasgow, where he was shortly afterwards seized with the small-pox. Illness often effects a moral cure, and Darnley, sick and lonely, began to regret his cruel and wayward behaviour, and sent to request Mary to go to him, which she hastened to do. A happy reconciliation took place, and Darnley begged Mary never to leave him. It would have been more fitting had Darnley undertaken never again to desert his wife;

but Mary was too happy at the change in his sentiments to quarrel with the manner of their expression. Towards the end of January, Darnley was sufficiently recovered to travel to Edinburgh; here—in order to avoid any risk of infection for the baby Prince at Holyrood—the King was lodged in a house in the south part of the town, called the Kirk o' Field. In this place, destined to be so fatal to him, Darnley was comfortably established, and here the Queen was with him constantly.

In these last days of his life, Darnley's better nature asserted itself, and there seemed a greater prospect of future happiness for the royal pair than had ever before been the case. But these hopes were not to be realised : Darnley's enemies had now matured their plans, and on the 9th of February the blow was struck. Shortly after midnight Edinburgh was startled by the sound of a terrible explosion. The house of Kirk o' Field had been blown up, and the lifeless body of the King was found lying within a few yards of the building. The precise manner in which Darnley met his death will probably never be known ; but from the fact that his body bore no marks of violence it is conjectured that he did not suffer in the explosion, but was intercepted and strangled as he was attempting to make his escape. Bothwell, whom we now know to have been the chief actor in this tragedy, brought the fatal news to the Queen, on whom the shock fell the more heavily that she had parted from her husband but a few hours before in good health and spirits.

In her grief, Mary showed all the energy of her character: her one wish was to discover her husband's murderers. She had also fresh cause of anxiety for herself and her helpless child, for she well understood that by Darnley's assassination the conspirators had gained another step in their secret warfare against the throne. Mary's feelings at this moment of trial are well summed up in a letter to her ambassador in Paris, to whom she expresses herself in these terms: "God has (we are persuaded) saved and preserved us in order that we should fittingly punish this horrible crime; for rather than leave it unpunished we would prefer to lose our life and our all. We are assured that, whoever may be the authors of this crime, the enterprise was in reality directed against our own person as well as against the King." As may be easily imagined, the discovery of the criminals was an impossible task, as they were themselves among Mary's most trusted advisers and officers, and their common danger united them in every endeavour to defeat suspicion.

Popular rumour, however, soon fixed upon Bothwell as the principal instigator of the crime, and darker whispers, accusing the Queen herself of complicity, were industriously circulated among the excited people. In thus for the first time coupling the name of the Queen with that of Bothwell, Mary's enemies were preparing the public mind for the irreparable disasters which were to follow. So far Bothwell's position had not been a very prominent one. As Warden of the Marches, his duties kept him absent from court, and he was better known as a warrior than as a courtier. He had hitherto proved himself a faithful subject, and was one of the few noblemen who were not in the pay of England; but his moral character was of the lowest, and his bad passions, aided by his boundless ambition, made him a fit tool for the designs of the conspirators. Aware of the Earl's ill-directed ambition to obtain the Queen's hand, they saw in this project an easy method of working the Queen's ruin and attaining their own ends.

Before their plans could be matured, however, Bothwell had to stand his trial for the murder of the King : if trial it may be called, where the judges were bound by the circumstances of the case to acquit the prisoner, their own accomplice.

Shortly after this farce of justice, we find Mary's chief nobility, headed by her brother, signing a petition to implore her to marry Bothwell. The Queen declined this extraordinary proposal; but Bothwell was determined to effect by force what he could not obtain by persuasion.

On the 24th of April (1567), accordingly, as the Queen was returning from Stirling, where she had been visiting her little son, Bothwell, accompanied by a large force, intercepted the royal party, and on the plea of having discovered some plot against the Queen, persuaded her and some of her retinue to take refuge in his castle of Dunbar. Here, instead of finding safety from danger, fresh perils awaited her, for she found herself the Earl's prisoner. These days must have been the darkest in Mary's life. What sorrows in the past or future could compare with the indignities which, according to Bothwell's own confession, were then heaped upon her! He did not hesitate to resort to violence to attain his end, and before the Queen was permitted to return to Edinburgh he had obtained her consent to the marriage. This step, so fatal in its results, has been so amply discussed by Mary's biographers that we feel a diffidence in approaching a subject to which it is impossible to do justice within the narrow limits of our sketch; but it will be well to draw attention to the following facts.

Mary's enemies would have us believe that the Queen had for some time already indulged in a guilty passion for Bothwell, and that she was an only too willing bride; but happily the simple facts of the case are a sufficient refutation of such a charge. We find that, after undergoing the insults we have mentioned, Mary, far from being a free agent, was virtually kept a prisoner till the day of the marriage. She was allowed to return to Edinburgh, but only under Bothwell's care, who kept her under strict ward and guard until she became his wife. That Mary was forced into the marriage sorely against her will is also apparent both from her own report of the transaction, and from the testimony of contemporary witnesses of high character. It is evident that, under the circumstances of the case, no other course was now open to her.

The second great charge against Mary, founded on the supposition that Bothwell's first marriage was a valid one, and that therefore she was consenting to an immoral and illegal union, can now by grave documentary evidence also be entirely disproved. Bothwell's marriage with Lady Jean Gordon was already annulled for the cause of consanguinity, both by the Pope's Legate in Scotland and by the Kirk; and that the Church sanctioned the Queen's marriage is made evident by the presence of the Primate and two other Catholic Bishops at the ceremony. The marriage took place on 15th May, and there were present, besides the Bishops alluded to, the Earls of Crawford, Huntly, and Sutherland, together with several other noblemen and gentlemen. Moray, as we know, had conveniently absented himself during this period of unusual trial for his sister; but his signature at the head of Bothwell's "Band" leaves no doubt as to his sentiments regarding the marriage. One important person refused to be a witness of an act which he deplored,—Du Croc, the French ambassador,—but he paid his respects to the Queen in the course of the day, and he tells us that he found her in the deepest dejection. She told him that she only desired death. Melville, her trusted attendant, corroborates this statement in even stronger terms. This unhappy union only lasted one month. Those who had built up, now hastened to destroy. The nobles who had urged the Queen to marry Bothwell, rose to deliver—as they said—their beloved mistress from his hands, and to execute justice for the King's murder, which was now openly laid at the Earl's door.

On 15th June the opposing parties met on Carberry Hill, and here, without a blow being struck on either side, Mary virtually lost her kingdom. The Queen, anxious to avoid bloodshed, endeavoured to come to terms with the rebels, and at length determined upon the fatal step of placing herself in the hands of the confederates, who protested their entire loyalty to her person. She first, however, required that Bothwell should be allowed to depart in safety. His late accomplices dared not refuse, and he left the field a free man, unhindered by the very men who had so loudly declared war against him. The Queen and Bothwell never met again.

As soon as the confederates had the Queen in their power, their true sentiments became apparent. Mary was subjected to every species of insult, and after being imprisoned for a night in Edinburgh, she was hurried to Lochleven Castle and consigned to the care of Sir William Douglas and his mother, from whom she could hope for no sympathy.

The Queen being thus safe in prison, the first object of the rebels was to give a colour to their proceedings. For this purpose they again signed a "bond," reiterating that they had taken up arms to deliver Mary from the "thraldom and bondage" to which Bothwell had subjected her; adding that they did so in "lawful obedience *to our sovereign*," as if Mary herself had given orders for her own imprisonment. Such a declaration needs no comment.

The position of the confederates seemed indeed full of danger. Their number was small, by far the greater portion of the higher nobility being still loyal to the Queen, while both England and France denied their support. For once Scottish rebels met with no sympathy from Elizabeth, who seems to have been sincerely horrified at the attack on Mary, and the outrages offered to her both as a woman and a sovereign.

In France, the young King Charles warmly

sympathised with his sister-in-law, for whom he had always had a real affection; and his sentiments would have taken a more active shape had not his mother, who had never loved Mary, interposed her influence to arrest the assistance he was willing to send. For the present, therefore, the amicable feelings excited on behalf of the hapless prisoner bore no fruit. Elizabeth's efforts to effect her liberation were steadily eluded, and at last entirely crushed, by the policy of her chief adviser, Cecil; and many months passed before the courage and devotion of some of her subjects brought about the Queen's release. In many ways this imprisonment, at the hands of her own ungrateful nobles, must have been far harder for Mary to bear than the long years of her captivity in England; but her faith and resignation, and her bright, hopeful spirit, helped her through the weary days. There was one person in whose affection the Queen still trusted, wonderful as it seems. She looked forward to Moray's return, in the belief that he had the will and the power to effect her deliverance. He, on his side, was hastening back to secure the prize he had so long desired, and in the meantime was endeavouring to strengthen his position by spreading a fresh report against his sister. It is from him that we now first hear of the famous "Casket Letters," as they are called. These letters, which purported to be written by the Queen to Bothwell, contain the only proof ever produced of Mary's complicity in Darnley's murder; and, if genuine, they would without doubt have established her guilt. The Queen's enemies, therefore, make much of them, even now, when the evidence of their being forgeries seems to be overwhelming. It is well to remember that Mary's own contemporaries did not believe in them; for when Moray, later on, took them to England to incriminate his sister, so little was thought of his pretended proofs, that he had to take back the letters, and we hear no more of them.

Meanwhile, grave events were occurring of cruel significance to the Queen. Before Moray reached home, Mary had signed the abdication extorted from her by force, and her young son had been solemnly crowned at Stirling. Before accepting the regency now offered him, Moray went through the farce of visiting his sister and endeavouring to win her consent and approval; but in this interview, Mary's eyes were opened as to his true character, and she utterly refused his request.

As the year of the Queen's captivity drew to a close, a gleam of hope and prosperity shone on her fortunes. By the aid of a few faithful attendants, Mary escaped from Lochleven, and was joined by the loyal Hamiltons and several other noblemen. For a moment it seemed as if she would be restored to her throne and the cause of loyalty triumph; but the disastrous battle of Langside destroyed these hopes, and Mary, regardless of the advice of her truest friends, took the most fatal step of her life, and determined to throw herself upon the mercy of the English Queen.

In entering upon this, the third and last period of the Queen's life, we must bid farewell to those episodes of earthly glory and happiness which, like golden threads, have hitherto been interwoven with her history.

The next nineteen years lie stretched before us in a long monotony of baffled hopes and weary captivity, until the end is reached at Fotheringay. Could Mary have foreseen what was in store for her when she entered England, she might well have applied to that country Dante's famous line, "Leave every hope, ye who enter here." We, who know the sequel, wonder how it was that the Queen could make the fatal mistake of trusting Elizabeth; but once more Mary's own loyal nature misled her, and this time the error proved irremediable.

Mary and her small retinue of faithful subjects landed at a point on the English coast, called to this day Maryport. Here she was received by the Deputy Warden of the Western Marches and conducted to Carlisle, where it was agreed she should remain until Elizabeth could be informed of her arrival. At first the English Queen's sympathies were aroused, and it seemed as if she would welcome Mary as became their mutual rank and relationship ; but the old jealous policy soon prevailed, and Mary, instead of an honoured guest, soon found herself the prisoner of her sister queen.

Now begin a series of political intrigues which ended only with Mary's life. Could Elizabeth and her Scotch confederates have proved to their own satisfaction that Mary was guilty of the great crimes imputed to her, their path would have been easy and Mary's fate would soon have been sealed ; but the proofs brought forward to criminate her failed, as we have said, to convince even those most anxious of being persuaded of her guilt. Unable to condemn Mary on these grounds, Elizabeth still, however, pursued her short-sighted policy, and determined to keep her cousin in her own power ; and in so doing she prepared for herself also nineteen years of misery. This was only natural. So long as the Queen of Scotland remained a prisoner, so long did her friends and adherents endeavour to procure her freedom ; hence the constant succession of plots and conspiracies both in England and abroad which distracted Elizabeth's reign, and brought with them ready punishment for her injustice.

During these years Mary passed through every

phase of trial and humiliation. Seven times her prison was changed, through some fear or fancy of Elizabeth's. The damp of these abodes and the sedentary life gravely affected her health; while the constant possibility of death by poison or secret assassination would have crushed the spirit of any ordinary woman : but Mary never lost hope or courage, and by her bright unselfishness cheered the failing spirits of the attendants who so faithfully clung to her fallen fortunes. If we seek for the source of Mary's heroism, we shall find it in the Faith which had always been her support. In all her trials she saw, and lovingly accepted, God's will for her. Prayer was her constant solace ; powerless as she was to work actively for God's glory, her thoughts and prayers were occupied with His interests and those of His Church, and she often expressed her desire to lay down her life for the Catholic Faith. In this little sketch it is impossible for us to attempt any connected history of the period of the Queen's imprisonment : we will therefore confine our attention to the last year of Mary's life, with its final trials ending in the death, which, ignominious in the sight of men, was welcome to her as the end of all her sorrows and the commencement of her true happiness.

The first days of the year 1586 found the Queen established at Chartley, in Staffordshire :

a welcome change from her last cold and damp prison at Tutbury. The new year also brought her fresh hopes of freedom. Spain was moving on her behalf, and her English friends were unfortunately not idle. We say unfortunately; because nothing more unhappy in its execution, or more disastrous in its results, can be imagined than the conspiracy known as the Babington Plot. This project had a two-fold object: the rescue of Queen Mary, and, side by side with this, a design conceived by a few desperate individuals for the assassination of Queen Elizabeth. The latter project was carefully concealed from Mary; but she knew, and, as was natural, keenly sympathised with the efforts for her deliverance. Walsingham, —now Elizabeth's Prime Minister,—through his innumerable spies, was aware of the conspiracy long before it was ripe, and determined to make use of it for his own ends. Hitherto no evidence had been produced against Queen Mary sufficient to justify her death in the eyes of the law; but now the Minister saw his way to destroy her by involving her in the plot against the person of Elizabeth. Through the treachery of some of the conspirators, and the connivance of Walsingham and Mary's jailor, Sir Amyas Paulett, an ingenious method of introducing letters to the Queen in prison, and of receiving her replies, was instituted, by which she was completely deceived. For some

Mary Stuart 285

time Mary corresponded freely with her friends abroad and her adherents at home. Each of her letters was opened and read by Walsingham and his assistants, resealed, and sent on to its destination with, we have every reason to believe, such additions and alterations as the Minister considered useful for his purpose. When the matter had progressed as far as it was deemed necessary, the blow fell. Babington and his associates, the comparatively innocent agents in the plot, were imprisoned to await a cruel death, while the Queen of Scots was hastily removed from Chartley, and her private papers seized, in the hope that they would contain the longed-for evidence of her complicity in the projected attack on Elizabeth. No such evidence, however, was forthcoming, and the position of Elizabeth and her Ministers became one of difficulty. From hatred of Mary's religion, and jealousy of her as next in succession to the crown, Elizabeth desired her cousin's death. She still, however, hesitated. To take the life of a sister queen was a crime from which even she shrank: she dreaded the opinion of her fellow monarchs, and she feared the judgment of posterity, but in the end jealousy prevailed. Supported by the wishes of her Ministers, she determined to bring Mary to trial for the pretended crime of conspiracy against her life.

On 25th September 1586 Mary was conveyed

to her last prison, the Castle of Fotheringay. This gloomy fortress—a fitting place for the tragedy which was about to follow—seems to have impressed the Queen with sad forebodings from the first. As her carriage entered the gateway, she exclaimed, "I am lost."

On 15th October the captive Queen, who lay ill in bed, was visited by three of Elizabeth's Commissioners, who had brought her a letter from that Queen, demanding her, in obedience to the laws of the kingdom, to answer the questions which should be put to her. Mary replied with dignity that, being a crowned Queen, she could not be judged by subjects, declaring at the same time that she was innocent of any attempt against her cousin. The Commissioners again endeavoured to persuade Mary to consent to the proposed trial, but with no greater success. Elizabeth, informed of this, wrote again to Mary, urging her to submit, and hinting at future assistance if she would consent. On receiving this letter, Mary yielded. Once more, relying on Elizabeth's sympathy and confiding in her own innocence, she placed herself at the mercy of her enemies.

Two days later the Great Hall at Fotheringay presented a strange spectacle. At one end was erected the throne and canopy of state, representing the absent Queen of England, close to which was placed an inferior seat for the royal prisoner. The judges and their attendant lawyers and notaries occupied the body of the hall. At nine o'clock in the morning Mary appeared, escorted by halberdiers and supported by her faithful master of the household, Melville, and her physician, Burgoing. When she saw all the preparations, she said sadly: "I see many advocates, but not one for me."

The Lord Chancellor opened the proceedings by declaring that, in bringing the Queen of Scotland to trial, his mistress was actuated by "her sense of duty, and the needs of God's cause."

In reply, Mary formally protested against the injustice of her trial. "If I consent to answer," she said, "it is of my own free will, taking God for my witness that I am innocent." The act of accusation was then read, in which she was declared guilty of having known of, and participated in, the plot against Elizabeth. In support of the accusation, copies of letters were shown purporting to be Mary's, but, as on all similar occasions, no original documents were forthcoming. The alleged confessions of Babington and the Queen's secretaries were also produced.

The trial continued for two days, during which time Mary, alone and unaided, defended herself with a dignity and vigour which confounded her judges. "I am innocent," she said: "God knows it. My only crimes are my birth, the injuries which I have received, and the religion which I profess. Of my birth I am proud; I know how to pardon the injuries; and as for my religion, it has been my hope and my consolation in my afflictions, and I am ready to seal it with my blood. I should be happy, at that price, to purchase relief for the oppressed Catholics." In the face of this defence, and in the absence of all real proof against the prisoner, her judges were silenced. Elizabeth hesitated once more. She then determined to preside herself at a fresh trial, but, true to her fixed resolve never to see her cousin, Mary was not suffered to plead her cause in person. The court reassembled at Westminster; here the documents were again produced, and this time Mary's secretaries were brought forward as witnesses. Here was strange justice: at Fotheringay, in the presence of the accused, no witness appeared; now, in her absence, they are allowed to appear. On this occasion, the result of the trial justified Elizabeth's hopes: every voice save one pronounced Mary guilty of death, and Parliament, hastily summoned for the purpose, confirmed the sentence.

On 19th November Lord Buckhurst brought the news to Mary. She received it with perfect calmness, and again protested her innocence.

Mary Stuart

When Buckhurst advised her to prepare for death, and offered to send a Protestant clergyman to assist her, she gently replied that she had never desired to change her religion for any worldly good, and would not now do so; adding that she would heartily welcome death. On the following day Paulett caused the Queen's canopy to be removed, telling her that she must now be considered a dead woman, deprived of all the privileges of royalty. Mary accepted the humiliation without complaint, and placed a crucifix where the canopy had stood.

Mary now looked for immediate death, but three months elapsed before the sentence was carried out. During this period of suspense, when the Queen had reason to fear she would be put to death secretly, she wrote to Elizabeth, begging her to allow her the grace of a public execution, so that her servants and others might bear witness that she died true to her Faith and to the Church, and thus prevent false rumours being spread by her enemies. This remarkable letter contains the following touching passage : " I pray the God of mercy and the just Judge that He will enlighten you, and give to me the grace to die in perfect charity, forgiving all who unite to bring about my death. This will be my prayer to the end. Do not accuse me of presumption if, on the eve of quitting this world, and while preparing myself for a better, I remind you that one day you will have to answer for your charge, as well as those who have preceded you."

It might have been supposed that Elizabeth would have listened to her cousin's appeal; but, on the contrary, she continued to wish that Mary, if possible, should be secretly murdered, in which case she flattered herself she could shift the blame on to others, and deny participation in the crime. Walsingham did not hesitate to inform Paulett of their mistress's hardly-concealed wish; but the latter, though rough and hard, was a man of honour, and utterly declined to be an assassin.

Elizabeth's Ministers, impatient of the delay, at last determined to put an end to the Queen's indecision, and took upon themselves to hasten the execution of the warrant. For this purpose the Earls of Shrewsbury and Kent, together with the Clerk of Council, named Beale, were despatched to Fotheringay, where they arrived on the 7th of February 1587. They at once demanded to see Mary. She was ill in bed, but, as the Commissioners declared that their business was urgent, she rose and received them, seated at the foot of her bed, and surrounded by her household.

Shrewsbury informed her that his sovereign, yielding to the wishes of her people, had decreed that the sentence of death should now be put into

Mary Stuart 291

execution, and he read aloud his commission. Mary made the sign of the cross, and calmly replied that she welcomed the news he brought her. "I am happy," she said, "to leave this world, where I am no longer of any use, and I regard it as a signal benefit that God wills to take me out of it, after the many pains and afflictions I have endured, for the honour of His Name and of His Church—that Church for which I have always been ready to shed my blood, drop by drop." Laying her hand on a New Testament, she added: "I take God to witness that I have never desired, approved, or sought the death of the Queen of England." Mary then asked for a short delay, in order to complete her will, and put her affairs in order; but Shrewsbury answered roughly that it was impossible—she must die the next morning, between seven and eight o'clock.

The Queen then petitioned that her confessor, who was imprisoned in another part of the castle, might be with her to help her to prepare for death; but this consolation was also denied her. Shrewsbury and Kent now urged her to confer with the Protestant Dean of Peterborough, but this Mary indignantly refused. Kent then told her that it had been concluded that she could not live without endangering the State, the Queen's life, and the Protestant religion. "Your life," he said, "would be the death of our religion; your death will be its life." Mary replied that she was far from considering herself worthy of such a death, adding that she humbly received it as a pledge of her admission among the chosen servants of God.

When the Commissioners had withdrawn, the Queen endeavoured to comfort her sorrowing attendants, and bade them rejoice with her that the end of all her trials was at hand. She hastened the hour of supper, as time pressed, and there was much to do.

Her servants came and went about her, striving to show their zeal and devotion, though overcome with grief. At supper, Burgoing, replacing Melville, who had been of late separated from his mistress, ministered to the Queen with hands trembling with emotion, and the tears falling. The only person who remained calm and cheerful was Mary herself. At times she seemed plunged in deep thought, or smiled to herself as if she possessed some happy secret.

After supper she called her household round her. The faithful companions of her misfortunes threw themselves at her feet, imploring her with tears to forgive them any offences of which they might have been guilty towards her. "With all my heart, dear children," she answered, with a gracious smile, "as I also beg you to pardon any injustice or harshness I may have shown towards you." She then begged them to pray for her, and exhorted them to remain constant to their faith, and to live united in Christian charity.

Mary then spent some time in dividing her wardrobe, jewels, etc., among her attendants, and entrusted them with little gifts for her son, the King and Queen of France, and others who were dear to her. She also wrote two letters: one to De Préau, her chaplain, begging him to watch and pray with her in spirit during this her last night on earth; and a farewell letter to her brother-in-law, the King of France. When all her sad duties were accomplished, Mary lay down to take some rest, while her sorrowing women watched and prayed beside her. Mary lay with her eyes closed and her hands clasped, looking so happy that she seemed, as one of her women touchingly expressed it, "to be smiling at the angels." The attendants noticed that she never slept, but was absorbed in prayer and contemplation.

At six o'clock the Queen rose and dressed herself with care, as if for some grand and joyful ceremony. She then entered her oratory, where she remained in prayer until Burgoing, fearing for her strength, ventured to disturb her, and implored her to take some food. This she did, thanking him gratefully for his thoughtful care of her. Almost immediately afterwards a loud knocking was heard at the door. It was the High Sheriff, who had been sent to conduct the Queen to the place of execution. "Let us go," said Mary, in a firm voice; and, leaning on Burgoing's arm, she led the way to the door. Here the Sheriff interposed to prevent her attendants from going farther. They loudly protested against this cruel order, and Mary gently observed that it was hard that they might not be with her to the last. She finally obtained leave for two of her women to accompany her to the scaffold.

At the bottom of the great stair Melville, her faithful old follower, was permitted to approach. When he saw his mistress, he threw himself at her feet in grief and despair; but she comforted him, bidding him rather rejoice to see her so near the end of all her sorrows, and commanded him to bear her last blessing to her son. The sad procession now advanced to the Great Hall, which was to be the scene of death. It was hung entirely with black, and at the farther end was erected the scaffold. Three hundred spectators were assembled in the body of the hall, while in the courtyard outside an immense crowd had gathered, guarded by two thousand soldiers, as it was feared a rescue might be attempted. Mary moved towards the scaffold, calm and majestic, her countenance serene, and her whole bearing that of one who was preparing for some great happiness. Arrived at the foot of the steps, she accepted Paulett's arm, thanking him pleasantly for this, the last service she would ask of him.

When the Queen was seated, Beale read aloud the sentence. Shrewsbury then turning to Mary said : " Madam, you hear what our duty demands of us?" "Do your duty," she replied simply ; and addressing herself to the witnesses of her death, she reminded them in touching words of her long and unjust imprisonment, thanked God who had given her the grace to die for her Faith, and once more protested her innocence of the crime imputed to her. When she ceased speaking, the Dean of Peterborough placed himself before the scaffold and urged her to listen to his exhortations. Mary gently declined, and, as he persisted, she turned away and prayed aloud, invoking the Holy Spirit, confiding herself to the intercession of the Blessed Virgin and all the Saints, praying also for her son, for Queen Elizabeth, and all the interests of the Church. Then kissing her crucifix, she exclaimed : " As Thy arms, O my God, were extended on the Cross, do Thou extend over me Thy arms of mercy ; graciously receive me, and pardon all my sins."

The fatal moment had now come. Kneeling against the block, the Queen waited for death. As she repeated the verse, " In Thee, O Lord, have I hoped, let me not be confounded for ever," the signal was given, and the soul of Mary Stuart passed to its eternal reward.

In writing this little memoir difficulties have arisen from the very richness of the material connected with this period of history. It has therefore been our object to draw attention only to the chief events of the Queen's life, and in especial to those which throw light on her character. All controversy on disputed points has been purposely omitted.

For the benefit of those who care to know more of Mary Stuart, we subjoin a list of the books consulted for this slight sketch.

Jebb, Sam. *De vita Mariæ, Scotorum Reginæ.* 2 vols. London, 1725, folio.

Labanoff, Alex. *Lettres de Marie Stuart.* 7 vols. London, 1844, 8vo.

Hosack, John. *Mary Queen of Scots and her Accusers.* 2 vols. Edinburgh, 1869, 8vo.

Chantelauze, R. M. *Marie Stuart, d'après le Journal inédit de Bourgoing.* Paris, 1876, 8vo.

The History of Mary Stuart by her Secretary, Claude Nau. Edinburgh, 1883, 8vo.

Mary Stuart: a Narrative of the first Eighteen Years of her Life. By the Rev. Joseph Stevenson, S.J. Edinburgh, 1886.

X

THE CHEVALIER DE FEUQUEROLLES[1]

(From the French)

But Thou, exulting and abounding river!
Making thy waves a blessing as they flow
Through banks whose beauty would endure for ever
Could man but leave thy bright creation so,
Nor its fair promise from the surface mow
With the sharp scythe of conflict,—then to see
Thy valley of sweet waters, were to know
Earth paved like Heaven; and to seem such to me
Even now what wants thy stream?—that it should Lethe be.
     Childe Harold, Canto iii. Stanza 50.

T was the eve of the Battle of Ramillies. I had the honour of serving the King in his company of men-at-arms who formed his bodyguard. We lay quietly encamped several miles from the Dyle, and did not anticipate an engagement. On Whitsun eve the King's Guard received orders to picket

[1] This is a true story. The main facts may be read in the records of the time (1706—*Campaign in the Netherlands*), while the details are furnished by the archives of the House of Feuquerolles.

their horses, and we then realised that the enemy was at hand. The next day, when we were at Mass, at daybreak, we suddenly heard the signal for mounting. I well remember that as the trumpet sounded, the priest, turning his pale face towards us, and raising his hands to heaven, said, "The Lord be with you!" We all mounted hastily. The priest's words rang in my ears for some moments, but soon the hurried movements of the army, the objects that passed and repassed, the approach of battle, the noise of the guns, the uncertainty, a something, I know not what, which seemed to give more light to the day and to open up the horizon beyond the limits of vision, made me oblivious of aught else. If moral drunkenness could exist, I should say I was inebriated in head and heart. My strength seemed to me immense, and my blood coursed with unusual rapidity. With my head held high, I spurred on my horse, calling to my companions and joking them. I was nineteen! and I longed to gain my spurs. Oh, how happy I was!

At last it had come! the longed for day of battle.. I saw the engagement commence, and soon it assumed colossal proportions. I could hear its thunders in the distance, and could see its action before me simple and sublime. Green trees, large fields clothed with shrubs, cottages scattered here and there, formed the surroundings, and in the midst of these moved the long columns of infantry and the serried lines of cavalry and chariots, while over all rose a strange sound of human voices mingled with the metallic crash of warlike instruments. I was wild with joy. I remember that for a moment I thought I saw my father before me, and not alone. I saw other fantastic figures, among them the face of my betrothed. My father seemed to address me. "Be a man of honour," I heard; and in the sad smile of the young girl I read Faith and Hope. Lifting my eyes from the sword that my father had given me to the scarf embroidered by Jeanne, the ends of which floated at my side, I murmured, "Always worthy of you." But a halt that we made at the village of Ramillies roused me from my happy dreams. The battalions were re-formed, and the King's household troops were taking position, when we were suddenly attacked by the enemy's cavalry. The men-at-arms sustained the first shock with their ordinary valour, but soon they were forced to yield to superior numbers.

The King's Guards were beginning to waver, when a squadron of the enemy, breaking their ranks, advanced upon us at full speed. Our company rallied and charged them, cutting the enemy to pieces, and forcing the survivors to fall back on their lines. I saw their captain fatally wounded by one of my friends. When the poor wretch let go the reins of his horse and fell back, his eyes, lit up with despair, fixed themselves upon me, and his lips, stained with blood, murmured some unintelligible words. When he fell, the noise of the fall made me again turn my eyes in his direction. His face seemed to distort itself, and he stretched out his arm as if he were invoking a curse upon us.

Soon other corpses fell above him, horses fought their way across the slain, and when I again passed the spot, out of breath, and maddened by the smoke, I could see nothing of the captain but the head and hand. The sight lasted but for a moment. As long as I live, however, in the silence of the night, that head and hand will haunt and pursue me. All around, in a terrible group, lay the dead and dying, men and horses, abandoned uniforms and arms, and everywhere blood. But this crowd, where all seemed dead, had a life of its own, from which arose in piercing accents a terrible mixture of prayer and blasphemy. In the midst of this shapeless mass a head and a hand seemed to detach themselves in brilliant outlines; the eyes were half open, and tears of blood had made their way down the face. I am told this is often the case after a violent death. The lips opened and showed teeth of a dazzling whiteness, and the damp hair was drawn over the side of the forehead, where the veins stood out black and swollen.

The hand closed convulsively over the blade of the sword. Those vacant eyes, the violet hue of the lips, and the tears of blood, I see still; I shall always see them. It will take much longer to read these lines than it took me to receive this terrible, ineffaceable impression. I was carried on by the rush of battle, attacking the enemy, defending myself, when, just as I was being swept beyond the sight of the head and hand, the crush forced me backwards upon the scene, and it seemed to me that the head moved, and that the hand pointed a finger at me, while I heard the word "malédiction." No doubt·the sound came from some other dying man, but still! could it be possible that the captain was thus addressing me?

Meanwhile, in the hottest of the fight, the light horsemen of the King's Guard were performing prodigies of valour; there was a brave rivalry between them and the men-at-arms. We were victorious at this point, but our success cost us the life of Prince Maximilian, who died like a hero. The buglers were sounding the retreat for our cavalry when we perceived that the enemy's cavalry had received a reinforcement and were attacking our right. Burning to drive them back, we charged furiously; but the enemy met us, pistols in hand, and killed many of our men. The Prince, who was commanding us, was wounded in the thigh; but though the wound was severe, he continued to fight and encourage us by his example. In the mêlée I received a cut on my head from a sabre; and, to add to our difficulties, we had to cross an almost impassable morass. The Marquis de Goufiers was one of the first to plunge into it, and perished in the attempt. My horse was almost engulfed, but he made such efforts, vigorously seconded by me, that we regained firm ground. In the distance I saw our standard surrounded by my few remaining comrades, for the men-at-arms had been nearly cut to pieces. I resolved to join them at all hazards, though I had to pass through the enemy's cavalry, which occupied the ground in detached groups. I galloped off, therefore, at full speed, under a smart shower of bullets. A few horsemen pursued me; but I had already distanced them, and was approaching our own people, when I was overtaken by one of the enemy, and before I could turn round to face him a pistol-shot deprived me of both my eyes. I fell, and was quickly surrounded. One of the soldiers recognised my uniform and exclaimed, " He belongs to the King's Household, give him no quarter," and another pistol-shot was fired at my head, crushing the skull. Even in my half unconscious state I realised that my only chance lay in showing no sign of life, so I remained perfectly still while the officers stripped me of my uniform and of my money and then remounted.

I could hear them riding away. A few minutes later I heard the firing of artillery, and supposed that our men had rallied and that the combat was recommencing.

Lying flat on the earth, suffering agonies of pain, and deprived of my sight, I still kept the instinct of self-preservation. All my faculties were concentrated on that thought : my life ! I wished to live—to live at any price. I was so young ! "and the May sun had shone so brightly upon me only that morning."

Soon, however, my senses became less acute. I felt a dull rumbling in my ears, and frightful pains assailed me. My mouth grew dry and hard. I tried to change my position, but at the slightest movement my head seemed to be separating itself from my body. I fainted—and then ! was it a dream, or was it the delirium of fever that brought this apparition before me? Of all my sufferings, this was the greatest. The head of the dead captain placed itself close to mine. I felt his burning breath on my lips ; his vacant, glassy eyes froze me with terror ; and his icy hand pressed mine. If I moved, he moved also ; and if I made a despairing effort to escape from him, his terrible hand seemed to strangle me. I know not how long this vision lasted—a minute, an hour, or a century it might be ! At last the noise of the musketry, the heavy rush of the squadrons, roused me to consciousness. It seemed impossible that I should not be crushed to death by the masses of men and horses. I could only pray, "O my God." I have since learnt that it was the Bavarian Guards who had come near the morass to disperse the enemy. A bloody engagement took place, and lasted long. Little by little the tumult ceased, and the firing died away in the distance. Each shot affected me painfully. My poor head seemed continually to echo the two shots which had injured me so terribly.

The combatants had hardly gone when I heard on all sides groans and cries, words of despair, and mournful prayers for mercy. The sighs of the dying sounded in my ears with an unknown horror. In towns we seldom hear the complaints of men, or if so, they are softened by the tender care of friends ; but on a battlefield, abandoned by all, dying perhaps in the full strength of manhood, the murmurs of the dying are infinitely sad. I could hear the heavy faltering step of those who attempted to rise, one man rose, fell, and again rose, only to fall at my feet. I heard one long sigh, and then the silence told me he was dead. I longed to fly, my youth and the strength of my constitution were in my favour, and after a long struggle I managed to kneel up, and stretching out my arms tried to feel my way. Then I tried to take a few steps, but at each step I tumbled over the bodies that lay round me. At times I fainted from pain and exhaustion, but directly I recovered consciousness I made fresh efforts to save myself. At last I could hear frogs croaking, and feared I must be near the morass, and knowing that death was inevitable if I fell into it, I stopped and lay still. I could tell by the cooler air that night had come. What a night of horror that was! I passed through successive stages of resignation, of impatience, of sufferings of all kinds. I could hear people moving about, whom I recognised by their language as peasants of the neighbourhood, and I called to them to have pity on me and to save me. For a long time my supplications were unheeded, but at last some of the peasants approached me; I described my sad condition, and implored them to take me from the battlefield. I said they should never regret their charity to me. I spoke of money, of humanity, of everything that could touch them. After listening to me quietly these people robbed me of my clothes, telling me they were very sorry for me but that it was impossible I could recover, and then left me, exhorting me to have confidence in God. The wretches dared to speak to me of the justice of God, yet did not hesitate to rob me of all that remained to me. After a time, having treated many others in the same manner, the peasants returned to my neighbourhood, and I made another attempt to gain their sympathy. In the name of their mothers, their children, and of all they held dear, I conjured them to have pity upon me, or at least to leave me something to cover me. I tried to rise and go towards them, but before I had dragged myself a few steps, I felt a haversack thrown over me, and then I was left alone. Presently, however, the men returned and said that if I felt able to accompany them to the village, which was a mile off, they would conduct me thither. This offer re-animated my courage. I assured them I would follow them joyfully if they would call to me from time to time to guide me on the road.

Exerting all my strength l managed to rise. For a moment they seemed almost touched by my state, but nevertheless they walked on without attempting to assist me. I was so fearful of being left behind that I made heroic efforts to keep up with my guides. From time to time the heavy booty they carried forced them to stop, and I profited by these little halts to rest, but one of these moments of respite proved fatal to me. During one of them I fainted, and the peasants fancying, no doubt, that I was dead, proceeded on their way, leaving me to my fate. I cannot describe my despair when I regained consciousness and found myself deserted. My position was now even more appalling than it had been on the battlefield, the intense loneliness and the failure of my hopes utterly crushed me, and I know not how I survived. I had no idea where I was, and I knew that if I was still far from the village, my death must be a slow and terrible one, either the birds of prey or wild animals would devour me, or I should starve to death. For the first time my heart cried out to God with the Christian's infinite trust. Oh how I pity those who, wishing to deny all religion, despise that faith which enables us to bear the sorrows of this life and blesses their patient acceptance. He is indeed miserable who in his extreme need cannot fix his hopes higher than this world.

I made no formal prayer, I used no words, but I lifted my heart to God and resigned myself to His Holy Will. "My God, may Thy Will be done." The soft night breeze came to me laden with perfume. The slow beats of my heart seemed like celestial music. I no longer cried for help to man, I placed all my trust in Him who forgives those who suffer and repent.

The night passed slowly, towards morning it began to rain heavily. In all my troubles I had fortunately retained the haversack, it protected me now, and I lay wrapped in it upon the ground, which I could feel was covered by soft thick grass. At length the singing of the birds told me that day was dawning, and soon I heard church bells ringing. Presently a confused murmur of voices reached my ear; after many ineffectual efforts to rise, I succeeded in standing up and made signals, calling faintly for help. The villagers came towards me, but were so appalled at my appearance that they could not speak, and soon turned away, one of them murmuring as he went, "Let the poor creature commend his soul to God, for he cannot live long." I called to them, imploring them to take me to the village, assuring them that my wounds were not mortal, but no answer came —I was again deserted.

Now began again a time of agony—yesterday at the same hour I had been so happy—I had gone into action full of ardour, longing for glory. My horse seemed to share my excitement, and my very sword glowed in the rays of the sun. Surrounded by cheery comrades I was rich in hopes for the future, which to my nineteen years seemed endless, and now what was life to me. Where was my horse, who loved me and neighed at my approach? Where was my sword, my father's gift? And Jeanne's scarf? . . . Oh Jeanne, my betrothed, whom I should never see again, and who could love me no more. . . . My God, my God, how wretched I am, I cried.

In my state of exhaustion and misery I know not how it was that the thoughts of the joys of this world, which I had hardly tasted as yet, and which I was losing for ever, should come before me. I remembered too that the previous summer one of my friends had lost his betrothed, and that at his desire I had visited the house of mourning. I could see the young girl, as I then beheld her, beautiful in death, with her hands clasped over the crucifix. My friend, standing by with bent head and sombre look, could only say these words, "May you never lose that which you love." And now I was losing everything—fame, fortune, my beautiful betrothed—my whole future. Why then should I wish to live? and yet I still clung to life, and as I heard people coming and going but always seeming deaf to my entreaties for help, a feeling of despair seized upon me. What had I done to these men that they should leave me thus to perish in their midst.

Towards evening I made another attempt, and walked a few paces, but the swampy nature of the ground made further progress dangerous. Again, therefore, I spent the night in the same circumstances, but this time a merciful unconsciousness stole over me, from which I was roused by the chill of dawn. For the second time the church bells and the singing of the birds told me that day had come, and soon I heard women's voices near me, and I thought that they at least would have pity on me, but my hope was vain. Uttering cries at my appearance, they also took flight, and then a terror which had not before presented itself to my mind took possession of me. I saw death before me, not the violent death with which the vision of the Captain's head had threatened me, not the death of the Christian, the thought of which had so consoled me, nor the thought of death made easier by the presence of some loved one, but a death horrible indeed, that of a condemned prisoner waiting in his cell for the fatal signal. I began to pray aloud, and then I called my mother's name. A burning thirst assailed me, and thinking that my agony was beginning I knelt up and made the sign of the cross. "Why, is it possible you are not dead?" said a voice in my ear; "take courage, then, and I will fetch a horse and take you to the village." It was one of the peasants who had encouraged me to follow him the first day. At the sound of his words all my hopes revived. I rose, and trying to seize his hands I implored him not to leave me to fetch the horse, assuring him I could go with him if he would assist me. I threw my arms round his neck and held him tightly, fearing he might again abandon me. Perceiving my fears, he swore he would be faithful to me, and spoke so warmly that I trusted him. After a few steps I fainted, but the good man carried me on his shoulders.

When I came to my senses I found myself in an

old, dilapidated château, surrounded by wounded men who had also taken refuge there. Fires were lit in the middle of each room, and stones placed round them for us to sit upon. The change from my previous terrible condition made me think my surroundings delightful. Some charitable souls came to assist us. One of these good women brought me a "bouillon" made with buttermilk, at any other time it would have disgusted me, but now I ate it with avidity. I had been for three days without food, but I had suffered so terribly in other ways that I hardly felt this privation. Later I was given some bread and an egg, and when evening came some one laid me on a bed of straw. During the early part of the night the noise around me was distracting; some of the poor creatures groaned, some cried aloud, or uttered blasphemies, while others disputed over their share of the straw or the fire. By the middle of the night there was comparative peace, however, interrupted only by the smothered groans or low murmuring conversations. Each one described his wounds, and it is a real alleviation to the sufferer merely to describe what it is he suffers. I confess I found immense comfort in the pity my sad state awakened in these poor sufferers. We spent the night in these mutual offers of sympathy, for it was impossible to sleep.

Early in the morning we heard carriage wheels

in the courtyard. It was a wagon sent from Namur by M. le Comte de Saillons, to take the wounded to the town. When the news came a perfect tumult raged around me, all those who could drag themselves along besieged the wagon. I tried to follow my companions, but no one thought of me, and I was knocked over by the crowd. A monk who had accompanied the cart came to me and implored me to have patience, assuring me that other carriages were coming; but I could not resign myself to waiting, I shivered with impatience, and tried to walk on. At last I begged the monk to take me to the wagon. He consented, warning me, however, that it was already overcrowded, but I seized his cloak and repeated that there must be room for me, and that I would incommode no one. With the gentleness and charity belonging to his vocation, the good monk took my hand and walked in front of me. Without his help I must have perished in trying to cross the drawbridge, which was falling to pieces, and full of holes.

When those who filled the wagon caught sight of me, they told me to stand back, that the carriage was already too full, as indeed was true; but my kind guide appeased them, and promised that I should be placed in such a position as would not inconvenience them. I was accordingly seated at the end of the vehicle, with my legs hanging over the door, and as the roads were rough and stony, I was tied in with ropes of straw. The good monk arranged for my comfort as far as possible, and said a few parting words suitable to my condition. We then set off, the shaking of the wagon added to the pain in my head, and I suffered intensely. From time to time one of my companions died and was thrown out on to the road. I could tell this by the noise of the body falling, by the cries of the survivors, and by the greater space in the wagon. When we reached Namur, we were three less than when we started. At the gates of the town we were met by a considerable number of priests and citizens, among whom were some charitable women. Seeing my pitiable condition, these took charge of me, and one of them gave me a biscuit soaked in spirits. Then a Capuchin monk took me on his shoulders and carried me to the hospital, where he placed me in one of the wards. Some one asked me who I was, and I gave my name. My voice reached one of my old companions, who was already an occupant of the ward, and he begged that I might be placed in a vacent bed next his. Poor De Grandmaison! What comfort his welcome gave me! and how much was implied by his long, silent clasp of my hand. He was the first of my comrades I had met, and between us words were unnecessary. His grasp of the hand meant tears and blood. Without speaking he said to me, "The King's men-at-arms are dead, and France is conquered."

When the surgeons came to inspect me, they seemed quite terrified at the sight of my wounds, my face was unrecognisable and they could not understand how I still lived. The nurses contented themselves with fomenting my head with spirits to bring down the inflammation, and promised to dress my wounds later. I was given food and fresh linen, and soon felt more comfortable; indeed, when I compared my present state with all I had gone through, I felt almost happy. The first night, however, was very dreary. In the first place the doctors forgot me, and my pains increased, then I heard around me nothing but talk of legs and arms which had been, or were to be, amputated, while the cries of those under operation pierced my heart. My heated imagination brought before me incessantly the terrible instruments which caused these sufferings, I seemed to see bodies without arms, or arms without bodies; I thought I saw death stalking through the ward and leaping from bed to bed, choosing his victims. My delirium had reached this point when something touched me and I screamed with terror—it was the surgeon, who had come to dress my wounds. Later, when I told De Grandmaison of my terrors, he laughed and said I had good reasons for my alarm—the light heart of the *gen d'arme* survived amidst all his sufferings.

I could not get over my horror of my surroundings, the mere idea of being in a hospital terrified me, and I determined to get away, cost what it might. Fortunately a good opportunity shortly presented itself. Two of our old comrades came to see De Grandmaison, and told him that they had heard I was mortally wounded. No doubt my friend made them a sign to be silent and pointed me out to them, for after a few moments they approached my bed, and one of them addressed me saying, "Courage, Feuquerolles, you will soon be all right."

"Oh my dear friends," I replied, "I am blind, and I shall certainly die unless you help me to get away from the hospital; I have an old friend in the town with whom I used to lodge, pray go to her and tell her of my state and implore her to take me in." My friends willingly accepted the commission, and accomplished it so successfully that my former hostess, not being able herself to come to the hospital, sent her son to say that I should be most welcome. Without waiting even to thank the young man I threw myself out of bed, and seizing his arm begged him to conduct me at once to his house. The poor man endeavoured to calm me, fearing the consequences of so rapid a move, and finally persuaded me to wait for a coach. As soon as it came we set off, after I had embraced poor De Grandmaison, whom I was not to meet again in this life. I will not weary the reader with the details of the long illness which followed; thanks to my good constitution and to the excellent nursing I received, I survived the terrible treatment necessitated by my wounds, and with returning strength my spirits revived. In spite of my blindness I rejoiced to live, and in contrasting my past misery with the kindness and comfort which surrounded me, I felt the deepest thankfulness.

I hesitate to mention my hostess or her home, well knowing her dislike to publicity of any kind. However, dear friend, you must permit me to linger for a moment on the memories which the thoughts of past kindness recall. As you will remember, I occupied your son's room overlooking the garden, from which the sweet-scented breezes reached me. The day I arrived your daughter was ill, and you concealed from her that a wounded officer lay ill in the house. Two days after she came to visit me, poor child, and I heard her voice. I was told she was beautiful, I know she was good—like an angel. Do you remember our talks, Madame? those were happy days in spite of my wounds, your daughter's companionship made me forget my sufferings. The day of departure came, alas! and I can recall every detail of that moment, the provisions you had prepared for my journey, the scent bottle you gave me, and which I still preserve as a treasure. Marie allowed me to embrace her, thank your child for me. The remembrance of your goodness, Madame, will never leave my heart, and the gratitude of the wounded soldier will end only with his life.

II

In trying to write the latter part of my short life's story I lose courage, the words I search for escape me, and I despair of expressing what I feel.

For me there is nothing left in life. No love, no smiles, no tears even. My days pass slowly and heavily. When my father's old servant has dressed me, when he has thrown a veil over me (for who could bear to look upon me) and placed me in the arm-chair, my day begins. When my mother speaks I can hear the tears in her voice, she has lost her son, the brilliant son of whom she was so proud, and hope has gone out of her life. I spend whole days in silence. I shiver with cold, and it is in vain that the rays of sunshine strive to warm my emaciated frame, and yet I am not twenty, and once I was as gay and brave a cavalier as could be! Before I joined the army I enjoyed everything, my sport, my long walks in the forest, all was pleasure, and when I returned home in the evening my high spirits cheered those dear ones who awaited me with impatience, and who would gently scold me for my long absences.

To-day! when I hear the rain dashing against the window I recall how in old days I depended on the weather, my spirits rose and fell with it, and now I have lost for ever both the grey days of November and the sultry days of August. I loved nature and the sight of the birds and flowers. What beautiful things have I not dreamt when watching the summer sunsets. The boundless horizon spread before me seemed a fit emblem of my life then, with its immense possibilities of happiness. But—a pistol shot has shattered the prism that reflected those brilliant colours.

Only a year ago, Jeanne and I were so happy, and now the thought of that time is more than I can bear. I have lost all my golden dreams; I am dead to glory, dead to love, dead to all I care for here below.

I was told that to obtain Jeanne's hand I must make myself a name, so I determined to join the army, but before I went, we saw each other every day. She would sit in the recess of the window working, with me at her side. Sitting there, sometimes talking, sometimes silent, I had delicious dreams. My great ambition was to conceal from every one—from Jeanne herself especially—how much I loved her. She, with her little moods, now gay, now sad, and her attempts at innocent coquetry, had complete power over me. I obeyed her in everything.

I can see Jeanne now as she looked then, with her head bent over her embroidery, her gold ringlets shading her face, to which the long dark eyelashes gave a special character. I do not know if she was beautiful, the charm of her expression was enough. We were very happy. Now, Jeanne weeps and prays for me in her convent.

But I am anxious to finish this sad story, and when my task is ended I shall wait calmly for death. I have only had courage to continue thus far through my strong desire to make known what a cruel fate that of a soldier may be. The pomp and pageantry of war hides from the spectators the suffering that lies beneath. In the towns, after a victory, when the bells ring, and the cannons fire, when the churches resound to the chant of the *Te Deum*, all hearts rejoice and the young men think only of glory—glory won, or to be won, and their wives and mothers share the enthusiasm. The old men even, uncover their heads to salute the King's young soldiers. Every one is proud of the warriors, whose glory is reflected upon them. But oh my friends, you prosperous citizens, industrious tradesmen, simple country people, you do not realise that the noise of the cannon and the pealing of the bells conceal from your ears the despairing cries of the wounded. Happy, prosperous world, will it ever be given to you to see among the folds of the conquered standards, amidst all the trophies of victory, the blood-stains of those who have died for their country?

Glory is a fine thing. It shines brilliant as a diamond, but also like the diamond it must be searched for underground. When on a monarch's forehead his people admire a costly gem, how few realise the fate of the multitudes who toil in the diamond mines of Brazil or Golconda? Yet it is not difficult to picture the life of the poor miner —working by the feeble light of a torch, bent with years and toil, far from his home and family, his whole life is given up to the search, often unavailing, of the precious gem, and for this jewel he has bartered health and liberty. This miner is the soldier. The diamond is fame.

One day I was walking with Jeanne—it is barely a year ago—and we were both sad and silent. At last Jeanne spoke—"Do not go to the war," she said; "remain with us, friendship is worth infinitely more than fame. Here we shall meet each day, and the present and the future, the sorrows and the joys of life will be ours to bear together." "But, Jeanne," I replied,

The Chevalier de Feuquerolles

"I must seek renown, I must earn some memories for my old age. I want to make a name for myself, so that the glory may be reflected back upon you. Jeanne, in a book you were reading to me the other day, Memory was spoken of as an angel, always young, always beautiful, in the shadow of whose wings we walk, and who smiles upon us each time we look back upon him. Well, we must claim that angel's care. We are very happy now, but we shall be far more happy when I return from the war. I shall be Captain Chevalier de St. Louis, possibly even Colonel, and I shall have won fame among men. I shall be constant to you, Jeanne, for nowhere, in other lands, shall I find your like." . . .

(At this point a sudden fainting fit, followed by a long illness, interrupted the Chevalier's story. It was not till two months had passed that he who had written so far under his dictation dared to remind Monsieur de Feuquerolles that his history was still incomplete. One evening he resumed his task as follows :—)

I was then (to follow my own adventures without further digression) just leaving my kind hostess at Namur on my return to France. Before my start I had, however, an unexpected pleasure. My father, about whose fate I was becoming anxious, sent me a messenger with a letter full of affection for me, and which contained some news of himself. He had been obliged to evacuate Brussels and occupy Liége, which he was now fortifying against the enemy, and as a siege was imminent he warned me to expect no further intelligence for some time. The first time I left the house at Namur it was to thank God for my wonderful recovery. I was taken to the church, and there, kneeling in one of the chapels, I tried to make a humble act of resignation to God's holy will—which for me consisted in a total renunciation of the joys of this world—accepting the desolate life which lay before me.

The next day I went to thank M. de Saillons, whose goodness to me had been untiring, and on the following morning started on my homeward journey under the care of two friends. At Arras, where we made a halt, some officers who were passing through the town called on us. They came from Flanders, and brought news of the war. One of these gentlemen described the gallant conduct of an officer who was defending a position of great danger, a bomb struck him in the side but he continued to fight, preferring to die at his post. Soon, however, a pistol shot shattered his leg and he was removed to Nieuport, where he expired. We asked the name of this brave man, and they named my father!

I fainted, and for long my friends thought I

must die. I cannot even attempt to describe my despair — some sorrows are too deep to bear utterance. My great weakness was in itself the cause of my recovery, I think. I was so crushed by misfortune that I bent before this new sorrow like a reed before the storm—often I could not even think.

At length the moment came in our sad journey when my friends told me they could see the towers of my mother's old château. We drove on in silence, broken only by the rattle of the carriage on the road. Presently this ceased, and I could tell we had entered the avenue and were in the shade of the great chestnut trees. I trembled from head to foot. The carriage stopped and some one lifted me to the ground : I could feel the turf under my feet. Here in old days my father used to meet me! I heard a door open quickly, and then I was folded in my mother's arms; her tears fell upon me, and I could hear her broken words, "My child! my child!"

We entered the house, where our relations and friends had assembled to greet my return, but soon they withdrew and left me alone with my mother. I threw myself on the ground beside her and laid my head on her knee. We spoke of my father and of his glorious death, and my mother's words sank into my heart. " Glory !" she exclaimed, "glory ! my son—oh how dearly has it been bought !"

Two years later.

My mother never recovered from the shock occasioned by our sorrows. Her funeral bells are ringing to-day. O Lord my God, have mercy on me and take me also. I belong now to You alone.

XI

WINIFRED, COUNTESS OF NITHSDAILL

THE name of this heroic lady is familiar to us all, and famous among those noble women whose virtue and courage have given them a place in their country's history. At first sight it might seem, indeed, as if any new sketch of Lady Nithsdaill's life were unnecessary; and of the great event with which her name will be for ever associated, this is doubtless true. The story of Lord Nithsdaill's escape from the Tower has been often told, and we have Lady Nithsdaill's own narrative—the plain, unvarnished account of her courageous deed—to refer to. Little, therefore, remains to be said on this subject, but of Lady Nithsdaill's domestic history and her later life abroad we find many interesting details in the family correspondence, which is little known, and it is on this aspect of our heroine's life that we propose to dwell more fully.[1]

[1] The material for this Article is taken from Mr. W. Fraser's admirable *Book of Carlavrock*.

Winifred Herbert was the fifth and youngest daughter of William, first Marquis of Powis; and, an exile even in her childhood, must have early learnt to suffer in the cause for which her husband was so nearly to lose his life. Lord Powis, a Catholic and a devoted loyalist, followed James the Second to France, and it was therefore in the melancholy court of St. Germains that Winifred's youth was passed — a fit training, perhaps, for a life never, it would seem, very bright, and destined to end, like her royal master's, in a mournful exile. No traits of Winifred's girlhood have come down to us, and we can only endeavour to picture to ourselves how her education was conducted, or whose task it was to impress on her young heart those lessons of virtue and self-sacrifice which afterwards bore such noble fruit.

Meanwhile in distant Scotland Lord Nithsdaill was growing up under the care of his widowed mother. William, fifth Earl of Nithsdaill, was born in the year 1676, and on the death of his father succeeded to the earldom at the early age of seven. His mother, a daughter of the house of Douglas, a clever and energetic woman, admirably fulfilled her office of guardian, and brought up her son in those sentiments of devotion to the Catholic faith and loyalty to the house of Stuart for which his family was famous. When he was about twenty-three, Lord Nithsdaill journeyed to Paris;

no doubt chiefly with the intention of doing homage to King James, but another motive soon arose to keep him at St. Germains. He there met and wooed Lady Winifred, and, as the attachment was mutual, was soon her accepted lover. Their marriage contract is dated Paris, 2nd March 1699; but the day of the marriage itself is not known, nor can we discover where the young couple passed the first year of their married life. By the month of October 1700, however, Lord and Lady Nithsdaill were established at their own beautiful home of Terregles in Dumfriesshire, where the Dowager Countess continued also constantly to reside, and where she seems to have managed the affairs of the house, greatly assisting her daughter-in-law, who suffered from delicate health.

Lord Nithsdaill's only surviving sister had married (in 1694) Charles, fourth Earl of Traquair, and an intimate and loving friendship united the families of Traquair and Terregles. Five children were born to Lord and Lady Nithsdaill, but of these three—Lucie, Robert, and George—died young. William Lord Maxwell and his sister Anne—still an infant in 1715—alone survived.[1] Up to this memorable date there is little to record of Lady Nithsdaill or her family, and few letters

---

[1] Lord Maxwell was probably sent abroad when quite young for his education, as there is no mention of his presence at home at the time of his father's misfortunes.

exist to help us to follow the comparatively peaceful, and possibly rather uninteresting, tenor of their lives.

When, in 1715, the standard of the Chevalier de St. George (James III.) was raised by his adherents, Lord Nithsdaill, impelled by his own Jacobite sentiments, and by the traditions of his house, hastened to join the English rising under Forster and Lord Derwentwater. Lord Nithsdaill was reported to have been followed to the field by many of his tenants; but, on the other hand, it is stated that, far from this having been the case, most of his people were zealous for the Hanoverian Government, and but few followed their master. And this Lord Nithsdaill's own statement corroborates. That his wife's entire sympathy was with the royal cause, we cannot doubt; and, if it is difficult to imagine with the poet that the stately Lady Nithsdaill and her sister ladies were "full loud" in their merriment on this occasion, or that they "sang in the parlour and danced in the ha'," we cannot but share the sorrow of the faithful bard when he describes his mistress's grief on hearing the fatal news :—

"Our Lady dow do nought now, but wipe aye her een—
Her heart's like to burst the gold lace of her gown;
Men silent gaze upon her, and minstrels make a wail,
O dool for our brave warrior, the Lord of Nithsdaill."

Deep, indeed, must have been the despair of the

poor Jacobite ladies when the tidings reached them of the disaster of Preston, and that the prisoner noblemen were on their road to London. Lord Nithsdaill wrote to his wife urging her to join him in town. He knew he would be kept a close prisoner, but perhaps then he entertained hopes for his life : hopes in which his poor wife could not join, for reasons to which a passage in her "Narrative" gives us the key. "A Catholick upon the Borders, and one who had a great following, and whose family had ever upon all occasions stuck to the royal family," could not, as she well knew, look for mercy, and it must have been with a heavy heart that she prepared to follow her lord. Her preparations showed the prudence and foresight which characterised her. Dismissing nearly the whole of her establishment, Lady Nithsdaill confided the care of Terregles to three trusty servants; and then, foreseeing that the house would probably be searched in her absence, she, with the assistance of a faithful gardener, safely concealed the family papers in a portion of the grounds, still pointed out by tradition. Then sending her dearest treasure, her infant daughter Anne, to the affectionate care of her aunt at Traquair, Lady Nithsdaill set out on her long and perilous journey to London.[1]

[1] Lady Nithsdaill was accompanied on the journey by her attached Welsh maid Evans, whose name frequently occurs in the correspondence.

Her letters give a graphic description of all she underwent on the road. The winter of 1715-16 was unusually severe. The Thames was frozen over, and the road to the capital was blocked by snow. Coaches were stopped, and Lady Nithsdaill was forced to perform most of her journey on horseback, and this with the greatest difficulty. She herself writes to Lady Traquair: "I must confess such a journey I believe was scarce ever made, considering the weather, by a woman"; but, as she goes on to say, "an earnest desire compasses a greate deal with God's help." And so the courageous lady pushed forward, undaunted by the cold, and reached town towards the middle of January. Here she lost no time in endeavouring to secure her husband's safety, and earnestly sought the assistance of those in power; but she received scant comfort, and it was plainly intimated to her that though mercy might be shown to some of the imprisoned lords, none need be expected for Lord Nithsdaill, who, from his position and character, was too important a personage to be spared. The poor lady was allowed to see her husband once or twice, before she was prostrated by the illness brought on by anxiety and the great bodily fatigue she had gone through. The only thing that consoled her during this period of forced inaction was the assurance that nothing could be done in her lord's cause until sentence should have been passed upon the prisoners. On the 19th January Lord Nithsdaill and five others were brought to trial, and, on the recommendation of their friends, pleaded guilty. We cannot think that Lord Nithsdaill's reply to the indictment accorded with his own dignity, or with the sentiments which had animated him to draw his sword in his master's cause; and that he was afterwards sensible of this, and regretted it, his "dying speech"[1] affords proof. As it was, all the hopes held out to the prisoners of saving their lives by pleading guilty were vain. They were sentenced to death on 4th February.

After sentence was passed, Lord Nithsdaill still cherished hopes that if a petition were presented to the King, his life might be spared. Lady Nithsdaill, though she could not share this illusion, determined to make the effort, in spite of the known difficulty of approaching the King, who had taken measures to prevent all personal appeals being made to him on behalf of the prisoners; and here we shall be pardoned if we quote Lady Nithsdaill's own account of the result.

"The first day that I knew he [the King] was to goe to the Drawing Room, I dreased myselfe in a black mantow and peticoat, as if in mourning, and sent to

---

[1] We refer to the address written by Lord Nithsdaill on the eve—as he believed—of his execution.

Mrs. Morgan, the same as went with me to the Tower afterwards, as before mentioned, for I did not know the Electour, and might have taken another for him, and she did, so would show me the right. I had another gentlewoman with me, but I forget who, but we went all 3 into the chamber that was between his closet and the drawing room; so that he was to pass the wholl length of the room to goe to it, and there being 3 windows in it, we sat ourselves upon the midle one, that I might have time to catch him before he could get by, which I did, and knelt down and presented my petition, telling him in French that I was the unhappy Countess of Nithsdaill, that he might not pretend he knew not who I was; but finding him going without taking my petition, I took hold of the skirt of his coat, that he might stay to heare me; but he endeavoured to get away, and I held so fast, that he drew me upon my knees almost from the middle of the chamber to the drawing room door; at last one of the Bleu Ribonds that was with him took me round the waist to draw me back, and another drew the skirt of his coat out of my hand, and the petition that I had endeavoured to put in his poket fell down in the strugle, and I almost swounded with the trouble."

The unfortunate petition was picked up by a compassionate bystander and given to Lord Dorset, who managed that it should be read to the King more than once, but without apparent success. On 18th February the warrant for the execution of the prisoners was signed, and the fatal day fixed for the following Friday, 24th February.

On 22nd February a general petition was presented to the House of Lords on behalf of the prisoners. The Peers agreed to intercede with the King for such Lords as should be considered deserving of the royal mercy. By this, as Lady Nithsdaill well understood, were intended only those who would consent to give evidence against their companions in the Jacobite rising. To this she was assured Lord Nithsdaill would never agree, and she felt that his doom was sealed. All London had, however, admired her energy and spirit, and possibly it was owing to the unceasing efforts made by her to secure her husband's pardon that his name was actually included in the list of the four lords afterwards reprieved. Lord Nithsdaill, little foreseeing that this mercy would be extended to him, was now devoutly and courageously preparing for death. On the eve, as he believed, of his execution he wrote a beautiful farewell letter to his brother and sister at Traquair, in which the following passage testifies to the feelings with which he regarded his wife's loving efforts to save him :—

"I allso most humbly thank you for your unparalelled goodness towards my dearest wife and children, whom I most earnestly recommend to you as what is most dear to me after my own soul. You have been informed by my orders of what has passed here relating to me, and what my dearest wife has done for me, so all I shall say is there cannot be enough said to her praise. Everybody admires her, everybody applaudes her and extolls her for the proofs she has given me of her love. So I beg of you, dearest brother and sister, that whatever love and affection you bear to me you will transfer it unto her as most worthy of it."

It is evident from this letter that the Earl now considered his case hopeless; but Lady Nithsdaill, whose courage rose in proportion as hope fled, was even now preparing her plan of escape. Her husband's place of imprisonment was in the house of Colonel D'Oyley, Lieutenant-Depute of the Tower; and the window, which looked out upon Water Lane, was sixty feet from the ground. Escape in that quarter seemed impossible, and inside even greater difficulties met her. The room was approached through the council chamber and the stairs and passages of the Lieutenant's house, while sentinels were placed everywhere— one at Lord Nithsdaill's door, two on his floor, several in the passages and stairs, and two more at the outer door of the house. The chances of an escape seemed desperate, but Lady Nithsdaill when visiting her husband had discovered that the discipline of the prison was relaxed, and that the wives and children of the keepers went in and out frequently. Her plan was to endeavour to disguise Lord Nithsdaill in female dress and to escort him out of prison herself, making as though he were a lady friend of her own who had accompanied her to bid farewell to the Earl. And here her greatest difficulty was to persuade her husband to avail himself of the means offered for his evasion. He was more inclined to be amused at his wife's device than to believe in any successful issue to the scheme. His wife, however, nothing daunted, proceeded to concoct her plan of action, in which she was assisted by her faithful Evans. Taking advantage of the consent of the Peers to petition the King, Lady Nithsdaill hastened to the Tower the same day, 22nd February, and, assuming a cheerful manner, told the guards she was hopeful of mercy being granted to the prisoners, justly judging that if they believed that a reprieve was about to be granted, they would relax their vigilance. She likewise gave them money to drink to the health of the King and the Peers, but was careful only to give small sums to avoid arousing suspicion. She did not return to the Tower until the afternoon following—Thursday—the eve of the fatal day. As she was starting for the Tower, and not sooner, she communicated her intentions to Mrs. Mills, with whom she lodged, and requested her to accompany her, and also her friend Mrs. Morgan. Her idea was that the Earl, disguised in woman's dress, might pass for Mrs. Mills, who was about his own height; and she requested Mrs.

Morgan to wear under her hood another she had provided for Mrs. Mills when the latter should have given hers to Lord Nithsdaill. The two ladies willingly agreed to assist Lady Nithsdaill as she proposed; and, to give them less time to think of the risk they were incurring, she tells us that she talked unceasingly during the drive to the Tower. On arriving, Lady Nithsdaill—who could only take in one person at a time—first went up to the Earl's room, accompanied by Mrs. Morgan, and this good lady having divested herself of the extra clothing intended for Mrs. Mills, Lady Nithsdaill brought her outside the room, begging her, in an audible voice, to send her maid to her. Speaking in this way, and referring to a petition to be presented by her that night on Lord Nithsdaill's behalf, Lady Nithsdaill conducted Mrs. Morgan partly down stairs, and there met Mrs. Mills, who, in her character of a friend come to take leave of the Earl, concealed her face in her handkerchief, with what seemed but a very natural emotion. As soon as the two ladies were safely inside Lord Nithsdaill's room, Lady Nithsdaill lost no time in disguising her husband. To conceal his black eyebrows she painted them yellow, to resemble those of Mrs. Mills, and provided him with a wig of the same colour. As there was no time to shave his beard, she covered it with white paint, and likewise coloured his cheeks with white and red paint. This accomplished, and Mrs. Mills having put on the hood provided for her by Mrs. Morgan, Lady Nithsdaill saw her safely out, imploring her also, in very audible tones, to hasten to bring her maid to her. The guards, willing to oblige Lady Nithsdaill, and grateful for the presents of the previous day, made no difficulty about letting her friends in and out, and this second departure was successfully accomplished. The decisive moment now approached; after seeing Mrs. Mills off, Lady Nithsdaill finished dressing her husband in all "her petticoats but one," covering the whole with a brown cloak having a hood attached.[1] It was now growing dark, and Lady Nithsdaill resolved to delay no longer. She therefore proceeded to lead her husband from the room, adjuring him, as her supposed friend, to make the greatest dispatch to bring the tardy Evans to her, and lamenting anew her delay. The guards, who suspected nothing, and had kept no very clear reckoning of the number of Lady Nithsdaill's friends, opened the door, and Lady Nithsdaill, with her companion, passed down the stairs. Here she took care that the Earl should precede her, fearing that

[1] It is said that from the cloak and hood worn by Lord Nithsdaill on this occasion, came the fashion of "Nithsdales," worn by the Jacobite ladies. The cloak itself is still preserved by the descendants of Lord Nithsdaill as a precious heirloom.

the guard behind might discover him by his gait. At the bottom of the stairs the faithful Evans awaited them, and under her care Lord Nithsdaill was safely conveyed to a place of concealment. But the heroic wife dared not yet leave the prison; hastening back to her Lord's room she took the needful measures to prevent the immediate discovery of his escape, and here we will quote her own words:—

When I got into my lord's chamber, I spoak as it were to him, and I answered as if he had, and imitated his voice, as near as I could, and walked up and down the room, as if we had been walking and talking together, till I thought he had time enough to be out of their reach. I then began to thinke it was fitt for me to get out of it also. So, I oppen'd the door, and went halfe out of it, holding the door in my hand, that what I said, might be heard by those without, and took a solemn leave of my lord for that night, saying that I thought some strange thing must have hapen'd to make Evans stay, she that never used to be neglectful, in the smalest thing, to make her so in a matter of this consequence, but I found there was no remedy but going myselfe : that if the Tower was still oppen, when I had done I would see him that night, but he might be sure that as soon as ever it was in the morning, I would be with him, and hoped to bring him good newse, and then before I shutt the door, I drew in to the inside a little string that lifted up a wooden latche, so that when the string was wanting in the outside, the door could not be oppened but by those within—after which I shut the door with a flap that it might be surely shut, and as I passed by, I told my lord's valet de Chamber, who knew nothing of the matter, that he would not have candles till he called for them, for that he would finish some prayers first, and so went down stairs.

Taking a hackney coach, Lady Nithsdaill first returned to her lodging. There she discharged the carriage, and sending for a sedan chair, proceeded to visit, first the Duchess of Buccleuch, and afterwards her other friend the Duchess of Montrose, changing her chair at each house to avoid being traced. To the Duchess of Montrose Lady Nithsdaill confided what had occurred, and the Duchess, warning her friend to conceal herself, as the King was already prejudiced against her, hastened to Court, to see what effect would be produced by the news of the escape. At first the King was highly incensed, but when his anger cooled, is reported to have made the good-natured remark, that for a man placed in Lord Nithsdaill's position, to escape was the best thing he could do.

For two days Lord and Lady Nithsdaill remained concealed in a small room in the house of a poor woman, "just before the Court of Guards." On the Saturday Lord Nithsdaill was conveyed to the Venetian Embassy — the Ambassador knowing nothing of the arrangement — and remained there concealed in one of the servants' rooms till the following Wednesday, when, disguised in livery, he accompanied the Ambassador's coach to Dover. From there he crossed safely to France in a small sailing vessel, making so rapid a passage, that the captain of the boat remarked that they could not have had a fairer wind, had they been flying for their lives. The good man little knew how applicable his words were to one of his passengers.

Leaving Lord Nithsdaill in safety we must return to his courageous wife. She remained in London until the good news reached her of her husband's arrival in France. Till then it had been supposed that she had accompanied Lord Nithsdaill, but when she made known through a friend that she was still in town, and requested permission to go about freely, she was informed that although no special search would be made for her, yet if she appeared publicly in either Scotland or England, she would be made prisoner. Under these circumstances Lady Nithsdaill's friends must have urged her immediate departure for France, and to rejoin her husband must have been her own dearest wish, but before she could think of her own safety, she had determined to attempt a journey to Scotland, to secure the family papers buried by herself in the gardens at Terregles, and which would, as she knew, prove of vital importance to her son hereafter. To use her own words, "as I had riskt my life for the father, I was resolved to run a second risk for the benefit of the son." Therefore, accompanied by the trusty Evans, and a faithful Scotch man-servant, we find Lady Nithsdaill making her way North, this time choosing the smaller and less frequented inns to avoid recognition, and at last arriving safely at Traquair, which must have seemed a very haven of rest to the weary lady. Here, under the affectionate care of Lord and Lady Traquair, and in the enjoyment of her little daughter's presence, Lady Nithsdaill ventured to rest for two days. She then proceeded to Terregles. Here she spent three days. Having dug up the precious papers, which she found in a state of perfect preservation, she despatched them to Traquair, and returned thither herself, just in time to escape a domiciliary visit from the Magistrates of Dumfries. Lady Nithsdaill seems to have spent some weeks at Traquair this time, and as we hear of no annoying visits on the part of the authorities, we may conclude that this was a period of repose and peace. A few letters exist written at this time by Lady Nithsdaill to her agent at Terregles, which are interesting, chiefly as showing her interest and practical knowledge in the various domestic arrangements, necessitated by her straitened circumstances. In the month of June apparently, she returned to London, taking the same precautions as on her former journey. On reaching town she found that great talk was being made of her Northern expedition, and she was told that the King was greatly displeased with her, and had ordered search to be made for her, declaring that Lady Nithsdaill did what she pleased in spite of him, and had done him more mischief than any woman in Christendom. Lady Nithsdaill remained concealed until the excitement had subsided, and then, warned of the danger of her position as long as she remained in Britain, and urged by her husband to delay no longer, she prepared to join him in France, taking the little Lady Anne with her. Lady Nithsdaill writes to her sister at Traquair on the eve of her voyage, 19th July, and the next letter we find is one from the trusty Evans, announcing the arrival of the party in Belgium. Lady Nithsdaill had indeed escaped her enemies, but the stormy sea passage nearly cost her her life. Seized by a dangerous illness, she had to be put ashore at Sluice, where she lay for some time unable to proceed. This must have been the more trying as Bruges was so near, and Lady Nithsdaill must have longed to be with her sister, Lady Lucy, then Superioress of the English convent in that town. The latter, apprised by Mrs. Evans of her sister's condition, sent a lay sister to Sluice, and all the comforts necessary for the invalid. A gentleman who had been Lady Nithsdaill's fellow passenger was fortunately going direct to "the place" where Lord Nithsdaill then was,[1] and undertook to communicate the news of his wife's illness to him. These details we learn from Mrs. Evans' letter, so graphically written, and so full of affectionate interest in her mistress, that we regret that it is the only one that has been preserved. About the middle of August Lady Nithsdaill was able to move to Bruges, and by October she and her husband were once more reunited. Of Lord Nithsdaill's movements during the months previous to this date it is difficult to speak with certainty, but we gather from a letter of Lord Linton's to his mother, Lady Traquair, dated Paris, May 1716, that Lord Nithsdaill was then on the eve of starting for Italy to join the Chevalier (James III.). The Prince had written to him in warm terms urging him to come to him, and assuring him that as long as he himself had a loaf of bread in the world he would share it with him. Possibly Lord Nithsdaill had been disappointed with the reception he received; at any rate his visit must have been a short one if he could accomplish it and the double journey by October, as it is certain that by the middle of that month he and Lady Nithsdaill were together at Lille. Here his wife was again prostrated by

[1] It is to be regretted that Mrs. Evans does not mention the name of the place where Lord Nithsdaill was. As will be seen, we believe him to have been then in attendance on the Chevalier, presumably in Italy.

illness, as we learn by one of Lord Nithsdaill's rare letters. On leaving Lille the Nithsdaills proceeded to Paris, and there Lady Nithsdaill was received with great kindness by her royal mistress, Mary of Modena, at whose court, as we know, she had passed her youth. But willing as the queen would have been to serve Lady Nithsdaill, she was herself in such straitened circumstances, that but little help could be expected. Unable to place Lady Nithsdaill about her own person, she, however, granted her a pension of one hundred livres a month. Lord Nithsdaill already received two hundred livres, but with his expensive habits he could not live on this sum. And now commences the constant reference to money matters, the struggles to make ends meet, and apologies for Lord Nithsdaill's demands for assistance from his relations, which occupy so large a portion of his wife's letters, and which offer a melancholy view of the petty trials and difficulties undergone during the weary years now before her, trials which, to a high-spirited woman like her, must have been peculiarly trying. When the wives of the other Jacobite Lords were granted their jointures by the English Government, Lord Nithsdaill's heroic wife was purposely excepted, and she and her husband depended for the necessaries of life upon the bounty of the exiled royal family, and on the kindness and liberality of the Traquairs. That the latter were unfailing in their assistance, the family letters bear abundant proof.

By the end of February the Nithsdaills quitted Paris. Lady Nithsdaill had persuaded her husband to return to the prince, where alone there seemed a possibility of his being able to fill a position at all suitable to his necessities; and she herself, forced to live with as little cost as possible, retired for a short time to La Flêche, where she could have the satisfaction of being near her son, who was pursuing his studies at the Jesuit College of that town.[1]

How much Lady Nithsdaill felt the fresh separation from her husband, and her anxiety about his pecuniary matters, may be gathered from the following words in a letter to Lady Traquair, dated 28th February 1717:—

All my satisfaction is, that at least my husband has twice as much to maintain himselfe and man as I have, so I hope when he sees there is no resource, as indeed now there is not, having sold all, even to the little necessary plate I took so much pains to bring over, he will live accordingly, which will be some comfort to me, though I have the mortification to be from him, which, after we mett againe, I hopet never to have seperated, but God's will be done; and I submit to this cross as well as many others I have had in the world, though I must confess living from a husband I love so well is a very great one.

---

[1] After her residence at La Flêche, Lady Nithsdaill apparently returned to Paris.

On 10th June Lady Nithsdaill tells her sister-in-law, that she has heard of Lord Nithsdaill's safe arrival in Italy, after a most dangerous passage. For five days the peril was so great that the seamen, in despair, left off working, and the ship remained at the mercy of the waves. It was mercifully cast upon the shore at Antibes, and Lord Nithsdaill was soon after enabled to join his royal master.

It was not long, however, before he became weary of his position near the Chevalier, and his letters to his wife inform her of the disappointments he meets with, and soon of his wish to leave the Prince and return to her. He then still clung to the hope that Lady Nithsdaill would receive her jointure from the English Government, and looked to that for their support. Lady Nithsdaill, more prudent, and zealous of her husband's honour, continued to urge him to remain with his master.

In answer to one of Lord Nithsdaill's desponding letters she writes :—

You may be sure, my dear lord, that having you with me, or neare me, would be the greatest natural satisfaction I could have in this world; but I should be a very ill wife, if to procure it myselfe, I would lett you run into those inconveniencys you would doe, if you follow'd the method you propose of leaving your master. For assure yourself, you will in following it, ruine your reputation and put yourself in a starving condition.

This letter was written in September 1717, and in her subsequent letters to Lady Traquair, Lady Nithsdaill refers to the uncertainty of Lord Nithsdaill's plans and his recurring wish to leave Italy.

In the following May she alludes to the report of the Prince's approaching marriage, and on 8th June is able to confirm the good news, and inform her sister-in-law that Lord Nithsdaill has had a most satisfactory interview with his master, who announced his marriage, and told him he specially desired to have him in his household. Lord Nithsdaill urged his wife to join him with as little delay as possible, but as usual, pecuniary difficulties were in the way. After quoting her husband's letter, Lady Nithsdaill continues—

But tho' he bid me loos noe time in writing to you about borrowing money, I would not doe it, because though he did not know it, my dear Mistress[1] who was underhand the occasion of furthering my promotion, and who, though it must never be known, was resolved I should be about her daughter-in-law, had promist me to give me notice when it was fitt for me to goe, and would have given me what was requisite to carry me, and writ to me four dayes before her illness, what she would have me write to her Son in order to it, which I did the first post, and sent it inclosed in a letter to her. But, allas! it arrived the day she dyed, some hours after her death. Imagine you whether her loss is not a great one

---

[1] Mary of Modena.

to me. I may truly say I have lost a kind mother, for she was truly that to me whilst I had her. I would not write to you, being sensible that you have already done a great deal, so that nothing but unavoidable necessity could make me mention any such thing. But allas! I am so far from being able to comply with my husband's dessire now, that I know not how to scarce keep myselfe from starving with the small credit I have here, being reduced to the greatest of straits. My pention never having been payd but by months, and the dangerous and long sickness of my little girle occasion'd my being in debt, even before my fateall loss. But had I not lost my deare Mistris, I know she would have supply'd me out of hir privat purse, for my pention was too small to have lived upon, without her unknown supplys, and even of that small pention I have not had one farthing since her death, and if I doe not doe what my husband desires me, all hopes is lost of our ever promoting ourselves, if we slipe this opportunity, which you will see by his other letter writ after he knew of the loss I had made, tho' he knows not yet how great it was to me. But if your husband's goodness and yours does not give a helping hand, I may not only loos all hopes, but even starve for what I see.

We do not learn whether, on this occasion, Lady Traquair was able to come to her sister-in-law's assistance, but it was the less necessary, as the Prince himself provided money for her journey, and so at last she was able to rejoin her husband in Italy. This journey was the last of any importance undertaken by Lady Nithsdaill. For the remaining years of their lives, she and Lord Nithsdaill lived in Rome, with the exception, perhaps, of some visits to other Italian towns.

And now we would fain have hoped that the valiant lady, who had already suffered so much, would close her days in peace, honoured and appreciated by all; but although, no doubt, Lady Nithsdaill had attained her greatest wish—that of being re-united to her husband—many trials still awaited her. The old pecuniary difficulties met her in Rome, and her husband's inability to make ends meet was a source of constant anxiety to her. It might at least have been supposed that at the Court of Prince James Lady Nithsdaill would have met with that attention which her own character, as well as her husband's known suffering in the cause, merited, but even here much disappointment awaited her. When Lady Nithsdaill had been some months in Rome, the auspicious event already alluded to took place. On 17th May 1719, Lady Nithsdaill, writing to Lady Traquair, announces the arrival of the Princess Clementina Sobieski, the Chevalier's bride. Lady Nithsdaill is charmed with her appearance, and describes her as "one of the charmingest, obliging, and well brede young ladys that ever was seen," and very pretty, and considers that the Prince cannot fail to be extremely happy with her.

Lady Nithsdaill's subsequent letters constantly refer to the royal family, and the following passage of a letter, dated 1723, gives a pleasing picture of the kindly feeling evinced by the royal pair towards their followers :—

I have no newse to tell you, but that last Tuesday, we had the honour of my Master and Mistris at supper with us, so that I never could hope to have my weading day so solemnly kept, and they were so obliging as to be truly merry, which favour I shall never forget.

This is the bright side of the picture, for Lady Nithsdaill had many slights to undergo in her relations with the Court. She and Lord Nithsdaill must have had enemies, or at least but cold friends, among those near the Prince, for there certainly seems to have been a certain coldness and constraint on his part and on that of the Princess towards Lady Nithsdaill on more than one important occasion. That she keenly felt the difficulties of her position is evident from her letters, but for the sake of her family she bore everything, and did not seek to withdraw herself from her position in the royal household. That her personal feelings of duty and affection to her master and mistress did not falter we may feel sure, and her letters show the tender interest with which she watched over the infancy of the royal child, whose melancholy destiny she could then happily little foresee, and the joy with which she greeted, a few years later, the birth of a second Prince.

And so the years passed, without any special event to mark their course. The correspondence with her sister-in-law seems to have been one of Lady Nithsdaill's chief comforts, a link, as it were, with home and kindred, and we can imagine her pleasure when her son's happy marriage with his cousin, Lady Catherine Stuart, united the families still more closely. On the same day that witnessed Lord Maxwell's wedding, his sister, Lady Anne, became the wife of John, fourth Lord Bellew. This marriage also gave great satisfaction to Lord and Lady Nithsdaill. At peace about her children, Lady Nithsdaill had yet one great sorrow to undergo, the greatest that could befall her loving heart. In 1745, a fatal and memorable year for all connected with the House of Stuart, Lord Nithsdaill died, and we who have followed his wife through so much sorrow, can guess what this crowning grief must have been to her.

After five years of lonely widowhood, Lady Nithsdaill died, like her husband, in Rome. Of her last moments we possess no record, nor can the place of her sepulchre be discovered, but this matters the less, as her name is one of those that never die, and the story of her wifely devotion will be told in all generations.

XII

THE RUTHWELL CROSS

> Thro the Cross each Christian
> may reach the Kingdom.
> (*The Holy Rood*. Cædmon.)

HE Ruthwell Cross, one of the most interesting of our relics of early Christian times, whose story I am about to tell as far as we yet know it, now stands once more in the church of Ruthwell, near Annan, in Dumfriesshire. From the year 1802 till the moment of its last removal, it stood in the manse garden, having been rescued from long neglect by Dr. Duncan, the then incumbent of the parish.

The history of this curious Runic stone has been given to us by the learned Professor Stephens in his pamphlet on *The Ruthwell Cross*, published in Copenhagen in 1866, and I purpose to follow his account of the historical events connected with it, and the famous poem engraved upon it. After some interesting remarks upon the position of the

Cross, from which he claims that it should be classed among the *English* Runic stones, as belonging to that part of Scotland which formed part of ancient Northumbria, Professor Stephens gives us the details furnished by Dr. Duncan of Ruthwell regarding the Cross. This information starts with the discouraging remark that "the later history of this remarkable column is not much less indebted to tradition than that of an early date." Nevertheless, the traditionary facts are very curious. In Sir John Sinclair's *Statistical Account of the Parish of Ruthwell*, the Cross is said by report to have been "set up in remote times at a place called Priestwoodside (now Priestside), near the sea, from whence it is said to have been drawn by a team of oxen belonging to a widow. This tradition is still common in the parish, with some additional particulars." These are as follows: The stone is reputed to have been brought by sea from some distant country, and to have been cast on our shores by shipwreck. While it was being conveyed into the interior in the way described above, the ropes which bound it to the oxen are stated to have given way, and the people, seeing in this a mark of the Divine will, erected the Cross on the spot where the stone rested, and the church which was built over it became the parish church of Ruthwell. In confirmation of this tradition, it is mentioned that the remains of an ancient road built on piles of wood, leading through a morass to the Priestside, still existed in the last century. However meagre these traditions regarding the first coming of the Cross to Dumfriesshire may seem, it is certain that it was erected at Ruthwell at a very early period, and there remained, highly venerated, till the Reformation; and even after that period of desolation the Cross continued to be wonderfully preserved from destruction, probably, says Dr. Duncan, owing to the influence of the family of Murrays of Cockpool (ancestors of the Earl of Mansfield), who, being chief proprietors as well as the patrons of the parish, had espoused the Episcopal in opposition to the Presbyterian faction. When, in 1642, however, the latter, triumphing over the Court and its party, rose in power, an order was passed by the General Assembly for the destruction of the Cross of Ruthwell. Happily this order appears to have been reluctantly and only partially obeyed. The column was thrown down, and broke into several pieces, apparently in the fall, and it was probably then that some of the Catholic emblems were nearly obliterated; but the stone was left in the church, and remained where it fell, beside the site of the altar, where it is supposed to have served as a seat to the congregation for more than a century.

The Ruthwell Cross

In 1722 the Cross still lay within the church, but soon after this it was removed to the churchyard, which, being nearly unenclosed, proved a very unworthy resting-place for it; and it seems to have suffered much injury, so much so that Dr. Duncan, to save it from further demolition, transferred it, as we have stated, to his garden. Before this was done, however, a curious discovery had been made. A poor man and his wife, having died within a day or two of each other, were to be buried in the same grave, which for this reason had to be made unusually deep. The grave-digger, while engaged in this duty, came upon a large fragment of sandstone, which proved to be one of the missing portions of the Cross. One side of this stone bore the figure of our Lord bearing a lamb, while on the other were engraved two human figures in the act of embracing. It is supposed that the stone had been, out of reverence, secretly buried in the grave of some Catholic.

The only large portion of the Cross which seems to be irretrievably lost is what formed the transverse arms. It was, however, evident at what part the arms must have projected, and Dr. Duncan determined to restore them.[1] This,

---

[1] On the re-erection of the Cross it was found necessary to insert several new pieces of stone, but no attempt was made to supply the place of the lost sculpture, save on the transverse limbs of the Cross as stated.

in 1823, he attempted to do, with the help of a country mason; "being guided," as he writes, "by the shape of the capital, which is nearly entire, and which, besides being in all probability a counterpart of the arms, contains, on two opposite sides, segments of a circle, corresponding with similar segments in the stone immediately below, evidently indicating that the circle on both sides was originally completed, and formed the centre of the transverse limbs of the Cross."

And now, in the absence of the large and striking illustrations of the Cross given in Professor Stephens's paper, I must endeavour to describe its general appearance. In form not unlike many of the Iona crosses, the Cross of Ruthwell stands about seventeen feet six inches high, and is formed of two pieces of hard sandstone, of a reddish colour inclining to gray, the upper stone being of a deeper hue than the lower.

The Cross is most richly carved and ornamented, and bears inscriptions in Latin besides the Runic poem. On the Roman sides it is divided into compartments of different sizes, separated from each other by a raised border from two to three inches wide, which is joined to a margin also raised, and of about the same width, which borders the edges of the pillar.

These borders, as it were, frame the sacred

The Ruthwell Cross

figures engraved on the cross, and bear on their surface the Latin inscriptions regarding them.

On the Runic sides there is also a raised margin, which borders the sculpture, of nearly the same breadth as those on the reverse. On this the Runic characters are carved *across*, with the exception of a few which run *along* the margin of the upper stone. The beautiful carving on this side represents "a scroll with fruit and foliage interspersed with animals, a quadruped, two birds, and two monsters appearing upon each."

There seems to be good reason for supposing that the stone was at first much shorter, and that the upper stone terminating in a cross was added. The arguments for this are based on three facts: (1) On the difference in colour of the upper stone, which is of a deeper tint than the lower. (2) The but, or border, of the lower stone, the position of which on the Runic sides points to the conclusion that originally the pillar terminated at this point. (3) The superior artistic beauty of the Runic carvings on the lower portion of the stone, as contrasted with those above, and as contrasted also with the figures on the Roman sides, while the Runic letters on the upper portion, which ran *along*, instead of *across* the border as below, are also more deeply and sharply cut than those of which it is contended they are an imitation.

Although the chief interest of the Ruthwell stone seems to centre in the wonderful poem engraved on the Runic portion, which we will shortly consider, the carving and medallions, so to speak, on the Roman sides are very striking. The chief of these pictures in stone are, on the east side: (1) St. John the Baptist bearing the Lamb. (2) Our Lord with his right hand uplifted to bless, "in His hand He holds the sacred scroll. He treads on two swine, the miracle of the possest swine, and emblematic of His triumph over all unclean things." (3) St. Paul and St. Anthony eating the loaf of bread in the desert. (4) The flight into Egypt. Our Blessed Lady with the Child on an ass. The head of St. Joseph, who is leading them, is seen in the upper corner.

On the west side, the chief scenes are as follows: (1) The Visitation, with figures of our Lady and St. Elizabeth. (2) St. Mary Magdalen washing the feet of our Lord, who holds a book (or box of spikenard) in His left hand, while He blesses with the right. (3) The Annunciation. Our Lady and St. Gabriel both standing. Both heads have the glory. (4) The Crucifixion, which is much defaced. The Cross remains, with sun and moon visible above it, and there are traces of figures.

On the north and south, or Runic sides of the Cross, the designs are very similar. A grape-bearing vine (emblematic of our Lord, the True Vine, or the Vine representing the Church) winds upwards, with birds, squirrels, and other creatures, devouring the fruit.

And now the runes, sharply and beautifully engraved, as we have said, on these sides of the pillar, and of which another fragment also remains on the upper part of the Cross, will tell us their meaning after so many centuries of silence.

It is perhaps useless to enter into the theories and suggestions of the various learned but unsuccessful inquirers who, until 1840, endeavoured to decipher the sense of the Runic verses. It is to Mr. John M. Kemble that we owe the discovery of their true meaning. In his essay on the *Runes of the Anglo-Saxons*, published in 1840, Mr. Kemble draws special attention to the Cross of Ruthwell. He shows that it was undoubtedly a Christian monument, and that the Runic letters formed "twenty lines, more or less complete, of a poem in old North English on the Holy Rood, the Cross of Christ."

Two years later, Mr. Kemble was enabled, in a very interesting manner, to confirm this statement through the discovery of a German man of letters. This gentleman, Professor Blüme, had in 1823, in the course of a journey through Italy, found, in the library of a monastery at Vercelli, an ancient and much injured skin-book in old South English of the tenth century, containing homilies and six poems, some of them of considerable length. When this interesting discovery was made known in England, the Record Commission entrusted to Mr. Thorpe the task of publishing the verses, which he ably accomplished. One of the poems, called by Mr. Thorpe, "The Holy Rood: a Dream," "attracted Mr. Kemble's notice in 1842. It describes the vision of the Cross to a pious sleeper, and gives the beautiful and sublime address of the Cross itself, picturing the Passion of our Saviour. Mr. Kemble was arrested by certain lines, and on comparison found that they were *the identical inscription which he had previously deciphered on the Ruthwell Obelisk.*"[1] So exact had been Mr. Kemble's version of the poem, that the discovery of this MS. copy only led him to correct about three letters.

It was now seen, therefore, that the poem was in substance a work of the seventh century, and had been originally written in the North English, or Northumbrian tongue, but its author still remained unknown.

In 1856, Father Haigh,[2] in a paper on the Bewcastle Cross and that of Ruthwell, stated that in his opinion the poem inscribed on the latter

---

[1] Professor Stephens's pamphlet.
[2] Father Haigh was a very distinguished convert, who became a Catholic in 1847, and afterwards a priest.

stone must have been written by *Cædmon*. Professor Stephens has had the honour of proving this theory to be true. By the help of some casts taken by Father Haigh, and of the Vercelli Codex, he has discovered the name of Cædmon cut in the stone itself. Thus, in its own quaint words, the Cross testifies to the author of the verses engraved on it—

Cædmon me fawed [made].

So runs the inscription.

Professor Stephens would have us hope that Cædmon also composed, or adapted, his grand poem expressly for the Ruthwell Cross, to the erection of which St. Hilda and her friends may have lent their aid. All the dates are in accordance with this view. The Cross cannot be later, says the Professor, than the latter half of the seventh century, for it bears a grammatical form so antique (the accusative *dual unqcet*) that it has hitherto only been met with in this place, while the art workmanship also points to the same period. St. Hilda's Monastery of Streaneshalch (Whitby) was founded in 655.[1] St. Hilda died in 680. Cædmon, however, may have survived her for some years; at least the beautiful verse beginning, "Rent are now from me my friends the mightiest," seems to point to this conclusion.

[1] See footnote to p. 18, Stephens.

Familiar as are Venerable Bede's words concerning Cædmon, we cannot refrain from quoting his account of the wonderful incident which led the venerable poet to the discovery of his true vocation.

Cædmon then, whose office in the monastery of Whitby was the lowly one of taking charge of the cattle, was, says Venerable Bede, "placed in worldly life, until the time that he was of mature age, and had never learned any poem." So much did Cædmon feel his lack of the talents needed for joining in social meetings, when "for the sake of mirth it was resolved that they all in turn should sing to the harp," that he would leave the company and go home. One night when this had occurred, he had a dream. A man stood by his side, and, greeting him, said, "Cædmon, sing me something." To this he replied: "I cannot sing anything, and therefore I went out from this convivial meeting, and retired hither because I could not." But the visitor insisted: "Yet thou must sing to me." "What shall I sing?" asked Cædmon. "Sing me the origin of things," replied the stranger. And Cædmon straightway began to sing "in praise of God, the Creator, 'Now must we praise the Guardian of Heaven's Kingdom,' and the rest." "Then he arose from sleep, and had fast in mind all that he sleeping had sung, and to those words forthwith joined many words of song worthy of God in the same measure." Thus began Cædmon's new life. He became a monk, and all that he learnt of the Sacred Scriptures he "turned into the sweetest verse," beginning with the Book of Genesis, the departure of the people of Israel from Egypt, the entrance into the Land of Promise, and many other histories of the canonical books of Holy Writ, of Christ's Incarnation, and of *His Passion*, and other sacred subjects.

There follows a beautiful account of Cædmon's death, after receiving Holy Communion. "And thus it was, that as he with pure and calm mind, and tranquil devotion, had served God, so he in like manner left the world with as calm a death, and went to His presence; and the tongue that had composed so many holy words in the Creator's praise, he then in like manner its last words closed in His praise, crossing himself, and committing his soul into His hands."

It is to be regretted that in a slight sketch like the present, we cannot give the beautiful poem of the Holy Rood. We may be, however, permitted to conclude with the verse from it with which we commenced, and to console ourselves with the thought that—

    Thro the Cross each Christian
    may reach the Kingdom.

Printed by R. & R. CLARK, LIMITED, *Edinburgh.*

www.ingramcontent.com/pod-product-compliance
Lightning Source LLC
Chambersburg PA
CBHW031422230426
43668CB00007B/402